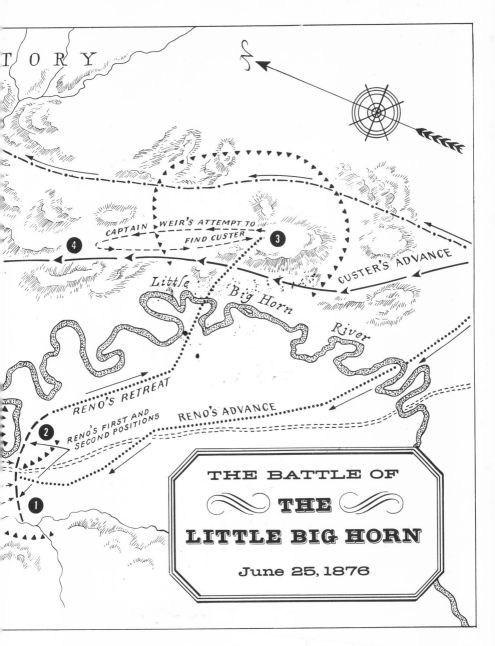

THE BATTLE OF THE LITTLE BIG HORN
June 25, 1876

1 Reno's first attack on the Indian villa[ge] where the
Indians began to outflank him • 3 and where
Captain Benteen's forces rejoined the [ ] of advance
reached during Captain Weir's attempt [ ] [dri]ven back to
the bluff by a strong Indian assault [ ] [Cust]er's forces
came down out of Medicine Tail Cou[lee] Custer's six
companies of cavalry made their famous la[st]

FAINT THE TRUMPET SOUNDS

FAINT THE TRUMPET SOUNDS

The Life and Trial of Major Reno

By

JOHN UPTON TERRELL

And

COLONEL GEORGE WALTON

DAVID McKAY COMPANY, INC.

NEW YORK

FAINT THE TRUMPET SOUNDS

LIBRARY OF CONGRESS CATALOG CARD NUMBER: 66-18622

MANUFACTURED IN THE UNITED STATES OF AMERICA

To
the memory of
Lieutenant Edward A. Walton, Jr., AUS—
killed in action—Cape Bon, Tunis—
May 8, 1943

Though faint the trumpet sounds,
Far in the years moved on,
Once blown a call forever lives.
It shall be heard,
Singing the truth that lips long
    silenced gave to it.
That way it shall be heard,
As long as men remember.

Song of the Little Big Horn

Acknowledgments

An historical biography cannot be the result of the author's efforts alone. It is the combined production of many persons, whose voluntary cooperation and assistance make the book possible. Often across a continent or ocean a stranger supplies a link of information that fits into the whole story like a missing tile in a mosaic. The thought of the many correspondents who helped to make *Faint the Trumpet Sounds* a reality gives me a warm glow of grateful satisfaction.

The actual writing of this acknowledgment, however, is difficult, for one starts with the realization that it would be impossible to include all who, in some measure, have contributed, and that a line must be drawn at some nebulous point. If I may revert to military parlance, this appreciation is in the nature of a commendation for voluntary services rendered far and beyond the call of duty.

Helen, my wife, through her encouragement, research—in which field she has no peer—editorial assistance and willingness to sacrifice all outside interest over a long period of time, contributed greatly. I also appreciate the professional assistance and interest of Hermalinda Renteria of the National War College.

The help and advice of Hugh W. Shick, Hollywood, California, and Barry Johnson, London, England, both of whom are Custeriana experts, saved me from many pitfalls as well as the pointless pursuit of false leads.

My two severest critics have been my sons, Major Frank and Captain Joseph Walton. I don't believe they will be convinced that this book will see the light of day until a copy is actually in their hands.

References to Carrollton, Illinois, were substantiated by its residents, Julia Pearson and Rollins Scott, and by Maude J. Miller of Nevada, Missouri. Brigadier General Henry Gross of Harrisburg, Pennsylvania, provided valuable sources of material of that city's early days.

Through the combined efforts of James E. Buchanan and Brandon Taylor, Jr. of Spartanburg, South Carolina, the history of that city and of Wofford College was made available. Roy P. Johnson of Fargo, North Dakota, and Gordon Guiness of Abercrombie were of great assistance in supplying information on Fort Abercrombie and the Dakotas.

I am indebted to Leona Postill, Historian of Waukesha County, Illinois, for her meticulous information on Cushman Kellogg Davis. W. Emerson Reck, Vice President of Wittenberg University, Springfield, Ohio, supplied interesting information about Brigadier General James M. Bell.

Much of the data on Robert Ross and Ittie Kinney Reno was supplied by Gertrude Morton Parsley, Morton B. Howell, Mary Stahlman, and Alice Stockell of Nashville, Tennessee. In addition, Lieutenant Colonel Tom Pickell of Washington, D.C., Brigadier General Philip P. Ardery, and Lieutenant Colonel C. S. Carter, both of Louisville, Kentucky, were very helpful in authenticating certain Kinney information.

Egon Weiss, Librarian of the United States Military Academy, Mary E. Snyder of the S. S. S. National Headquarters Reference Library, George J. Stanfield, Librarian of the National War College, Katherine Howell of the Wilmington, N.C., Public Library, and Camille Hannon, of the National Archives Library, extended patient assistance over a period of several years. Milton K. Chamberlain, Sara D. Jackson, and Michael Sims were tireless in fulfulling the almost daily requests for material in the National Archives. Finally, I must thank my colleagues: Cora Ford, Neil Tulloch, Sara Louise Owens; and Colonels Joseph Blum, William Brooks, Isaac Perry Cocke, T. Craig McKee, Robert M. Rankin, and Sergeant Thomas M. Reihm, 3rd. All contributed in various helpful ways to my endeavor.

I would be more than remiss if I did not extend my appreciation to my many friends, especially Colonel and Mrs. Charles E. N.

Howard and Dorothy Patterson, who have had the forbearance over four long years to endure my frequent conversational references to Marcus Reno and the Indian Wars. Their tolerance and patient interest have resulted in bringing this volume to its final conclusion.

To all concerned, I am grateful.

GEORGE WALTON

Preface

*M*ajor Marcus A. Reno was a victim of vicious Army politics. The incompetence, egotism, and stupidity of glory-seeking George Armstrong Custer pushed him into the spotlight of American history.

Mark Reno's life was, almost from beginning to end, a series of disappointments, frustrations, and tragedies. We have made a sincere effort to understand him, both as a human being and as an officer. It was far from a simple task, for his character had many facets, and frequently his actions were deeply puzzling. Indeed, to understand him at all one must also achieve an understanding of the times in which he lived, his environment, and the circumstances under which he served.

As a student and writer of western history, I long ago formed the opinion that no American officer had been so unjustly treated, so greatly maligned and unfairly discredited as Mark Reno. Both my own research and that of Colonel Walton unequivocally support this contention. Yet complete accuracy demands the additional comment that, although Major Reno was a brilliant, dedicated, and admirable field officer, although he was maliciously persecuted, he was also in many ways his own worst enemy.

JOHN UPTON TERRELL

FAINT THE TRUMPET SOUNDS

1

*W*hen Major Reno arrived at Fort Leavenworth with his wife and small son early in August, 1869, most of the troops regularly stationed there were away on campaigns and patrols in the high plains country. Brutal, relentless heat seared the valley of the Missouri River, and the post buildings had the drab and forlorn appearance of useless ammunition boxes discarded about the perimeter of the burning parade ground.

Reno was tall, dark-haired, and stockily built with piercing dark brown eyes and a thin mustache that framed a long, firm, full-lipped mouth.

At Regimental Headquarters of the 7th Cavalry, the major was promptly escorted into the presence of Colonel Samuel D. Sturgis. Although he had never served with the colonel, he had long known his reputation and his character, and each was celebrated in ways that lifted it out of the realm of the commonplace.

There were few men on the frontier with more combat experience than Sam Sturgis. Almost continuously since he had graduated from West Point in 1846, he had been on fighting fronts. Captured at Buena Vista, he had returned from the Mexican War to campaign for more than ten years against the Apaches, Cheyennes and Comanches. He was instrumental in keeping Missouri in the Union, and he saw action at Bull Run, South Mountain, Antietam, Fredericksburg, and in a score of less decisive battles, emerging from the war a brevet* major general. He was not destined to enjoy for long the blessings of peace. The West was

---

*A brevet was a commission conferred upon an officer in addition to, and higher than, the rank he held. He was entitled to wear it when off duty. Brevets were awarded in the Mexican, Civil and Indian Wars, for gallantry or meritorious actions.

aflame, and he was soon back in it engaging Indians. He had been commanding officer of the 7th Cavalry only four months when Major Reno arrived at Fort Leavenworth.

Short and thickset, Colonel Sturgis had a large head of black curly hair, and his weathered face wore a perpetual expression that suggested an abiding disgust for life in general and all forms of humanity. He was pompous, arrogant, almost childishly possessive, excessively serious about his rank and success, and given to assuming a Napoleonic posture in the presence of his staff.

If he was pleased that Mark Reno, an experienced and capable officer who also held the brevets of a general, was to join the 7th, he gave no sign of it. He greeted him with a cold, quick handshake, showing no more enthusiasm than he might have displayed had he just learned the thermometer had passed the hundred mark. In a few minutes, the major and his family were being shown to their dreary quarters by an orderly whose two stripes appeared to increase rather than destroy his desire to be of service and his good manners.

Hot and uncomfortable as the rooms were, Mary Hannah Reno was thankful to be in them, and she wasted no time getting herself settled. It might be some weeks before their own furniture, dishes and linens arrived from their house in Harrisburg, but with a few purchases in the post store . . . possibly the major would have an opportunity to take her to Kansas City.

Mary Hannah was slight, dark-haired and frail in appearance. She had a sweet disposition and spoke gently at all times. Her physical limitations curtailed her activities and made the rigors of Army life difficult for her to endure.

Traveling always depleted her energy, and the long journey from Portland to Panama and up to New York seemed to have exhausted her to an unprecedented extent. Even the weeks at home in Harrisburg, when the major was on leave, had not served to bring a full recovery. Then they were off again for Kansas, and she carried hope that the major's assignment to the 7th Cavalry might result in providing them with a home in which they could reasonably expect to remain for more than a few months. Her first sight of Fort Leavenworth had done nothing to endear it to her, but if they could remain there in a settled condition for even a whole year, she would gratefully commend the Commanding General of the Department of Missouri, gruff old John Pope, in her prayers.

A few scorching days and insufferable nights comprised the entire lifetime of Mary Hannah's hope. It was abruptly destroyed by orders which General Pope, unaware that he was to be the target of a ladylike oath instead of the beneficiary of a blessing, dispatched to Regimental Headquarters. They directed Major Reno to proceed at once to Santa Fe. He had been detached for duty on a General Court-Martial, an assignment expected to last several months.

The major's cheerful assertion that at least the weather would be salubrious in the high New Mexico country, and the scenery would be interesting, did nothing to alleviate Mary Hannah's despair. She cried to herself as she began to pack the luggage emptied only a few days before.

It was early on the morning of August 25 that a squad of enlisted men, followed by an ambulance which had been converted into mobile quarters, stopped at the door. The trunk containing the best clothes of Mary Hannah and 5-year-old Ross, and the uniforms of Major Reno, was carried out by two troopers. The carpetbags, valises, and boxes went next.

"There you go, my boy," a corporal said as he lifted Ross to the front seat. "Right beside the driver so you can see it all." He had a strong Irish accent. "Ma'am," he murmured politely as he assisted Mary Hannah into the ambulance, "comfortable you'll be, I hope."

A trooper led the major's horse forward, and he mounted. His order to start came with a nod to the corporal. Scattered small spirals of dust rose in the sunlight from hooves and wheels as the little detachment passed along the parade ground and out the gateway of Fort Leavenworth. The major acknowledged a sentry's salute.

Low hills, rolling like amber waves, marked the edge of the

grass sea, the interminable plains that swept onward for hundreds of miles until they broke against the western mountains. Mary Hannah closed her eyes, as if to shut out the thoughts of the days ahead.

2

*T*he major had not revealed to his wife the misgivings which had arisen in him when he had been assigned to the 7th Cavalry. He had himself long looked forward to being permanently attached to a Regular Army regiment of which he could be proud and in which he could rise to command, but the 7th had never come within the purview of his considerations. Had he been given a voice in the matter, the 7th probably would have been the last he would have chosen.

His disappointment in no way stemmed from the fact that the 7th had been in existence only three years. He would have welcomed an opportunity to participate in whipping a new regiment into shape, molding it into an efficient and formidable fighting force. That, however, was not a task he would have to face. It already had been ably accomplished by the 7th's first commanding officer, Major John W. Davidson, and his successor, Colonel Andrew Jackson Smith. Smith, whom Major Reno had known at Fort Walla Walla, had resigned to become Postmaster of St. Louis.

From colleagues Major Reno had heard of the ordeal Davidson and Smith had undergone. The original recruits of the 7th had represented virtually every stratum of society, the larger part low on the human scale. Nor were the original officers, with the exception of a handful, deserving of a higher classification.

If this was a regrettable situation, it had not been confined to the 7th Cavalry. Following Appomattox the Volunteer Army had been mustered out of service with all possible speed, while at the

4

same time Congress had determined that the Regular Army should be increased from its prewar size of approximately 16,000 to 57,000 officers and enlisted men. There were to be sixty regiments —ten of cavalry, four of artillery, and forty-five of infantry—as well as a thousand Indian scouts. It was obvious that to carry out such a plan the officers corps would have to be expanded. There were not enough regular officers available, nor would the annual graduating class of the Military Academy provide sufficient lieutenants to meet basic requirements. The necessary number of commissioned men would have to be acquired by other means.

Neither moral scruples nor a genuine desire to serve his country to the best of his ability were profound concerns of Secretary of War Edwin M. Stanton. The problem of integrating and completing the new Army Congress had ordered was his responsibility, but in undertaking the task he gave little consideration, if any, to either the caliber or the ability of most of the men he commissioned. Although originally appointed to office as a Democrat, he was fanatical in his support of the Radical Republicans. In making appointments, either military or civil, he held the view that a candidate's political affiliations were more important than competence as an executive, field experience, or the ability to command. With even less concern for the future of the Army or the welfare of the nation it must protect, Stanton had permitted the continuance of the pernicious Civil War practice of commissioning almost any foreign adventurer who claimed to have seen service abroad. It was nothing less than a phenomenon that despite this senseless discrimination and favoritism several military strategists marked with genius and a considerable number of brilliant field officers found their way to high posts in the new Army.

Forty-one initial appointments were made to the 7th Cavalry. Among them were foreign frauds, incurable alcoholics, fugitives from justice, crooked gamblers, and moral degenerates. Because reliable information to the contrary was absent, it was assumed by the few old-line troopers on the staff that most of their colleagues were disciples of Stanton's political faith.

Desertions, courts-martial, and forced resignations aided in the gradual relief of the odious condition. By the time Major Reno received his transfer from the Inspector General's Office at Fort Vancouver to the 7th, most of the undesirables had disappeared. He joined what he understood to be for the most part a hard corps of competent officers. Although men of greatly diverse natures, they had received training in the field, they had known the terror, bloodshed and death of combat; their loyalty to the Army, their courage, and their understanding of their duties were never open to question.

Yet, for all their common ability and the commendable qualities they shared, the officers of the 7th remained a dangerously divided group. The situation was not a mystery to Major Reno. He understood the reasons for it, and he had no wish to become involved in it. That, he felt, could only bring injury to himself.

The schism was the result of a tragic occurrence for which one man had been responsible. In the minds of many officers throughout the country, it had placed on the record of the 7th Cavalry a disgraceful and ineradicable stigma. Others, notably one faction of the 7th, retained a less stringent opinion. As a consequence, controversy that often became acrimonious and created bitter enmity between men obliged to share the same camps and tables continued without any sign of possible abatement. Morale frequently sank to a level that seriously menaced routine affairs and even threatened the efficient conduct of field operations.

Major Reno could look back through the years and recall numerous occasions on which he had met Lieutenant Colonel George Armstrong Custer. Some of them had been in the pleasant environment of social functions, and some of them had been under the grueling, terrifying conditions of Civil War campaigns.

Custer had been a plebe in the Military Academy in 1857, the year Major Reno graduated. The two men had not then met, but it was not long after the start of the war before they found themselves on common ground. From that time on, Custer had the advantage. Dashing, reckless, handsome, and with numerous friends in high office, he rose fast in rank. The "boy general" he was called, not always in a complimentary sense, and had not the war ended when it did, his gallantry and courage, combined with the influence of his sponsors, in all probability would have brought him even greater renown and position.

If Major Reno had never thought much of Custer's ability as a military strategist, he willingly acknowledged his bravery, and he harbored no resentment that Custer had been, in the span of a few years, promoted above him in permanent rank. That was the way of the Army, and Major Reno was too sensible to complain unduly about a system which he had learned through painful experience was indestructible. There was nothing to be gained from butting one's head against the stones of the Washington political wall. He had long before resigned himself to carrying out his assigned duties as best he could, and leaving the course of his career to the inexplicable whims of Fate.

Major Reno had reached Fort Leavenworth with no animosity for George Armstrong Custer, but he had not gone there without knowledge of the situation he would be called upon to face. That knowledge was possessed by the entire United States Army. He could do no more than hope that he might find a means of taking a middle road, of avoiding open partisanship. The chances of maintaining such a position for any length of time, however, he admitted to himself, were extremely poor.

Several of the officers of the 7th, Major Reno was aware, had served with Custer during the Civil War, and their esteem and admiration for him were without bounds. It was not extreme to say that they literally worshiped him, refused to admit that he could make a mistake, and were instantly antagonistic to those who did not hold similar feelings.

There were numerous others whose feelings were quite different for various reasons. Some questioned Custer's professional ability, some disliked his personality, some resented his nepotism, some were annoyed that their commanding officer was younger than they were. While it had existed from the moment Custer joined the 7th, the controversy, however, had not reached a stage verging on violence until the grievous events which took place immediately before and during the 1868 campaign against the Cheyennes and Arapahoes.

7

Lieutenant Colonel Custer's cruelty had led him into serious trouble. He had been ordered to stand trial on charges that he instructed his junior officers to pursue and shoot down several deserters, bringing none back alive. The court-martial found him guilty and suspended him from rank without pay and allowances for a year.

Temporary command of the 7th fell to the senior officer then on duty, Major Joel H. Elliott, a man of small stature with the appearance and characteristics one might expect to find in a schoolteacher, but who possessed the courage and tenacity commonly attributed to a bulldog. He had served ably in the Civil War, rising from the ranks to become a captain of the Indiana Cavalry. Mustered out, he became superintendent of the Toledo, Ohio, schools. Longing for Army life, he had taken an examination for a commission with the hope that he might secure a lieutenancy. He had scored an almost perfect paper, and to his astonishment had been commissioned a major.

In the summer of 1868, with eleven companies of the 7th, Major Elliott had set out on an expedition commanded by General Alfred Sully, the son of the famed portrait painter, Thomas Sully, to punish Indians who had raided white settlements along the Walnut and Solomon rivers.

The raiders were successful in evading the troops, and the campaign ended in failure. Sully thought Elliott had been remiss and had not shown proper enterprise, but General Philip Henry Sheridan, commanding the Department of Missouri, did not agree with this view. Because of the seriousness of the situation, Sheridan had gone into the field himself, and he had soon reached the conclusion that enterprise was not the only thing needed to combat the Cheyennes and Arapahoes. Mobility and men who could fight in the manner of Indians were more likely to bring success.

Elliott was a competent officer, but he had been handicapped, as any other officer in his place would have been, by the necessity of transporting his own supplies and relying for his strategy on inadequate intelligence, if not inefficient scouts.

It was futile to attempt to pursue the Indians, who were thoroughly familiar with every hill and gully and who could live indefinitely off the country, without an unwieldy force and cumbersome trains. Following this line of reasoning, Sheridan approved the formation of a volunteer battalion of experienced frontiersmen under Major George A. Forsyth to scout the Indians.

If the idea of sending out a force that could travel fast and employ Indian tactics was good, its execution was bad. It was thought that fifty veteran fighters, armed with repeating rifles, could accomplish the desired end. The fallacy of this belief was soon demonstrated. On the Arikaree River the battalion was very nearly exterminated by Cheyennes.

By the fall of 1868 Sheridan had decided that a winter campaign would bring better results. The assignment would require leadership by a man of spirited determination—better termed recklessness—and extraordinary boldness. He settled on George Custer, and to get him he secured the remission of the balance of Custer's sentence, and returned him to command of the 7th Cavalry.

From the start Custer lived up to Phil Sheridan's opinion of him. In a raging snowstorm on November 23, with the regimental band blaring "The Girl I Left Behind Me" through blue lips, Custer led the 7th out of Camp Supply, on the frozen plains of Oklahoma, to remove the blots which had tarnished his renown and regain the glory he so greatly loved.

It was on Thanksgiving Day, 1868, that Major Elliott, while on a scouting patrol, came across an Indian trail leading southward. Leaving the supply wagons in the care of the regiment's Quartermaster, Captain James M. Bell, Custer dashed in hot pursuit of the quarry. At nightfall, in the valley of the Washita River, he came upon a sleeping Indian village.

During the night hours Custer fashioned a fateful pattern. He made no attempt, which he might well have done through his Indian scouts, to determine whether the village contained friendly Indians or the hostiles he had been sent to subdue. He made no reconnaissance to learn what strength he was facing. He divided his command, sending contingents far out beyond his control.

As the sun appeared on the horizon of the wintry plain, he ordered the band to play "Garry Owen," his favorite song, and he waved and shouted his men into action. Major Elliott, with Companies G, H, and M, attacked the village from the left. From the right came Companies B and F under Captain William Thompson.

The direct attack from the front Custer selected for himself, and he charged with A, C, D, E, I, and K Companies, and Cooke's Sharpshooters. To his dismay, he met with no organized resistance. A few Indians, roused from their blankets, fired at the onsweeping cavalcade. Obviously they did not know the troops were coming, and they had no reason to anticipate a surprise attack.

The Indians were a friendly village led by Black Kettle, and they were a party to the Treaty of Medicine Lodge. As a reward for affixing their marks to this declaration of peace and friendship, 103 of their warriors were shot to death without warning by Custer's guns. The colonel did not bother to count the many women and children who were slain.

The 7th Cavalry suffered only one fatal casualty that cold November morning. He was Captain Lewis Hamilton, a grandson of Alexander Hamilton, and one of Custer's most loyal friends.

The information that he had murdered nearly two hundred men, women, and children who had placed their faith in the integrity of the Great White Father and the honor of the United States Army appeared to disturb George Custer not at all. He ordered Major Elliott to take a patrol of nineteen troopers and ride in pursuit of some villagers who had managed to escape.

As he started off with his men, Joel Elliott called out: "Well, here goes for a brevet or a coffin."

A scout reported that Indians could be seen gathering on bluffs along the Washita, and Lieutenant Edward Godfrey approached Custer to say he had been informed there were more villages down the valley.

Custer appeared unconcerned by the intelligence. He had watched closely as troopers carried out his order to herd the remaining villagers, most of whom were squaws and children, some of them wounded and injured, before him. Everything was to be destroyed—tepees, food, weapons, blankets, clothing—and the fires were being lighted.

Spasmodic shots came from Indians on the bluffs, and platoons dashed after them. Troopers dropped to the ground and attempted to pick off the swiftly riding warriors. One company rode in a circular sweep, a mile outside the burning village, but the Indians vanished like wraiths before them. Cavalrymen had rounded up eight hundred Indian ponies and were holding them a short distance away along the river bank.

Custer ate and lounged beside a warm campfire. Twice during the morning Lieutenant Godfrey stopped before him to report that Major Elliott had disappeared over a ridge two miles from the camp, and that firing had been heard in that direction. Godfrey suggested that Major Elliott and his men might be in trouble. On each occasion Custer ignored him. At last Custer took up a sporting rifle. It was time to have a little fun. Inasmuch as the Indian ponies had to be destroyed, why not show the dirty squaws and their brats some real and fancy shooting? He ordered the ponies to be herded along the creek.

Frederick William Benteen was the senior captain of the 7th, a quarrelsome, incredibly courageous, blunt, remarkably capable veteran. He was to write a letter from Fort Cobb, Indian Territory, to a friend in St. Louis which would give to posterity a condemning record of Custer's actions that day on the Washita River in Oklahoma. His friend, William J. De Gresse, would take the letter to the St. Louis *Democrat*, which would publish it without a signature, and it would be reprinted in the *New York Times*. Benteen graphically described the scene to De Gresse·

. . . little has been done save the work of the first hour. That which cannot be taken away must be destroyed. Eight hundred ponies are to be put to death. Our Chief exhibits his close sharpshooting and terrifies the crowd of frightened, captured squaws and papooses by dropping the straggling ponies in death near them. Ah! he is a clever marksman. Not even do the poor dogs of the Indians excape his eye and aim, as they drop dead or limp howling away. . . . The plunder having been culled over is hastily piled; the wigwams are pulled down and thrown on it, and soon the whole is one blazing mass. . . . The last pony is killed. The huge fire dies out; and as the brave band of the Seventh Cavalry strike up the air, 'Ain't I Glad To Get Out Of The Wilderness,' we slowly pick our way across the creek over which we charged so gallantly in the early morn. Take care! do not trample on the dead bodies of that woman and child lying there! . . . But surely some search will be made for our missing comrades.

No search was made for Major Elliott and the nineteen troopers who had vanished over the ridge with him. Custer led the regiment back to the supply train, which had been left with Captain Bell twenty miles from the Washita.

On the 11th [December], [William Benteen wrote in his letter] we camped within a few miles of our "battle of the Washita," and Gens. Sheridan and Custer, with a detail . . . went out with the view of searching for the bodies of our nineteen missing comrades, including Maj. Elliott.

The bodies were found in a small circle, stripped as naked as when born, and frozen stiff. . . . They lay scarcely two miles from the scene of the [village] fight, and all we know of the manner they were killed we have learned from Indian sources.

Major Elliott and his troopers had suddenly found themselves surrounded by a greatly superior force of Cheyenne warriors. They dismounted. There they fought to the death.

"Who shall write their eulogy?" William Benteen asked in his letter. He and Joel Elliott had long been close friends. He was indignant, angry, and heartsick at Custer's criminal indifference to the two reports of Lieutenant Godfrey, and his unconscionable act of leaving the field without making any search for the missing men.

The 7th was still at Fort Cobb when Custer received a copy of the St. Louis newspaper in which the Benteen letter had been printed. Shaking in fury, he sounded officers' call. He paced up and down in his tent, a rawhide whip in his hand. When the officers were before him, he brandished the paper in their faces, shouting that the letter could only have been written by one of them, and threatening to "cowhide" the culprit, if he could discover him.

Captain Benteen took a step forward. "I wrote the letter, General," he said.

Blood rushed to Custer's face. His words came in a stammer. "Captain Benteen, I'll see you again, sir."

None of the officers of the 7th Cavalry ever heard Colonel Custer speak again of the Benteen letter.

A short time later, Captain Benteen received word that his child had died and his wife was critically ill. He requested an immediate leave, and prepared to depart. The leave was refused, and Colonel Custer ordered him to report without delay to Fort Dodge.

Major Reno had never discussed in detail with Mary Hannah the unbridgeable chasm between the 7th Cavalry's two factions. Life would be strained enough for her without the pressure of that burden. Although not gregarious, she made friends easily, and she had already demonstrated her diplomatic ability. He hoped that she would find pleasant companionship among the wives of other officers to alleviate the dullness of the long days and nights when he would be in the field.

Nor had he revealed to her before they started for Santa Fe that a few days after their arrival at Fort Leavenworth he had made a strenuous effort to secure a transfer. The opportunity had arisen when he had unexpectedly met an old friend, Major Samuel F. Chalfin. After twenty-two years of service, Chalfin, an assistant adjutant general, was retiring.

Under Army regulations, officers were permitted to exchange positions, provided they obtained the sanction of the Secretary of War. When Chalfin readily agreed to make the exchange with him, Major Reno wasted no time sending a telegraphic request to Adjutant General Edward D. Townsend at Washington. Within a few hours a reply was received. "If General Schofield recommends, I do not object," it said.

Major Reno was delighted. He was unaware that Chalfin, being an amiable man, had also expressed a willingness to transfer with Major Lewis Merrill, who was as eager to escape from the 7th as was he.

Merrill and Reno had graduated from the Military Academy in the same class. The first assignment of both had been with the 1st Dragoons. Both had received the same brevet promotions during the war. The matter of the transfer, however, at once superseded all considerations of their old friendship. A bitter contest, largely carried on by telegraph, ensued, and even manners and dignity were forgotten. Merrill charged Reno with a breach of good faith in wiring directly to General Townsend instead of going through proper channels. Reno countered with the assertion that Chalfin had not committed himself irrevocably to Merrill, and intimated that he considered Merrill wanting as a gentleman, if not guilty of deception.

General Townsend, shaking his head in dismay, took advantage of his rank and delegated the argument to an assistant, Colonel James B. Fry. No one was more skillful in the use of red tape than Colonel Fry. He merely penciled a note to his superior which expressed the opinion that under new regulations the exchange "would violate the spirit of the law which forbids the filling of any vacancy in the Department without the approval of Congress, and I think Congress would be exasperated."

General Townsend carried on, quashing the applications of both Merrill and Reno with the statement that he did not "for a moment believe that the Senate would confirm the nomination of any Major transferred to Colonel Chalfin's place under the circumstances."

Major Reno left for Santa Fe with mixed emotions which he felt it would be both unwise and unfair to explain to Mary Hannah. He was really grateful for the detached duty which took him away so quickly from the inauspicious atmosphere of Fort Leavenworth. On the other hand, he could not avoid the realization that he would soon have to return. Perhaps he had better begin at once to reconcile himself to living with the 7th and its problems. It would not be an easy thing to do, but that also was a subject which simple kindness precluded him from adding to the concerns of his wife.

3

*A*t the age of thirty-five, when he was assigned to the 7th Cavalry, Major Reno had been a soldier of the Regular Army twelve years, but in looking back through his entire life he found justification for the assertion that he had lived always in or near the smoke and thunder and tragic destruction of war.

He was born on the fifteenth of November, 1834, in Carrollton, a village which had nothing to distinguish it from a hundred others in the rolling black-loam region of southwestern Illinois. A stage line gave it access to the outside world by way of Springfield to the northeast and through St. Louis to the south. Two days' ride would take one to the mouth of the Missouri River, and that was the gateway to the western wilderness. Steamboats had pushed their way up the great waterway, but they had not brought civilization to the western Indian country. That was still half a century away, and when Marcus Alfred Reno was an infant a man would not have had to journey far to hear the drums of a Scalp Dance, and the time of the great Indian Wars was just beginning.

In settled country and yet close to the frontier, Carrollton displayed the characteristics of both. Situated as close to the pro-slavery South as it was to the abolitionist North, its residents, and those of the surrounding country, were sharply divided in their political, economic, social, and religious doctrines. Tolerance was not a virtue of any faction, bitterness frequently led to violence, and rarely was a reconciliation achieved among those whose roots were in the South, the New Englanders, and the German and Scandinavian farmers and merchants. Mark Reno was a small child when in nearby Alton an editor with abolitionist leanings was murdered by a mob, and a prominent businessman who had signed an antislavery petition saved himself from another crowd of angry citizens only by climbing the steeple of the Baptist Church.

Slavery was not the only issue that drove men to murder and arson. Prohibition was just as fanatically supported and opposed, and blood not infrequently smeared whiskey bottles. During Mark Reno's boyhood the Prohibition Party steadily gained strength. There were men in Carrollton who had seen with their own eyes the horrors caused by the fur traders' liquor in the Indian country. They knew that the troubles of the wilderness had come in the main out of kegs, and if the frontier had been pushed westward beyond the Mississippi, the sources of the evil had remained behind.

The unexpected often came as a logical consequence, but the seemingly contradictory just as often concealed a strange compatibility. For example, the people of Carrollton appeared to believe in an indestructible Union, but they were widely split on the issues, such as slavery, high tariffs, and questions of States' rights, which created a deep gulf between the North and the South. They sympathized with the struggles of the trade unionists against the antilabor policies of industrialists and eastern financiers, and they professed to believe in religious freedom, but engaged in bitter denominational fights.

Young Mark Reno knew paradoxes and conflicts in his own family and in its branches. His mother, Charlotte Hinton, whose patriotism was unqualified, made no effort to conceal the pride she held in her British ancestors. She was the granddaughter of James Hinton,* whose distinguished service to the Crown had brought him the reward of a large tract of land in North Carolina. The defeat of England in no way tarnished the splendor in which she painted him. This attitude, and her superior education, did not endear her to the plain, illiterate women of Greene County whose forebears had been largely ragged privates in the Revolutionary Army.

*Although British Army records show no record of a General James Hinton, the family claimed that he was a general.

16

Her father, James Hinton, Jr., had not cared for life on a Carolina plantation, and as a young man had moved westward with the growing tide of emigration. He had selected Carrollton as an auspicious place to settle and rear a family. If western Illinois did not develop in the way or to the degree he had anticipated, nonetheless he remained. In addition to Charlotte, he left two sons, Alfred, who studied law and became a judge in Kane County, and Oscar, who acquired wealth as a stage coach contractor.

Charlotte was a young widow with one daughter, Harriet, when she married James Reno. Marcus Alfred was the fifth of their six children. Preceding him were three daughters, Eliza, Cordelia, and Sophronia, and a son, Leonard Warren. The youngest was Henry Clinton.

The hotel James Reno built was named the Hinton House as a tribute to his wife's family. James not only liked the role of innkeeper, but he played it well. He was friendly, good-natured, convivial, set a good table, and enjoyed circulating among the guests, especially those who frequented the tavern room. He held no inordinate pride in his ancestry, as did his wife, but he was not above reminding her on occasion—probably in self-defense —that the French blood in his veins was touched with blue, that he was a great-nephew of Phillippe François Renault, who had journeyed to America with the Marquis de Lafayette. Somehow the name Renault had become Reno, but that, he maintained, did not in any way impair its distinction.

An enterprising businessman, James Reno formed a partnership with an energetic and capable young physician, James M. Simpson, to open Carrollton's first pharmacy. Dr. Simpson combined the practice of medicine with strenuous religious activities and leadership in the Prohibition Party. The drug firm of Simpson and Reno prospered, and the doctor increased his ties with the Reno family by marrying his partner's stepdaughter, Harriet. Thus he became James Reno's stepson and Mark Reno's stepbrother-in-law.

The Black Hawk War had ended two years before Mark Reno's birth, but for several years afterward its repercussions were felt, and these were among his first memories. As a youth he watched men going off to fight Indians, and then he saw other men leaving to help Texas. After that came the Mexican War.

Several times he saw a gangling, tall splinter of a man stretching his legs in the small lobby of the Hinton House. The man was Abe Lincoln, a young lawyer from Springfield, Ill. Another young lawyer also visited Carrollton and stayed at the Hinton House. He was short and stocky, and both his voice and manner were full of fire. His name was Stephen A. Douglas. They both were there during the court sessions, and they were often pitted against the most prominent member of the local bar, one Edward D. Baker.

Every schoolchild in America would be told about Lincoln and Douglas, but Baker would be remembered mostly by historians. He was to wear a colonel's uniform, and was destined to die in the Battle of Ball's Bluff, a hero. If Carrollton and Greene County respected Abe Lincoln as a counselor, he was rejected as a politician. When elections came Carrollton and Greene County turned him down, and helped to send the little giant Stephen A. Douglas to the United States Senate.

The celebrated evangelist, Lorenzo Dow, called himself the "eccentric cosmopolite." Some of the persons whose souls he sought to save spoke of him irreverently as "Crazy Dow." He had won a certain international fame as the first man of the cloth to conduct American-style revival meetings in the shadows of the Catholic churches of Ireland and the cathedrals of the Church of England. Dow died the year Mark Reno was born, but he had cut a wide swath through Greene County, and he had not been forgotten. People reminisced for years about the old man with the long beard and flowing locks with the result that Mark Reno felt he had known Dow.

Townspeople never failed to chuckle at the remark that Crazy Dow had helped to lift the Methodists to the level of the Baptists. If true, it was a feat of major significance in a community that had a population of six hundred, four established churches, and six resident preachers.

Charlotte Reno drilled her children. She sat them down and made them learn to read and to count numbers, she lectured them on their proud heritage, and she was ruthless in her determination that they would go out into the world as educated young men and women.

Itinerant teachers came to Carrollton now and then—there was no public school there in Mark Reno's time—but none of them stayed long. They set up classrooms and collected their fees, but always something happened to cause them to leave.

Of the Reno children, Mark was the most alert, learned faster than the others, retained the knowledge he acquired, and gave the most promise of applying himself diligently in some professional career. He was timid and retiring, a sturdy, handsome, dark-haired lad, but he possessed an innate perseverance and refused to acknowledge defeat, either by a mathematical equation or in a fist fight. He might fail to solve a problem and be beaten by physical superiority, but he never thought of himself as having lost.

He watched the annual muster of the Greene County militia with great interest. When he was thirteen he saw seventy-five of Greene County's young men leave for the Mexican War, and it was then he announced for the first time that he would be a soldier.

Two youths he knew had left for West Point. Jimmy Fry had gone in 1842. He was the son of Colonel Jacob Fry, who had fought in the Black Hawk War, and he would become a major general and provost marshal of the United States. Bill Carlin had gone in 1846, and he would also wear the insignia of a major general.

President Van Buren appointed James Reno Postmaster of Carrollton, and he was confirmed in the waning hours of the Twenty-sixth Congress. The Democrats lost the next election, and James Reno expected to be ousted at any moment, but the new President, William Henry Harrison, died a month after his inauguration, and he was succeeded by Tyler, a Democrat, and James Reno held the post. The Reno and Hinton families were becoming prominent and prosperous. Uncle Alfred Hinton was elected a township trustee in a runoff with J. E. Walker. Each had received twenty-nine votes. Dr. Simpson was being urged to run for the state legislature.

Mark Reno not only knew the feeling of being close to war; he knew the tragedies war caused, and as a boy he knew the meaning of death. His eldest sister, Eliza, was the first to be placed in the family plot at the edge of the village. He was seven when his half-sister, Harriet Simpson, was laid to rest in a nearby grave. Dr. Simpson soon left for his old home in Virginia. He returned with a new wife, Jane Hopkins Simpson.

When Mark was eleven his father died suddenly, at the age of forty, on July 3, 1845. Charlotte Reno carried on, holding classes for her children, managing the Hinton House as efficiently as her husband had done. The drugstore also brought her an income. If he was excessively religious and a fanatical prohibitionist, Dr. Simpson was honest. He paid Charlotte her full share of the profits.

With Charlotte's death in 1848 came the end of the Reno family home, and the loss of the guiding hand of a devoted and capable woman. The Reno children were not penniless orphans, but there was no way they could be kept together. Uncle Alfred Hinton, the lawyer, was named their guardian, and he found homes for them. Mark was sent to live with the Simpsons.

It was a crowded household. Jane Simpson had given birth to three children in rapid succession. Her sister, Mary, her brother, Sam, and a cousin, Martha, had come out from Virginia to live with her and the doctor. Mark could claim no blood relationship, and he always felt himself an intruder. Dr. Simpson was by nature austere, he was bigoted, and he made of his home a virtual branch of the Baptist Church and headquarters of the Prohibition Party.

As a youth of sixteen Mark was lonely and retiring; he had developed a profound dislike for all formal religions, a detestation of clergymen, and an abhorrence for cant. That year he was offered a permanent clerkship in the drugstore, and he went to work, but he had not lost his determination to secure a college education, and he had not forgotten his ambition to be an officer in the United States Army.

On October 1, 1850, he wrote the letter that was to establish the course of his life. It was addressed to the Secretary of War, Hon. C. M. Conrad:

Sir, I have the honor to request of you information in relation to the qualification of a candidate for admission to the U. S. Military Academy. . . . I desire to receive an appointment as Cadet . . . as my Father and Mother are both dead and it is not within my power to obtain an education at my own expense. I can give the required recommendation in regard to moral character and intellectual capacity.

The information came. A cadet shall be over sixteen years of age but under the age of twenty-one; at least five feet in height; free from any disfigurement, disease, or infirmity; write a fair and legible hand without material mistakes in spelling; perform with facility and accuracy the ground rules of arithmetic: reduction, simple and compound proportion, vulgar and decimal fractions.

Under the law of 1843, each Congressman was privileged to submit the name of one candidate.

Quickly a letter went forward to Congressman William Alexander Richardson. It was dignified and restrained, yet its words reflected the profundity of a young man's hope and the fervor of his dreams. Mark Reno was unaware how strongly in his favor were the political winds, for he had little regard for politics, and he had in him none of the common attributes of the politician.

That could not be said of Representative Bill Richardson. He practiced law in Shelbyville and Quincy. After serving in the Illinois House of Representatives and the State Senate, he had been elected to the U.S. House of Representatives to take the place of Stephen A. Douglas, whom the legislature, rejecting the candidacy of Abraham Lincoln, had sent to the United States Senate. Richardson often had stayed at the Hinton House during sessions of the Greene County Court, and he had been a friend of James Reno. He was closely associated with Judge Alfred Hinton, Mark's legal guardian. Dr. Simpson, in whose home Marcus Reno lived, was a pillar of Richardson's church, an eminent physician and businessman, a leader of the rapidly growing pro-hibition movement, therefore a man to be politically courted.

On May 31, 1851, Representative Richardson sent to the Sec-retary of War the nomination of Marcus Alfred Reno as a cadet at the United States Military Academy.

4

One hot August afternoon in 1851, Mark Reno stood on the open deck of the little steamer on which he had traveled down the Hudson from Albany as it approached the newly erected South Wharf of West Point. He was still awed by the immensity of the world he had seen on his first long journey from Carrollton, and he knew a sobering fear that caused him to wonder if he had not made a mistake in putting so far behind him the only environment, the only way of life, he had ever known. The stark, rocky cliffs and the somber, stone buildings ringed with mountains only served to increase that apprehension. Beyond them was a vast unknown. The fear was relieved to some extent by admiration of the rugged beauty of the scene as he trudged, with five companions, up the road to the West Point plain, and his attention was caught by the imposing array of structures which spread before him; the turreted Elizabethan library and observatory, the Grecian chapel, the immense stone Academic Building, and beyond the drill plain the new Cadet Barracks. He stared long and thoughtfully at the barracks, for he had read that it had cost the fabulous sum of $186,000. It was four stories in height, contained 176 rooms and a central heating system, and, even more amazing, had complete bathrooms in the basement.

Along the northwest side of the plain were the duplex houses in which officers lived with their families. Eastward could be seen the summer camp of the Corps of Cadets, the tents standing in precise gleaming white lines, rifles stacked neatly along the gravel walks on which sentries paced.

The little group, conspicuously marked by the ill-fitting clothes of young men from small towns, followed the rigid back of a noncom. Ahead they could see Roe's, the square stucco hotel which recently had acquired a new wing, and in which they were to live until they had passed their entrance examinations and were formally accepted as probationary cadets. Mark Reno reassured himself by touching the wallet he had pinned to an inside pocket of his jacket. It contained the eighty dollars he would pay to the adjutant as a required entrance deposit, and a few extra dollars which he had saved from his wages in the drugstore. His income would be twenty-four dollars a month, but there would be little of that, if anything, left to be spent for his own pleasure. Out of it he would have to pay for his rations, his uniforms, and his mattress.

In the following days the discipline, not the spelling, the French, the gunnery, the engineering, or the vulgar fractions, was the hardest to learn. The unyielding, inviolable, never-ending discipline became torture and brought nightmares to the young men who had never known a prescribed, rigid way of life. Willingness and eagerness to obey were insufficient. It was response, performance, that counted. Idiosyncrasies, inherent characteristics, habits were not tolerated. A young man's life was no longer his own. It belonged to the rule book and the verbal order.

Of the sixty-six cadets of the Class of 1855, which was the first to know the luxury of barracks bathrooms, thirty-one would be sent away on the steamers to New York and Albany, never to return. The young men with whom Mark Reno was the most companionable would be among the failures. One would be James A. M. Whistler, whose father had graduated in the Class of 1819. A hundred and thirty-six demerits, received in a single term, followed young Whistler's name on the roster. When he was asked to define silicon, and he identified it as a gas, the end soon came. He was to say: "If silicon *had* chanced to be a gas, I probably would have been a major general." To which Mark Reno was to add: "Yes, but then no one would ever have heard of your mother."

One class member would die in his hard barracks bed. Two would be killed as second lieutenants in Indian combat soon after graduating. Three from northern states would fight for the Confederacy alongside three of their classmates from the South. One would become a general and make good use of the talents of a major named Reno. Two others were destined to influence the course of Marcus Reno's life.

It was in chapel on Sunday mornings that one had the best opportunity to glance in awe and admiration at the great, the distinguished, and the famous. In the fifth pew one could see the imposing figure of Lieutenant General Winfield Scott, Commander of the Army of the United States, hero of the Mexican War, a gigantic man in a gold-embroidered, full-dress uniform. There were visiting Senators, other generals, Cabinet members, and an occasional foreign statesman or soldier, and there was Captain Henry Brewerton viewing his charges with proud eyes, the commander under whom the Academy had grown and had become world-famous. He would leave West Point a major, breveted a brigadier general. If the Civil War was marked throughout with the work of brilliant military strategists, it was because many of the officers who planned and executed the battles and campaigns of both sides had been trained under the administration of Henry Brewerton.

During Cadet Reno's second year, a colonel of engineers was assigned to replace Brewerton. His name was Robert E. Lee, and he was a Virginia aristocrat. Thin and standing an inch under six feet, his countenance beamed with gentleness and benevolence. Lee was a member of the Class of 1820, the first and only cadet to graduate without a demerit. If he loved West Point and looked back on his years there with fond memories, he was not happy about his appointment. "I learn with much regret," he wrote, "the determination of the Secretary of War to assign me to that duty, and I fear I cannot realize his expectations in the management of an institution requiring more skill and more experience than I command."

His words were both accurate and prophetic. If academic standards and discipline were maintained at acceptable levels, it was not so much Lee's accomplishment as that of his dedicated staff. "I wish boys would do what is right," he said to his son one day when they came upon three cadets far beyond limits. "It would be so much easier for all parties." His son could have told him the names of the disobedient cadets, but he forbade him. If he didn't know their names, he could not report them.

Lee constructed the Riding Hall, the largest building in America devoted to equestrian exercises, and he built fine new cavalry stables southeast of the library. Cavalry tactics that were to win battles for both the North and the South had their origin and were studied under Lee's supervision. One of the most attentive and able students of cavalry warfare was Cadet Reno.

August 22, 1852, was a hot sunny day. A sentry on duty in a secluded area beyond the drill plain paused beneath the shade of a tree, mopped his brow, and succumbed to the temptation to sit down. While sitting he took out a penknife and carved the initials "MAR" in the tree's trunk. As he completed his artistic work he looked up into the face of the Officer of the Guard.

For the first time Cadet Mark Reno was placed under arrest, charged with failing to "walk his post in a soldierly manner" and "wantonly destroying a shade tree which was his duty to protect." For nine days he waited dejectedly for the court-martial that he understood would result in his dismissal from the Academy. It never came, but four hours of extra guard duty each Sunday served to make the infractions unforgettable. He had been saved by his good record.

His first love was the cavalry, and his respect and admiration for his instructor, Lieutenant George H. Thomas, were unbounded. He was morose for several days upon learning that Lieutenant Thomas had been assigned to other duties. The new cavalry instructor was First Lieutenant Fitz-John Porter, and within a short time after his arrival the last fragment of Mark Reno's morosity had vanished. His admiration and respect for the dapper Porter soon equaled that which he had held for Thomas. Moreover, Porter proposed astonishing tactics that were not in the manual. He talked of such radical things as aerial reconnaissance, and he advocated that every division of the Army be assigned balloon companies for observation purposes, subjects that stirred sharp young minds with their daring departures from standard established techniques.

Two years had passed during which he had seen virtually nothing of the world beyond the drill plain, two years of relentless discipline and study. Suddenly on June 1st he was freed. He prepared, with other cadets, to take the boat for Albany on the only leave he would receive until he graduated.

Colonel Lee apparently was somewhat apprehensive as to the manner in which the departing cadets would conduct themselves, for he appended a personal note to the standard form of the leave orders. "The Superintendent places full reliance upon the deportment of the cadets now granted a leave of absence," it said, "and trusts that while away from the Academy, they will be guilty of no act calculated to reflect discredit upon themselves or the institution of which they are members."

In the case of Cadet Reno it was a needless admonition. He had only one desire in mind. It was to stroll along the main street of Carrollton, resplendent in his uniform, and he trembled inwardly with excitement as he held a vision of himself greeting old friends in front of the drugstore and in the lobby of the Hinton House.

On July 1st he was back in an immaculate white tent on the drill plain, back to days in which every minute of every hour was filled with scheduled duty, duty from which there could be no escape without disaster.

Spirit and defiance, the surge of hot blood, fires unquenchable by human will power, were given a brief outlet. Cadet Reno slipped away to Benny Haven's Tavern on the evening of July 3, 1854. The forbidden luxury of cheap whiskey was always available in Benny Haven's back room, and sometimes girls strayed in, perhaps a pair of floating flossies who rode the river boats or inhabited the bordellos of Albany. It was rousing to match wits with them, even if one had no money with which to engage their charms.

Tattoo sounded as he raced panting up the road. He was ten minutes late at his tent, and he was placed under arrest and confined to quarters. Extra sentry duty came with the order for his release on July 11. Once again his creditable classroom record had saved him, but he was soon to understand that he had paid a high price for those extra minutes of freedom. As he began his fourth year at West Point, Mark Reno was soberly informed that more than half the allowable number of demerits had been recorded against his name.

The handicap was too great to be overcome. He moved high in his class in cavalry tactics, but on two occasions appeared with a button undone. He received satisfactory grades in mathematics, but left lint in the bore of his rifle. He was complimented for his work in ballistics, but twice was fifteen seconds late at formations.

In March, the Academic Board recommended that Reno be dismissed for deficiency in conduct. Cutting initials in a tree, sitting down while on guard duty, leaving buttons undone, being guilty of tardiness measured in seconds and minutes that could be counted on the fingers, failing to remove lint from a rifle bore— these were the crimes which were to destroy nearly four years of study, diligence, and accomplishment. It brought no satisfaction to Cadet Reno to know that several of his classmates who had received grades above his own were to suffer the same fate for disciplinary infractions. In his misery he wanted no company.

Compassion was a pronounced quality in Secretary of War Jefferson Davis, and he could look back, if not with pride with profound understanding, to his own fourth year as a cadet. In that period he had suffered the ignominy of 137 demerits. With this memory guiding his pen, he modified the recommendations of the Advisory Board. The seven cadets would leave the Academy at once, but they would have permission to return on July 1, 1855, at which time they would be assigned to the next graduating class.

Cadets Vinton, Weitzel, Bascom, Williams, Harmon, Landis, and Reno packed their few personal belongings and went their separate ways into the civilian world. Three vanished and Mark

Reno never again heard of them, but in years to come he was to remember the other three and recall clearly the roads down which destiny had sent them. Vinton and Weitzel, like himself, would attain brevet general officer status in the Civil War, and Bascom would be killed in action in Val Verde, New Mexico, in 1862.

Dispirited and chagrined, Mark Reno went back to Carrollton in April, to live through the seemingly endless weeks of that spring and early summer. On the last day of June he was trudging once again up the road from the South Wharf, once again admiring the rugged beauty of the stark cliffs on which the forbidding stone buildings stood, once again filled with the hope and desire he had so long harbored, and which were impregnably based upon a new and indestructible determination.

Changes had taken place at the Academy during his absence. Colonel Robert E. Lee had been assigned to the Cavalry arm of the service, and had been succeeded by Captain Jonathan Gross Barnard, a Mexican War veteran who was to rise to prominence as General Grant's chief of engineers. With the advantage of repeating the fourth year courses, Cadet Reno easily maintained passable grades, and experience aided him in avoiding demerits that would make his position precarious, but the fall days of 1855 dragged on in a monotonous parade.

With the passing of the year-end holidays, during which he spent lonely hours in his quarters, he knew the relief of the start of his final term. He had no reason to fear that he would not reach the graduation days of June with a record somewhat above the average.

Then came the fateful night of January 23, 1856. He was on guard duty in the barracks, but even that boring assignment could not dampen the high spirits that surged through him. In less than five months the ordeal would end, he would wear the uniform of an officer, he would travel and command and be accorded respect. As he paced his post, he burst spontaneously into song. Suddenly, he heard a footfall behind him. The voice of First Lieutenant William H. Wood, a tactical officer, was unfriendly as he ordered Cadet Reno to stop singing on duty.

Marcus Reno had been lost in happy speculations on the fu-

28

ture, and the transition to the role of an obedient, sober, and soldierly cadet was slow in coming. The respectful reply of "Yes, sir," which Lieutenant Wood expected to hear eventually came, but it was preceded by a gay smile and an impertinent question. What regulation, Cadet Reno inquired, forbade sentries from singing on duty? He knew of none. Lieutenant Wood's explanation came in the form of an order for his immediate arrest and a recommendation that he be given a court-martial.

The trial court, presided over by Colonel Joseph Plympton, an aged veteran of both the War of 1812 and the Mexican War, convened early in February. Reno entered a plea of not guilty, and in his defense he was successful in having a charge of contemptuousness stricken from the specifications. This had the effect of reducing his misconduct to the category of disrespect for an officer, but if he had eliminated the possibility of permanent expulsion, he had not saved himself from severe punishment. On February 14 the court ordered that he be released from arrest and proceed at once to his home. On July 1, 1856, if he so desired, he would be permitted to re-enter the Academy and join the Class of 1857.

It was not a friendly Mark Reno that Carrollton knew that spring. If the pride and spirit he had previously displayed had not been killed, they were at least submerged beneath an impenetrable soberness and a cold detachment. He appeared to be totally uninterested in the social events to which he was invited, and the formal attitude he presented during his hours behind the counters of the drugstore and the desk of the Hinton House, where he earned enough to pay for his board and room in the Simpson home, aroused in those who had long known him the conviction that he had become afflicted with an excessive egotism.

The same manner, the same attitude, the same coldly sober countenance were shown as he trudged up the road from the South Wharf to begin what he had believed on two previous occasions would be his final year at West Point.

Once again he found that changes had occurred during his absence. Captain Barnard had been succeeded as superintendent by the dignified and aristocratic Major Richard Delafield. Gas lights had been installed. A bell and clock tower was being erected. Fort Clinton, a relic of the Revolution, was being restored as an historical shrine. The Rev. John W. French had become chaplain and would teach ethics.

If Cadet Reno found his studies monotonous the previous year, their repetition for the third time was almost unbearably tedious, but he was undeviating in his methodical pursuit of them. He displayed no brilliance in any subject, no unusual aptitude, and when the final examinations had been completed he stood twentieth in a class of thirty-eight graduates.

A headless drum on a pedestal in the chancel of the chapel held the diplomas. Presiding over it was Superintendent Major Delafield in full-dress uniform, with heavy bullion epaulets, his Roman nose spanned with glasses that gave him the look of a wise old eagle. Beside him stood his Adjutant, First Lieutenant James B. Fry of Carrollton, Illinois. As each graduate was called forward to receive his diploma and a stiff handshake from the resplendent superintendent, he was informed what branch of the service had been chosen for him. Marcus Alfred Reno was assigned to the cavalry.

That afternoon he started back to Carrollton to await his orders. He also had the problem of acquiring the money to pay for the uniforms he would need. Perhaps he could manage to borrow it from Uncle Alfred or Dr. Simpson.

As he stood on the open deck of the Albany steamer, he knew a slight resurgence of the spirit that had been so long subdued. He gazed up at the stark cliffs and the old buildings standing against a clear June sky, and a smile, somewhat grim in its tautness, moved his lips.

5

*O*ne day near the end of October in 1862, when Captain Reno was on a special mission in Harrisburg, he received an invitation to a dinner party at the home of Mrs. Mary Haldeman Ross. He had several friends in Harrisburg, since his first assignment after graduating from West Point in 1857 had been to the Eastern Remount Station at Carlisle Barracks, only eighteen miles from the Pennsylvania capital, but he had not, to the best of his recollection, met anyone named Ross or Haldeman.

The name of Haldeman was known to him, as, indeed, it was to anyone familiar with Harrisburg. The stately three-storied red-brick Haldeman mansion, located at 227 North Front Street, was pointed out to all visitors. The Haldemans were a family of wealth and distinction.

The financial and industrial society of Harrisburg was rigidly dominated by a small group of families. The Rosses were neither the wealthiest nor the most distinguished of this select coterie, but they had long enjoyed a secure position in it. In normal times the luxurious and exclusive houses would have been closed to a young man of Marcus Reno's background, but doors had been opened by the war, and the closer the conflict came to the valleys of southern Pennsylvania, the more Harrisburg's elite vied to entertain the ranking officers stationed in the city and at Carlisle Barracks. Ancestry and position were overlooked, and the only qualifications required for acceptance in gracious drawing rooms and at elaborate dinners were those of the common garden variety—ordinary politeness, good table manners, and normal dignity.

Mark Reno had more to offer than that. He was a graduate of

West Point, therefore presumably a gentleman. He had won brevets on the field of battle, therefore if not exactly famous he was at least a hero. Besides, he was entertaining, had a good :sense of humor, and was an excellent storyteller.

Mary Hannah Ross had her own reasons for seeing to it that Captain Reno was invited to a series of dinners and parties and for choosing him as her escort to functions in the homes of friends. Standing five feet eleven, with a strong face, broad straight shoulders, striking dark eyes, a full closely cropped mustache, and a vigorous manner, he was a handsome and most presentable companion.

No more than a few weeks had elapsed before whispers were heard that she and Reno were in love. This gossip was given substance in fact after Captain Reno paid a formal call on her mother, Mrs. Mary Haldeman Ross, and announced his intentions.

Grief and suffering had recently struck in the Ross household. Shortly after the start of the war, Mary Hannah's elder brother, Jacob, had died suddenly. This loss was followed in less than five months by the untimely death of their father from a heart attack.

Mary Haldeman Ross had determined to carry on as they had always lived—the banking and industrial shares Robert James Ross had left her made that possible—permitting neither her own sorrow nor the burdens of the tragic losses to affect adversely the lives and happiness of her children. She encouraged her daughters to give parties, perhaps not altogether unselfishly, for she found that the responsibilities social affairs entailed and the presence of gay guests, especially the officers, helped to ease the pain in her own heart.

It was difficult enough to realize that the time was not far distant when they would be gone to live lives of their own. She could be thankful that Robert was too young for military service, but Roberta was sixteen and already thought of herself as engaged to young Wilson Orth. Mary Haldeman Ross admired Marcus Reno, and considered him fully acceptable as a son-in-law. She made only a single request of Mary Hannah. She asked her to wait until the war had ended to marry. The promise was given.

For a young officer, Captain Reno had seen an extraordinary amount of action and had been trusted with uncommon responsibilities. The Rosses and their friends soon came to look upon him as an authority on the past and present conduct of the war, and they pressed him for opinions and advice. This was not altogether a hardship on him. He was not averse, especially in the presence of Mary Hannah, to telling about his experiences and expounding his views.

Recalled from the northwestern frontier at the start of the war, he had been sent in command of a cavalry company to bolster the defenses of a panicky Washington. He remarked with wry sarcasm that at first glance the capital seemed hardly worth saving from the Confederates. Hundreds of shacks had been erected to house the wartime population. The uncompleted dome of the Capitol Building stood against the sky at the head of Pennsylvania Avenue in a maze of scaffolding. Chuckholes, hub-deep mud, garbage and refuse made passage along the streets precarious and unpleasant. Out of debris which littered the Mall the unfinished Washington Monument rose in an ugly stub. When the wind came from the south and west, as it did much of the time, it spread the sickening stench of the Potomac sewage marshes over the city and the surrounding countryside.

War had come swiftly to Washington, with threats of Confederate raids and streams of sick, wounded, and dying Union soldiers returning from the battlefields. Twenty large hospitals were soon filled beyond capacity, and long rows of cots, between which there was hardly room for the weary nurses and exhausted doctors to pass, lined the corridors of the public buildings. Even so there were not enough facilities, and convalescent camps had been established in outlying areas. Thousands of casualties had shivered through the first winter in canvas shelters, without adequate food or blankets.

General George B. McClellan, Little Mac the Perfectionist, had driven fear from the city, and he had made an army out of an ill-organized mass of men, men demoralized by defeat and ready to run at the first shot. He weeded out many of the incompetent officers, replacing them with regulars with field experience, trained men who had been baptized by fire in the war with Mexico and on the western frontier. He held the respect of rank and file alike, and he inspired new courage in all.

Forts soon surrounded Washington, and confidence that the city would be saved returned; if Little Mac had his way, there would be no more Bull Runs, no more untrained youths thrown into battle to die to appease men like Horace Greeley. The cry of "On to Richmond" was now seldom heard. A well-trained, disciplined Army of the Potomac would move when it was ready. While Little Mac's men loved him, the politicians he did not hesitate to criticize despised him. They needed a victory, and they ranted at his caution, his thoroughness, and they forced him to move his army into Virginia against his better judgment.

In Washington, Reno was assigned to command Company H of the 1st Cavalry, hardly more than a mob of raw recruits. He had difficulty obtaining the bare necessities for his men, and there were insufficient horses, but he trained them on the mounts available, and he trained them on foot. He made cavalrymen of them, and on the thirtieth of March, 1862, he led them, not without pride, across the Potomac to Alexandria to join the Army of the Potomac. Three days later they boarded small schooners and sailed for Old Point Comfort and Fortress Monroe. They reached there April 4. On the sixth, Company H moved to Kentucky Farm, where there were sufficient grazing pastures.

Richmond was both the symbol and the keystone of the Confederacy, and it was generally believed by northern strategists that if it fell the rebellion would end. President Lincoln and Secretary Stanton argued for a direct land assault, but McClellan contended it should be made by a water approach on a route down the Potomac, through Chesapeake Bay to the peninsula between the James and York rivers. The President and Stanton reluctantly gave their consent to McClellan's plan.

McClellan had started his Peninsula advance on the day Reno reached Old Point Comfort. On April 11 all eight companies of the 1st Cavalry moved to Chessman's Creek, in the vicinity of

Yorktown, where they joined the main Army of the Potomac.

Faulty intelligence was an ever-present weakness of the Peninsular Campaign. The professional sleuth, Allan Pinkerton, had been assigned to the Army by Stanton. He continually overestimated the strength of the enemy, and fed this misinformation to McClellan. The general's maps were equally inaccurate, failing to show, for example, the true course of the Warwick River or that it was a formidable obstacle.

McClellan had expected to find defenses around Yorktown, but he did not expect that his troops would be stopped by fortifications that extended completely across the Peninsula. This line of defense was thinly held by General John Bankhead McGruder, who made up for his military deficiencies by being an accomplished actor. Constantly shifting his troops and moving units across the front, he was able to convince Pinkerton, and thereby McClellan, that his force was much greater than its actual strength.

McClellan decided to bring up big guns and lay siege to Yorktown. This move not only resulted in surrendering the initiative to the enemy, but the loss of a month's time. The interim was well utilized by the Confederates, who brought General Johnson's troops to the Peninsula and strengthened the defenses of Richmond.

In a siege there is little for cavalry to do, and Reno saw little action until the night of May 3. Then Johnson, using General J. E. B. Stuart's cavalry to cover his rear, began a withdrawal toward Richmond. The evacuation was quickly discovered by Professor T. S. C. Lowe from an observation balloon in which he and the Union General, Samuel Peter Heintzelman, had ascended to observe the enemy.

The following morning Union troops, including Company H of the 1st Cavalry, under command of General Edwin Vose Sumner, were sent in pursuit of the retreating Confederates. In deep mud and driving rain, they soon made contact, and forced Stuart's contingents toward Williamsburg. There the Confederates, now commanded by General James "Pete" Longstreet, took positions in strong entrenchment which had been prepared previously by McGruder. On May 5 Union forces, by seizing and holding several redoubts on the Confederate left flank, endangered Longstreet's line of retreat, and he was forced to withdraw up the Peninsula.

Reno and H Company arrived before Williamsburg May 5, remaining there until the eleventh, when the march started toward Richmond. Reaching West Point on the twelfth, they were at New Kent Courthouse on the thirteenth. From St. Peter's Church they continued their northern movement, reaching Tunstall's Station, seven miles from Richmond, on the twenty-third. When the month ended, they were encamped in Walnut Grove.

McClellan's move up the Peninsula had been agonizingly slow. Still believing Pinkerton's faulty intelligence, he now rested before Richmond. Lincoln had promised him General Irvin McDowell's forty thousand men, who would proceed to join him over a land route from Washington. Thus McClellan took his time. The battle of Fair Oaks had been fought to an inconclusive end before McClellan learned that McDowell's I Corps was not coming. Major General Thomas J. "Stonewall" Jackson had so alarmed Mr. Lincoln and Secretary Stanton by his Virginia campaign that they refused to weaken the troops guarding Washington.

At Mechanicsville June 26, along the banks of Powhite Creek, Reno and his men had their first real baptism of fire. He had been given the routine duty of protecting divisional artillery. Rebels made a deep penetration of Federal lines, and Company H fought as infantry until they had driven back the attackers and re-established the front.

On the next day, at Gaines Mill, Reno and Company H had a full opportunity to display their mettle. All day they had been part of the cavalry reserve under Colonel William N. Grier. Steadily the Confederates had pressed forward. By late afternoon the steady crack of small firearms, the din of heavy artillery, and cries of the wounded became too much for General Fitz-John Porter's infantry. They broke and began withdrawing. A counterattack failed with heavy losses, and the Union troops were ordered to fall back and occupy a point six hundred yards to the rear of their former position.

A small group of infantry had rallied at the bottom of a hill, and while engaged in holding the Confederates in check became trapped. Reno and his company were ordered to their support. He was successful in covering the surrounded infantrymen until they had withdrawn across a small creek and reached the safety of the main army.

Of the 125 men Reno had led to the rescue, one officer and twenty-three men had been killed. Reno was personally mentioned in Colonel Grier's report for "prompt and cheerful assistance given in the field." Grier also mentioned the "coolness and steadiness of the officers and men" of Company H, "under a heavy enemy fire."

Only two of McClellan's corps had thus far been engaged, and both had done extremely well. Yet, inexplicably, he ordered a withdrawal to the James River.

The retreat continued to Harrison's Landing on the James. It afforded ample space for the entire Army of the Potomac. Supplies were brought up the James. Most of the contingents took advantage of the opportunity to rest and re-equip, but not the cavalry.

On July 3 Reno was sent with a detachment toward the Charles City Road to locate enemy guns. He found them, and drove back the Rebel force that was manning them.

A few days later, Mr. Lincoln journeyed down to the James "to see for himself." McClellan told the President that with additional forces he could take Richmond. Lincoln made no promises, and went back to Washington. Obviously, as later events demonstrated, he had not liked everything he had seen.

Richmond did not fall. McClellan was damned by the politicians and armchair strategists in Washington. In the crowded bar of Willard's Hotel, Senator Zachariah Chandler of Michigan shouted out for all to hear that McClellan was a coward. The accusation was more than an outburst by a drunken politician. It suggested the attitude of the Administration, for Chandler was the "Mr. Republican" of his day.

Upon returning to Washington, President Lincoln made the incredible mistake of appointing Major General Henry W. Halleck commander in chief and McClellan's superior. Popeyed, flabby, seedy and crafty, Halleck was one of the most disliked men in Washington. Secretary of the Navy Gideon Welles said of him: "He has suggested nothing, decided nothing, done nothing, but scold and smoke and scratch his elbows."

Halleck ordered McClellan's Army of the Potomac to move north to Aquia Creek, Virginia, not far south of Washington. Once more Reno loaded his men and horses on schooners and sailed back to Alexandria. He did not arrive in time to take part in the Second Battle of Bull Run, but was assigned to the defenses of the national capital.

The terrible defeat of the Union forces at Second Bull Run brought a new threat to Washington. There was still an Army of the Potomac, but it was once again disorganized and part of it actually existed only on paper.

It was fully expected by the Administration that Lee, with Richmond no longer menaced and a great victory at Bull Run behind him, would carry his assault to Pennsylvania Avenue. The morale of the North was at its lowest ebb.

Lincoln defied his advisers and reached the conclusion that only one man, after all, could achieve the Union triumph so badly needed, and that man was General McClellan—Little Mac.

Little Mac was eating his breakfast when a servant announced that the President of the United States was at the door. Before nightfall the word had spread throughout the Union forces that McClellan was once more in command, and soldiers and officers cheered themselves hoarse. Swiftly the Army of the Potomac became a formidable fighting force. By September 13 the Antietam Campaign was under way.

Captain Reno rode out of Washington at the head of four veteran companies of the 1st Cavalry. He drove into Maryland, seeking the enemy. At Crampton's Gap he joined General William Buell Crampton's corps and aided in sending Confederates under General Lafayette McLaws into retreat.

Next he was sent as a part of General Alfred Pleasanton's

Union cavalry to scout the right flank of the Union forces. On September 16 it was learned that General Jeb Stuart's cavalry was guarding the left, or northern, flank of the Confederates under Longstreet, along a little stream called Antietam.

The Battle of Antietam began at dawn on September 17. The savage charges and counterattacks over the scarred cornfields, the desperate struggle at the Dunkard Church, the carnage at Bloody Lane, and the vicious fighting for the Stone Bridge combined to make the day the bloodiest of the war. At night two exhausted armies faced each other, but Lee had been stopped.

The Union cavalry had moved southward early in the day and first struck the enemy at Middle Bridge. Captain Marcus Reno led his men in a crossing under heavy fire, and at noon had established a position on the Sharpsburg Road. Scouts detected a weakness in the Confederate line before Sharpsburg, and Pleasanton urged an attack, but McClellan declined to exploit the opportunity.

The terrible carnage at Bloody Lane left the Union forces in control. A vigorous general attack along the line might have brought an overwhelming Federal victory. It did not come.

McClellan was not a leader with imagination. Early in the Antietam Campaign he had again demonstrated his inherent overcautiousness, and he had allowed the badly dispersed Confederates to unite. The Union soldiers had fought well, the cavalry and artillery had been superb, but McClellan had elected to fight the battle in stages. For example, on the final day, instead of being permitted to smash through the demoralized Confederates at Sharpsburg, Reno and his cavalry companies, as well as Sykes' infantry, had been held east of the town on the turnpike.

Still, the Union had gained a partial victory, largely because of its superior forces. Through September 18, Lee remained in his precarious position, gaining a moral victory out of a lost battle. All through the eighteenth the shattered gray defenders waited for waves of blue to move toward them. McClellan didn't advance. During the night Lee made a skillful escape, crossing the Potomac at Boteler's Ford, and the battle was over.

It was not the great Union victory Lincoln had wanted, but it served to bring new hope to the North. Lee had been stopped. The Emancipation Proclamation could be issued.

McClellan sat north of the Potomac feuding with Halleck by telegraph, but it was a time of action for the cavalry. Captain Reno and his companies were part of the cavalry under Pleasanton sent to harass the retreating Lee. The irrepressible Stuart led his men on a daring ride completely around McClellan's army, and Reno made a forced seventy-five-mile ride in an attempt to cut him off.

For several weeks there were running fights through the hills of northern Virginia, Reno several times emerging the winner of sharp clashes. He smashed into Charles Town, driving the Confederates out and holding an important salient. He demonstrated his ability as a strategist and showed initiative and courage in his raids that brought mention of him in dispatches to Washington.

By October, 1862, the horses of the cavalry attached to the Army of the Potomac were nearing exhaustion. Many of them could no longer hold up under the punishment of long and swift dashes. Many had sore mouths, and troopers were refusing to torture them. McClellan sent an urgent request to Halleck for remounts.

In reply he received an ill-tempered telegram from the White House. President Lincoln wanted to know what McClellan's horses had done since Antietam that had so fatigued them. Every effort to get McClellan to cross the Potomac and engage the enemy had failed. Little Mac courteously protested the reflection on his troopers, and respectfully informed the President that his cavalry had been picketing 150 miles of the Potomac River against Confederate raiders. The request to purchase two thousand remounts was approved, and on October 20 Captain Reno was sent to Pennsylvania with an order to obtain them.

Before the Ross fireplace in Harrisburg, Mark Reno could hold the rapt attention of Mary Hannah, her mother, and their many guests with accounts of his experiences. With becoming modesty he mentioned that his commander, General Pleasanton, had told headquarters that the portion of the 1st Cavalry "did good service under Captain Marcus A. Reno." Nor did he overlook the opportunity to disclose that he had been cited by General Hancock, with five other officers, as "deserving of special mention" for his fighting in northern Virginia.

The war was close to the people of Harrisburg. Its grimness and terror were well understood by persons who gathered at the Ross home. Reno was only one of numerous officers stationed in or near the city who had faced death in battle, but there were few, if any, who had been for more than three years in the wilderness of the far Northwest, few who could talk knowledgeably about such places as Walla Walla, Owyhee, Umatilla, Klickitat, Yakima, or about Indian chiefs called Yellow Hawk and Howitchwampum.

Fort Walla Walla had been established only two years before Reno arrived there. It was his first view of a true frontier post. A collection of rough log buildings grouped about an open area, called a parade ground, the whole suggested a bleak existence.

Only a handful of troops comprised the garrison, and Reno learned the reason for the paucity of men when he reported to his commanding officer, Major Edward Jenner Steptoe. The previous May, Steptoe had set out with a detachment of 150 men to punish Indians who had killed two white settlers at Fort Colvile. Near Ingossoman Creek the troopers had been ambushed by a force of some twelve hundred Indians. Steptoe had been able to hold out until nightfall. Then, by abandoning some of his wounded and traveling ninety miles, he had reached friendly Nez Percé Indians. In the ambush twenty-one troopers had been killed.

Steptoe was bitter, telling Reno: Those chair-borne soldiers back at the Department of Columbia sitting on their backsides in plush headquarters just don't know what we in the field are confronted with. In retaliation they sent Lt. Col. George Wright with about five hundred men, two six-pounders, two howitzers, two pack trains with thirty days' rations and more ammunition than you ever saw. Then Wright took two hundred and fifty of my men, almost all I had on the post, and set off. Hell, with all that, anyone could lick Indians. What really burns me is that they are calling it the "Steptoe massacre." It was not a massacre —just an engagement in which I was outnumbered and successfully withdrew.

A few days after Reno's arrival word was received that Wright had been victorious in several encounters with Indians, and had won their complete surrender at Coeur d'Alene on September 15, 1858.

Reno was delighted to find that his West Point classmate, Second Lieutenant Robert Anderson, was post adjutant at Walla Walla. Anderson told Reno: "You're lucky. You're assigned to Company E, and Lieutenant Sweitzer, its CO, has been on sick leave. So you will command your own company on your first assignment. Not many in the class will do that."

On October 5 the victorious Wright expedition returned to Walla Walla, and Reno took over command of Company E. Without a commanding officer for two years, and newly returned from the field, the outfit was in poor condition. Delighted with the challenge, Reno soon had it organized and functioning with efficiency.

In November word was received at Fort Walla Walla that two white men had trespassed on lands of friendly Indians under Chiefs Yellow Hawk and Howitchwampum. Reno was ordered by Major Enoch Steen, the post commander, to take four troopers, go to Yellow Hawk's camp and arrest the white men and bring them to the post. The mission was carried out without difficulty, and the two trespassers were escorted out of the country.

On April 4, 1859, Reno was named post adjutant to succeed his friend Anderson. A staff job had no appeal for him. Plans were being made at the time to send out an expedition to protect emigrants who were flooding over the mountains from the East, and Reno applied for permission to accompany it. He was named acting assistant quartermaster for the Wagon Road Expedition.

Setting out on May 19, under command of Captain Henry D. Wallen, it consisted of eighty-five dragoons, Company H of the 4th Infantry, and a detachment of engineers. Few Indians were encountered during that summer, and there was no fighting. All told, the expedition marched more than nineteen hundred miles, reaching as far east as Fort Boise (near the city of the present name in Idaho). Reno returned with the last of his contingent to Fort Walla Walla in November.

The winter of 1860 was quiet. Lieutenant Sweitzer returned from sick leave and resumed command of Company E. Reno became his executive officer. In April, 1861, Sweitzer left for duty with the mounted recruiting service, and on May 1 Reno became commander of the company.

The summer of 1861 was spent in protecting emigrant trains, and Reno was attached to patrols along the roads crossing the mountains. In September he was ordered to the Nez Percé Indian reservation to take command of Company C of the 1st Dragoons. He returned to Fort Walla Walla in November, remaining there until February, 1861.

At that time word was received that white settlers had been murdered by Indians on Umatilla, Willow and Bitter creeks. Two forces were immediately dispatched, one to the Umatilla, and the other, under Reno, to cut off hostiles attempting to escape up the Columbia River.

Reno succeeded in capturing two Indians who were known to have participated in the killing of white settlers. He hanged them.

A month later Reno was back at Fort Walla Walla, and was granted his first leave since arriving in the Northwest. He went to San Francisco, and returned to duty in late May. Several officers, including his classmate Anderson and Colonel Steptoe, had resigned and had departed to fight for the Confederacy. In April Reno was promoted to first lieutenant. Once again the summer was spent in patrolling the emigrant roads.

The orders long expected came on October 9, 1861. Reno was ordered to leave Fort Vancouver on November 16 with his C Company for Fort Sprague, one of the hastily established training grounds at Washington, D.C.

He arrived in January, 1862, to begin his duty in the Civil War. At Camp Sprague he was elated to learn that even before he had left Fort Vancouver he had been promoted to the rank of captain. He was twenty-eight years of age, and he had achieved a rank which many officers of the pre-Civil War Army did not reach in a lifetime of service.

They could not have imagined at those pleasant Harrisburg soirées Mark Reno as he had been in his last year at West Point. He was friendly, quick to laugh and smile. If he appeared exceedingly mature for a young man of twenty-nine, it was the war, the closeness to suffering and terror and death he had known, that had made him sober and reflective. He was no longer a young man who walked alone, who shunned company, whose spirit was on the verge of despair.

Yet he displayed an air of detachment that discouraged familiarity and caused those who met him not to presume upon him in any manner. This was not because of bitterness he held, nor was it coldness. It was because he was prepared to stand alone if need be, because of his inherent courage and determination—the qualities that had taken him back to West Point to face for the third time the rigid discipline and hard work of the fourth-year class.

Mary Hannah, more than anyone else, understood these things, for she demanded to know every detail of his life, demanded the right to look into his thoughts and his heart, and questioned endlessly the man she loved and with whom she expected to spend her life.

Mark Reno's humor was at its best when he talked of his experiences as a young officer facing his first assignment. Upon leaving West Point he had requested to be attached to the 2nd Dragoons, not because it was considered one of the finest regiments, but because it was the wildest, most reckless outfit of hard drinkers in the Army. It was scattered all through the Southwest, and its units were almost constantly in combat with Indians.

"The request was ignored," he said. "Undoubtedly I wasn't hard enough, although I certainly could have qualified as a drinker. I was assigned instead to the staid old First Dragoons." He shook his head, as if the memory still filled him with sadness.

"The First Dragoons, a regiment of gentlemen. Well, I did the best I could to make them think I was one."

Upon receiving his initial orders as a second lieutenant, he had written the Adjutant General that he couldn't report to the commanding officer of the 1st Dragoons because he had no idea where the regiment was stationed. That was not surprising. It was stationed at a place called Fort Walla Walla. If it had been in China, it would not have been as difficult to reach.

Actually, he was filled with pride to be a member of the 1st. Its record as a fighting unit was incomparable, and its roster contained many of the most illustrious names in military history—such as Stephen W. Kearny, Henry Dodge, Jefferson Davis.

Mary Hannah was moved to the verge of tears when she learned that before leaving for Walla Walla he had been stationed a short time at Carlisle Barracks, so near to her, and she had not been aware of it.

6

*O*n the night of March 16, 1863, General William Woods Averell led 2,100 men, among them Captain Reno's 1st Cavalry companies, toward Kelly's Ford on the Rappahannock River. They reached the crossing at dawn. A company of Confederates guarding it was driven back after a sharp exchange of fire, and Averell pushed on half a mile to a wooded area. He carried orders to meet and destroy the Confederate raiders led by the bold and aggressive General Fitzhugh Lee, and he had expected to meet them near Culpepper Courthouse. Instead, he found them advancing toward the woods in which he had stopped to rest.

Averell deployed his men along a stone fence and met the oncoming Rebels with a strong fire. They were stopped. Averell at once made two charges. Lee's men broke and began a disorganized withdrawal, closely pressed by the 1st Cavalry.

As Captain Reno rode at the head of his men, his horse was shot, and in the sudden fall Reno was pinned beneath it. He knew at once that he was badly injured. Slowly and in extreme pain, he managed to extricate himself, and it was with great difficulty that he mounted another horse which a trooper brought to him. Stoically enduring the punishing agony of his injury, Reno continued to ride with his men.

Although they had been victorious in driving the Confederates from the field, Averell's force had suffered severe casualties, and he withdrew across the Rappahannock to the protection of Federal lines, with Reno's troops covering the orderly retreat. In reporting to his commander, General Joseph Hooker, more commonly known to the men of the Army of the Potomac as "Fighting Joe," Averell cited Captain Reno for gallantry in action and recommended the awarding of the brevet rank of major.

The report which Captain Reno received in a hospital tent was less pleasant to contemplate. He had suffered a serious hernia that would incapacitate him for some weeks. Treatment was not possible in the field, and he would have to be sent north to obtain it and to recuperate. A surgeon suggested Baltimore, but Captain Reno quickly assured him that he was well acquainted with a physician in Harrisburg who specialized in abdominal injuries, and that facilities for his convalescence would be readily available to him there.

He did not add that the facilities were in the home of a young lady named Mary Hannah Ross. A week later, after a slow and painful journey by ambulance and jolting railroad cars, he was comfortably ensconced in a large bed in a pleasant room overlooking the Susquehanna River. Women fluttered about bringing him broth and tea and little cakes, and the Ross family's physician was in daily attendance.

A sense of honor, if not almost complete recovery, soon forced him to abandon the role of an invalid. With no little regret he announced his intention to return to duty, but the attentive Dr.

46

J. W. Wilson discovered that an abscess had formed in his groin. A report of this new affliction brought a fortnight's extension of leave.

When the respite neared an end, Dr. Wilson found new reasons to oppose his patient's departure, and forthwith he sent a letter to the Adjutant General of the United States in which he certified that Captain Marcus A. Reno would be unfit for vigorous cavalry duty for a period of two to three months. Captain Reno appended a missive of his own to the medical certificate. It requested that he be assigned to recruiting duty in Harrisburg, pending the improvement in his physical condition which would permit him to return to the 1st Cavalry without danger to his good health. Somewhat enthusiastically he pointed out to the Adjutant General that the first enlistment of many Union soldiers would soon terminate and that he believed he could induce a good number of them to re-enlist. While convalescing he could be of useful service in this respect. It was perhaps incidental that with such an assignment he could also draw commutation.

The Adjutant General agreed, but accord was not among the vicissitudes of war decreed by the hand of Fate.

Up the Shenandoah Valley came the Army of Northern Virginia, the benign and gentlemanly Robert E. Lee leading it on to its manifest destiny of glory and death. Intelligence and rumor, equally without foundation, had it that Lee had set his sights on the Pennsylvania capital. Overnight Harrisburg was thrown into a frenzy, and the situation was hardly less confusing at headquarters of the Department of the Susquehanna.

General Darius Couch was frantically attempting to erect adequate fortifications. General William Farrar Smith, more familiarly known as "Baldy," was trying with equal desperation to fashion battle-ready troops out of rag, tag, and bobtail contingents of untrained New York Guardsmen and Pennsylvania Militia suddenly thrown at him by frightened strategists in Washington. He was unabashedly delighted to see Captain Marcus Reno appear without warning and offer his services in the crisis. Competent and experienced young officers were what he needed most, and he was well aware of Marcus Reno's military record and competence. He had taught Cadet Reno mathematics at West Point, and they had seen action together in the Peninsular Campaign. Without hesitation he appointed Captain Reno his chief of staff.

North and east of Harrisburg the roads were crowded with fleeing civilians and herds of cattle, sheep, and horses being driven over the mountains beyond the reach of the invaders by southern Pennsylvania farmers. Captain Reno advised Mary Hannah and her mother to take a train to either Pittsburgh or Philadelphia, but they refused to leave. He insisted that their household and personal valuables be buried behind the house. If Mrs. Ross felt the precaution extreme, she was more convinced of its soundness when she saw her neighbor, William Bigler, former governor and United States Senator and then President of the Philadelphia and Erie Railroad, in his shirt sleeves digging a similar pit in his garden.

Robert E. Lee was not interested in sacking Harrisburg. He sent General Richard S. Ewell with the 17th Virginia Cavalry toward the capital, and dispatched other raiding contingents through the area, but he was looking for bigger game. He continued on toward a little crossroads village, where, his intelligence reports informed him, Union forces were concentrating. The name of the village was Gettysburg.

It was on the first of July, 1863, that Jeb Stuart, with 3,300 troopers, swept up to Carlisle and ordered the town to surrender. Baldy Smith, with Captain Marcus Reno beside him, and surrounded by a frightened mob of recruits, curtly refused. Stuart sent a second flag of truce forward. Again the answer was an unequivocal *"No."* Stuart opened fire with seven artillery pieces.

Carlisle was fiercely ablaze when Stuart received orders to leave it and join the main army of General Lee. Lee had been badly in need of Jeb Stuart's cavalry at Gettysburg, and the defiance Stuart had met at Carlisle from Reno and Baldy Smith had been costly to the Confederates. In fact, some Civil War historians contend that Jeb Stuart's absence represented the difference between victory and defeat for the Union forces at Gettysburg.

Baldy Smith and Marcus Reno, following instructions received

48

soon after their courageous stand at Carlisle, set out with six thousand men to strike at Lee's flank. They moved toward Cashtown, and for the next ten days wandered, much of the time aimlessly, about the Pennsylvania countryside. Order after order from higher headquarters, each one contradicting its predecessor, kept them in confusion. Many of their men were without shoes, many had no blankets, and none had adequate food. Contacts with retreating Confederate troops were frequently made, but pursuit in most cases had to be abandoned because ammunition supplies failed to arrive.

Orders from Washington deprived Baldy Smith of the services of his chief of staff. Captain Reno was directed to return to his recruiting assignment and, in addition, to assume the duties of inspector of horses purchased in the Pennsylvania area.

He returned to Harrisburg to find that Mary Hannah also had plans for his immediate future. She had persuaded her mother to relieve her of the promise not to marry until the war had ended. Preparations had been made for a quiet and unostentatious wedding.

A leave was not obtainable, but Captain Reno found it necessary to make a trip to inspect horses in eastern Pennsylvania. He and Mary Hannah left immediately after the ceremony on a crowded, dirty troop train. At the end of a wedding trip of three days in Philadelphia, Captain Reno did take time to inspect some horses, and they returned to Harrisburg. Mary Haldeman Ross was delighted to have them make their home with her, and set aside a suite for them. They had hardly time to arrange the rooms to their liking and to feel settled before the letter Mary Hannah had prayed would never come arrived.

On October 8, 1863, Captain Reno once more took over command of Company H of the 1st Cavalry at Elk Run, Virginia.

Throughout the fall and into the winter the Army of the Potomac and the Army of Northern Virginia reeled and maneuvered like weary, punch-drunk fighters. Meade forced the passage of the Rappahannock, and Lee established a strong entrenched position at the Rapidan. If the Confederates were on the defensive, they were far from being decisively beaten. The war had become a supreme test of endurance.

For weeks in dismal wetness and icy cold, Captain Reno and his company had been on scouting patrols and picket duty without sight of the enemy. He was much of the time in acute pain from sciatica and lumbago. On December 24, 1863, he was sent to Washington for a medical examination. An Army surgeon, Dr. Basil Morris, pronounced him unfit for duty. Once again he was able to secure permission to take treatment and recuperate at Harrisburg. He arrived there three days after Christmas. Dr. Wilson was quickly on hand, and he found the captain's sciatic nerve badly inflamed. Back and abdominal muscles had been severely strained. Pounding from the saddle, long hours in dampness and cold, exposure to rains, improper rest, and an inadequate diet had left their marks. Dr. Wilson superintended the arranging of a bed in a manner that would relieve tension and support the tortured tissues. Weeks of rest would be necessary.

It was late in February, 1864, when the Cavalry Bureau at Washington inquired if Captain Reno would be available for a mission to purchase horses in New York State. Dr. Wilson gave his consent. Mary Hannah was in the sixth month of pregnancy, and Reno expressed concern about leaving her. The doctor ordered him to take her with him. They left for Elmira, New York, early in March. It was their first trip together since their brief honeymoon in Philadelphia.

Dr. Wilson's ministrations and medication had done their work. When, with the completion of his mission in New York State, Reno received orders to report immediately to his regiment, he left Harrisburg at once. He had hoped that he might be with Mary Hannah when their child was born, but that event was not scheduled until late in May or early June.

7

A plain man who often went about camp in rather baggy trousers, a short blue coat, and a slouch hat had come out of the West. He talked as much as he thought a situation demanded, but he was never chatty, except when he was among intimates. Persons who thought that a great man, a military genius, should look something like one were disappointed when they first saw him, but the fallacy of this notion soon became apparent to them. Somehow, whenever he appeared on the scene, things began to happen. He improved discipline with no more than a grunt and a stern glance. Spirit was born anew whenever he went among his men; plans came to life, all things seemed suddenly to have been given meaning and reality. Moreover, there was motion, action, and accomplishment. His name was Ulysses S. Grant.

General Alfred Archimedes Torbert, veteran of the Peninsular Campaign and Antietam, where he had been severely wounded, had been given command of the 1st Division of the Cavalry Corps. When he had discovered that Captain Reno was off somewhere buying horses, he had made a request for him. He wanted Captain Reno because he knew his caliber and his ability. Regular officers of Reno's competence and experience were at a premium. Major General Philip H. Sheridan approved Torbert's request.

In the warm sunny days of spring, Grant's great efficient machine moved south through the hills of Virginia. The Rapidan was crossed May 3, and near Chancellorsville the advance through the Wilderness was begun. Lee attacked and Grant was unable to defeat him, but maintained his ground, and Union columns rolled on toward Spotsylvania Courthouse.

General Torbert's troopers met the Confederates along the Mattaponi, drove against entrenched infantry at Milford Station, and gained a bridgehead across the stream. Lee moved back to the North Anna River, and Grant's men reached him there, but the fighting was inconclusive, and at the end of three days Grant pulled out, moving across the Pamunkey River at Hanover Town. Lee established a strong position behind Totopotomoy Creek, covering all the approaches to Richmond from the Pamunkey River crossings.

The cavalry of Hampton met Torbert's 1st Division at Haw's Shop. Captain Reno was at the head of the Union charge. For the second time, his horse was shot from under him, but he managed to jump clear of the falling animal and was not injured.

Cold Harbor began as a cavalry engagement. The divisions of General David M. Gregg and Torbert took the little town. Then the two great armies collided. Torbert received orders to hold the village at all costs. The troopers worked through the night building fortifications, knowing the onslaught they would be obliged to meet with the coming of daylight.

They were right in their estimation of Lee's intentions. Having received heavy reinforcements, Lee planned to recover the initiative. He sent a strong force to retake Cold Harbor, preparatory to a general Confederate attack to roll up Grant's left flank.

In the early morning the Confederate armies of Generals Richard Anderson and Robert F. Hoke bore down on the cavalry divisions of Torbert and Gregg. The troopers stood before the onslaught in their makeshift defenses. Although greatly outnumbered, they had the advantage of breech-loading and repeating carbines, fire superiority over the infantry muskets of the attackers.

Hoke's men, having suffered heavy pummeling only the previous day, displayed little ferocity, but they pushed ahead with slow determination. Anderson's leading brigade wavered before the cavalry fire, then suddenly broke to the rear.

Meanwhile, a fortnight had passed since the time for the birth of Reno's child, and he was tortured by anxiety. He had been named inspector general of the 1st Cavalry Division, and in that administrative post he received both dispatches and mail with a minimum of delay; but when he still heard no word from Harrisburg, his advantageous position only served to increase his concern for Mary Hannah. He was thankful when his division was ordered to rest and reorganize near Bottoms Bridge on the Chickahominy River. Perhaps while they licked their wounds a letter would catch up with him.

The 1st Division was riding toward Charlottesville when the long-awaited letter arrived. Mary Hannah had been successfully delivered of a son, who had been christened Robert Ross Reno. The relieved father scarcely had time to give a cheer before a clash had begun with Confederate cavalry in a heavily wooded area.

A young brigadier general named George Armstrong Custer swept into the thick of the fight with his division. He drove between two Confederate cavalry columns, quickly capturing eight hundred horses of an enemy supply train. Recovering swiftly, the Confederates soon recaptured their mounts and wagons, and took several hundred Union prisoners. The "boy general" managed to hold Trevilian Station, and his daring maneuver had disrupted the Rebels, but neither side could claim a victory in the day's fighting.

Sheridan led his badly bruised and wearied troopers to rest quarters at Lighthouse Point. There they received fifteen hundred sorely needed remounts. Before July had ended they were back on the pikes to Petersburg and Richmond. The 1st Cavalry Division drove along the Darbytown Road. Cavalry were of little use in the siege of Petersburg, but Grant had new plans for them. He gave Sheridan command of the Army of the Shenandoah. Torbert became commander of the Cavalry Corps, and at once named Captain Reno his chief of staff.

The Shenandoah Valley, varying in width from ten to fifty miles between the Allegheny and Blue Ridge Mountains, stretching from the Potomac to below Lexington, had been since the start of the war of immense strategic and logistic importance to the Confederacy. Grant understood that he must drive the enemy from it, and he gave Sheridan the job.

Early in August at Harpers Ferry, Phil Sheridan looked over the army he had assembled. In it were the VII Corps, a division of the XIX Corps, two divisions from West Virginia, and the 1st and 2nd Cavalry Divisions. A third division of cavalry, assigned to him, had not yet arrived. Altogether Sheridan could count 26,000 men, not a very large force for the Herculean task facing him. He dismissed that concern, for his orders were clear and they called for action. He began an advance toward Strasburg. A message came from Grant that the Confederate general, Jubal A. Early, then in the valley, was being reinforced from Petersburg. Grant estimated that Early would soon have forty thousand men.

Marcus Reno had not yet celebrated his thirtieth birthday when he became General Torbert's chief of staff. The post, in addition to the administrative and technical burdens it brought to him, placed him in a position to exercise considerable authority over various division and brigade commanders. It also made him a target for the criticisms of men who, even though they wore the insignia of higher rank, were obliged to carry out his orders.

Borne on the winds of jealousy and resentment, the criticisms came, but Captain Reno justified the faith General Torbert held in him. He avoided controversies that would have been injurious to the efficiency and progress of the campaign, but he had no means of halting rumors that were without a shred of foundation. One of them which was frequently heard was that he had had a serious clash with George A. Custer, who had been made a brigadier general, and that violence had been narrowly averted. The story was completely false. Reno and Custer had no trouble, but on the contrary remained on good terms. In reality, the fabrication was perpetrated not so much by enemies of Captain Reno as by officers who hated Custer.

Custer, with his high political connections, had risen in meteoric fashion in the cavalry, while most of his colleagues of the same age, training, and length of service continued to wear the insignia which had adorned their shoulder straps at the start of the war. In their zeal to injure and malign the "boy general," Custer's enemies made Captain Reno an innocent victim of their envy and malice.

Offensive and counteroffensive scarred the valley of the Shenandoah. Winchester, Cedarville, Halltown, Williamsport, Leestown and Kearneyville were blackened by fire, torn with the destruction of the guns. Cemeteries charted the flow and ebb of the blue and gray waves. The leaves were turning, as if reflecting the color of the blood on the fields, when the wearied and torn forces met at Opequon Creek and Fishers Hill. Jubal Early was broken.

Methodically Phil Sheridan began his destruction. Crops, orchards, granaries, mills were laid waste. Cattle, sheep, and swine were shot. Those which could be eaten were butchered, and the others were left to rot where they had fallen. Only the homes and the persons of helpless civilians were spared. From Staunton to Winchester the valley of the Shenandoah was a scene of desolation and devastation. The bread basket of the Confederacy had been destroyed beyond possible recovery, and Sheridan could rejoin Grant at Petersburg.

Although he had been a staff officer burdened with heavy administrative responsibilities, and might have remained at cavalry headquarters in the rear, Captain Reno had taken every opportunity to ride at the head of the troops.

He exposed himself recklessly to enemy fire, led charges against Rebel detachments holding strong positions in woodlands, and relentlessly pursued Confederate troops until they were either killed in close fighting or had become so badly disorganized that they were ineffectual and no longer to be feared. For his gallantry he was cited and awarded the rank of bevet lieutenant colonel.

The last weeks of the Shenandoah Campaign had inflicted heavy casualties on the regular cavalry, and replacements from the Mounted Recruiting Service had been inadequate. Instead of moving with Sheridan back to Petersburg, Captain Reno was ordered to Carlisle Barracks to speed the flow of recruits. It was an assignment he undertook with great enthusiasm, and in the middle of December he saw his son for the first time.

55

Promotion came to most officers of the Regular Army with aggravating slowness. One way of attaining higher rank with greater speed was to secure command of a volunteer regiment, but that could be achieved only through appointment by a state governor. Captain Reno had given the matter considerable thought, but he had concluded his lack of influential friends would defeat any attempt he might make. He knew no one in high office in Springfield; indeed, he had been gone so many years from his native state that he had no idea of the political situation there. Harrisburg proffered little more in the way of possible assistance. The Haldeman and Ross families, although among the city's most wealthy and influential, were ardent Democrats. Pennsylvania's Governor, Andrew Gregg Curtin, was a Republican. Turning to Washington would have been futile without the advantages of the kind enjoyed by George Custer. Custer's father was a close friend of Secretary of War Stanton. With the stroke of a pen, Stanton had made the callow and dashing Lieutenant Custer a brigadier general.

If he had thought the issue permanently closed, however, he found that it was very far from that state when he arrived in Harrisburg late in December of 1864. Mary Hannah and her mother had been enlisting the assistance of friends in proposing him for a regimental command. Their campaign had been aided by his own good Army record and the esteem with which many people held him. It had not been forgotten how he and Baldy Smith had refused to surrender Carlisle to a greatly superior Confederate force. Businessmen, factory owners, and shopkeepers were especially grateful. Impressed by the number of personal recommendations in his behalf, and the prominence of the solicitors, Governor Curtin ignored the political affiliations of the Ross family and asked that Captain Reno call at his office.

Captain Reno wasted no time in complying with the Governor's request, and a brief audience ended with his being offered the command of the 12th Pennsylvania Cavalry. He accepted without hesitation. Governor Curtin sent off his request to the Adjutant General in Washington, and Captain Reno was relieved temporarily from Regular Army duty to become Colonel Reno with his own regiment.

The 12th Pennsylvania Cavalry had a highly creditable war record. Organized in 1861, its first assignment, after six months of training, had been guarding the Alexandria and Orange Railroad, a vital supply and communications line south of Washington. It had been badly mauled at both the Second Battle of Bull Run and Antietam. Made a part of the Army of the Shenandoah, it had seen action in the majority of battles of the valley campaign. The man who had led it through three years of combat, Colonel William Pierce, had become seriously ill, and it was the vacancy created by his resignation that Marcus Reno was to fill.

At the time Colonel Reno assumed command, in January, 1865, the 12th Pennsylvania Cavalry's mission was to guard the rebuilt railroad running from Harpers Ferry to Winchester. Although the big armies had gone south, bands of Rebel raiders were operating in the Shenandoah Valley. Skirmishes with these Confederate cavalry detachments occurred almost daily.

As was the case in many volunteer regiments, political appointments brought into power men without military training who were poorly suited to command troops. Colonel Reno found the 12th Pennsylvania Cavalry was not an exception to the general rule. Several of its most able junior officers had been killed in the last months of the Shenandoah Campaign, and others whose competence and courage had been tested and found commendable had been forced by injury and illness to withdraw from active service. Their replacements were generally without the qualities he thought mandatory in men charged with the grave responsibilities warfare placed on them.

He began at once to enforce the rigid discipline and customs of the Regular Army, the value of which he well understood. Several members of his staff were severely punished for infractions which might have been considered minor under other circumstances. Two resigned rather than bow to his will, and wrote derogatory letters about him to Governor Curtin and the Secretary of War. The few Regular Army officers attached to the regiment, however, gave him their unstinted support, and at the end of a month he could note that improvements in both the morale and the efficiency of his first command had been achieved.

Yet he was far from satisfied. Drastic changes remained to be accomplished. This was made tragically apparent in February when the regiment was moved into West Virginia to protect the Baltimore and Ohio Railroad. Colonel Reno made his headquarters in Charles Town.

Word soon reached him that a band of Rebels had derailed a train near Keyes Ford. A civilian spy informed him where the raiders had gone into hiding, and he quickly dispatched two details of fifty men each, under the command of Lieutenants Guild and Chase, to capture them.

Lieutenant Guild was given orders to attack the hideout, while Lieutenant Chase was to guard nearby roads to prevent any of the Rebels from escaping. After leaving camp, Lieutenant Guild decided to disregard his orders and approach his objective by a route of his own choosing. As a consequence, Lieutenant Chase, obediently carrying out his assignment, mistook Lieutenant Guild's detail for the raiders, and opened fire on them. One trooper was shot. The Rebels, hearing the firing, fled to safety in the hills.

Colonel Reno placed Lieutenant Guild under arrest, and recommended he be dishonorably discharged. "I do not design that he be court-martialed," he said in his report to Washington, "as that would occupy more time than he is worth. He is entirely unfit for a commission inasmuch as he takes no pains to improve himself, nor does he study to render himself worthy of his position . . . when not stupefied with whiskey, he is with opium. His performance last night is sufficient evidence against him to hang him." Lieutenant Guild's brief career as a soldier was abruptly terminated, and he returned to the world of corrupt politics, his neck saved only because a busy and responsible commanding officer did not wish to waste the time a court-martial would consume.

The hills and valleys through which the 12th Pennsylvania Cavalry regiment patrolled in the spring of 1865 were a center of maximum guerrilla activity. It was called by soldiers, more often soberly than with humor, "Mosby's Confederacy."

John Singleton Mosby, a thorough gentleman, who practiced law in Bristol, Virginia, achieved fame as a raider without peer. He and his men had become a scourge to Union supply lines. Employing unprecedented commando tactics, they struck and ran, dispersed into fast-moving small groups virtually impossible to trail and capture, came together at appointed rendezvous, struck and ran again. Mosby repeatedly eluded elaborate and carefully planned traps devised to capture him. He rode through the hills and valleys like a wraith, well deserving the appellation "Gray Ghost."

Colonel Reno's troopers were often on Mosby's trail, even sighting him on numerous occasions, but always he slipped away from them, vanishing like a wisp of smoke in the greening Virginia hills. The colonel himself led offensives against Mosby guerrillas at Upperville, Hillsboro, Purcellville, Leesburg, Lovettsville, Waterford, and Wheatland. Riding into the Quaker village of Hamilton one bright spring day, he was astonished to see the Gray Ghost himself sitting his horse among a small group of men a short distance away.

Colonel Reno raced forward at the head of his troopers. The pursuit took them along the road to Middlebury, passing a heavily wooded section. Suddenly Colonel Reno and his men were met with a devastating fire. Twenty-one troopers fell and Reno was obliged to order a retreat. Reassembling his confused men, he led a charge toward the trees from which the firing had come, but the Rebels had vanished, and with them had gone the Gray Ghost.

Marcus Reno learned a lesson he never forgot that day. With five hundred troopers behind him he had raced down the Middlebury Road in a mad pursuit of his quarry. It had not occurred to him that Mosby, operating with no more than a comparatively small number of guerrillas, would attempt to attack such a formidable force. But Mosby had purposely let himself be seen in Hamilton, and he had led Colonel Reno on past a thick woods in which he had concealed more than a hundred guerrillas.

On the fifth of April, only four days before Appomattox, Colonel Reno was given command of a provisional brigade. Under ordinary circumstances the assignment would have been accompanied by a promotion to brigadier general, but Washington was too excited about the approaching end of the war to give consideration to such routine matters. Reno had been given his volunteer regiment too late, but he was not yet aware of that pending disappointment as he led his brigade down the Shenandoah Valley, his destination Lynchburg.

At Edinburg on April 12, he had a sharp engagement with the enemy. He was successfully driving the Confederates before him, taking prisoners as he advanced, when he received the dispatch which told him that Lee had surrendered to Grant three days before at Appomattox, and the war was over.

Weary weeks of idleness followed. For more than a month Colonel Reno's brigade was held in camp near Mount Jackson. His only assignment was to stop and parole any Confederate soldiers returning to their homeland by way of the valley. At last orders came to march back up the Shenandoah to Winchester. When Colonel Reno arrived there on June 11, he received notice that for his outstanding service he had been breveted to colonel of the Regular Army and to brigadier general of Volunteers.

Another month was passed in almost intolerable boredom. At last, on the twentieth of July, 1865, Colonel Reno and the 12th Pennsylvania Cavalry were mustered out of service. He was wearing the brevets of a general when he leaped from a railroad coach a few days later at Harrisburg, into the waiting arms of Mary Hannah.

8

*O*nce again Captain Reno stood on the open deck of the little steamer from New York looking up at the rugged, forbidding cliffs of West Point. It was August, 1865, and he had come back to the Academy, not as he had gone back before, a profoundly concerned cadet, but as a man of rank, holding the brevets of a brigadier, a man whose gallantry and distinguished service had won him an appointment to the faculty.

Captain Reno's assignment as an instructor at West Point had come as a complete surprise. If they had been given the privilege, neither of them could have conceived of a more suitable and delightful place in which to establish their first home. Moreover, the duty was a plum many officers sought and few received. Mary Hannah's joy matched her husband's satisfaction as they were driven up the road from the wharf. Her eyes reflected intense interest as he pointed out the turreted library, the chapel in which they would worship each Sunday morning, and Roe's Hotel, its stucco looking sadly stained and weathered, in which he had spent his first night at the Academy. Her eyes lingered on the duplex houses beyond the plain in which, Captain Reno explained, officers with families were quartered, and she remarked that they appeared to be quite spacious and comfortable.

The unending frustrations and disappointments of life in the Army were unknown to Mary Hannah. She experienced them for the first time an hour later, and they struck her with brutal reality. Captain Reno had known them well, but even he had not anticipated anything like the painful shock which came with the sight of the building in which they were to live.

There had been no funds available for construction during the war years, and West Point, its Cadet Corps and faculty steadily increasing, had become crowded far beyond capacity. The four small rooms to which Captain Reno and his family were escorted were in an old dilapidated barracks. The advantage of illuminating gas, which had been installed with little effort to conceal the pipes, was offset by a wood range which stood beside a tin sink in a cubicle that was meant to be a kitchen. Mary Hannah was unable to hold back her tears. She sank down on a hard horsehair sofa. Captain Reno stood with his hand on her shoulder, his face stony with resentment. Suddenly he turned and went out.

The protest he wrote in the office of the superintendent was duly registered, noted, and filed. It expressed in clear and precise language his conviction that as an officer with more than eight years of service, and as a captain with three Regular Army brevets received in combat, he was deserving of better accommodations for himself and his family. Then he returned to Mary Hannah, knowing the futility of his protest but feeling somewhat better for having made it. They had no alternative but to make out as best they could until better quarters became available. That, indeed, might mean a wait of a year or two, until new buildings had been constructed. He wondered with rising concern if a young woman who had never known anything but a gracious and large mansion beside the Susquehanna River would be able to endure the ordeal. It was anything but a pleasant matter to contemplate.

Captain Reno was cheered by the attitude Mary Hannah displayed the following morning. West Point would be an interesting place to live, she asserted, despite the inconvenient and inadequate quarters, and she optimistically predicted that an opening would soon occur in the more desirable houses beyond the drill plain.

His rising spirits were dashed, however, when he reported for duty. After eight years as a cavalry officer, a branch of the service in which he had distinguished himself and in which he had become highly proficient—his records both on the frontier and in the war attested to that—he had been assigned as an instructor in infantry tactics.

It was incredible, and he left the office utterly astounded. Infantry tactics! Knowing little about them, hardly much more than he had learned as a cadet, it would be asinine for him to pose as an expert. He would make a fool of himself. Anger, chagrin, and utter disappointment blended in a wave that surged through him and left him sick at heart.

Superintendent George Washington Cullum registered no little surprise himself that afternoon when he read a letter placed before him by an aide. The letter had been left at the office by Captain Reno himself, and it was a vigorous protest against his appointment to the infantry department.

If he suspected that Captain Reno had suffered an aberration, Superintendent Cullum showed no inclination to be sympathetic or patient. One of the greatest honors an officer, young or old, could receive was to be named a member of the Academy faculty. Since the very day West Point had been founded there had been a long waiting list of Regular Army men requesting the duty. A protest of the kind Captain Reno had registered was unheard of. Superintendent Cullum quickly prepared a dispatch for the Secretary of War in which he requested that Captain Reno be immediately relieved.

Mary Hannah postponed her plan to have furnishings sent from Harrisburg. Four weeks passed while they waited with no little apprehension for a reply to the superintendent's request. It was received on September 29. Captain Reno was ordered to report forthwith to his regiment in New Orleans.

The Secretary of War had expressed no opinion in the matter. Captain Reno hopefully sent a letter to the Adjutant General acknowledging receipt of the orders and requesting permission to stop in Washington en route to the South to make a personal explanation of the situation which had prompted his dramatic actions. He would, he informed the Adjutant General, await an answer in Harrisburg. He and Mary Hannah packed to go home. When they boarded the New York steamer, he found a place for her and his son in a cabin. Then he went out on the open deck and stood there watching the grim cliffs of West Point until they had faded into the blue haze of the fall day.

The Adjutant General's answer was waiting for him when they arrived in Harrisburg. It bluntly refused him permission to appear in Washington, and reiterated in stiff language the instruction to report before the month's end in New Orleans.

Reno harbored very serious doubts as to the wisdom of taking his wife and infant son with him. The South, suffering the aftermath of the terrible war, its wounds still bleeding, economically decimated, filled with confused blacks suddenly given a freedom they could not comprehend, and bitter whites whose government and way of life had been disrupted, whose property had been destroyed or taken from them, was a pitiful, dangerous, oppressed land. He recalled reading that New Orleans was considered an unsafe city for Northerners. Only the previous July it had been torn by riots and scores of persons had been killed.

Captain Reno might have spared himself his concern. Mary Hannah had no intention of remaining in Harrisburg. If the West Point experience had somewhat dampened the enthusiasm with which she had looked forward to Army life, it had not diminished in any way her determination to remain with the man to whom she was completely devoted. He and their son came before all other considerations, and she was resolved to make a home for them under whatever arduous circumstances his assignments presented. It would have been no problem for him to have entered business in Harrisburg. Their influential friends would have been only too willing to find him a suitable post. She quickly rejected the idea as unthinkable, and said nothing about it to her husband. Resigning the commission he had struggled so many years to achieve, and of which he was inordinately proud, would have been excruciatingly painful to him. She understood that he loved the Army, that it was his world, and she would have been despicably selfish to have asked him to abandon it.

By the thirtieth of October they were settled in a two-story frame house with a small walled courtyard shaded by a chinaberry tree at 32 Carondelet Street in New Orleans. Upon reporting to headquarters of the Division of the Gulf, Captain Reno had been appointed Assistant Judge Advocate of the Military Commission governing the city.

Brevet Major General Absalom Baird was Assistant Commander of Louisiana and Chief of the Freedmen's Bureau. A dedicated and honorable man, he was highly dissatisfied with the Volunteer officers under him who permitted their personal prejudices and politics to influence their work. Baird was looking for Regular Army officers, and when he heard that Captain Reno was in New Orleans he at once requested that he be assigned to the Freedmen's Bureau as Provost Marshal.

The Bureau of Freedmen, Refugees, and Abandoned Lands had two primary duties: to protect newly freed Negroes from unscrupulous persons and to provide relief for both Negroes and whites who had been impoverished by the war.

Captain Reno found his assignment as Provost Marshal far more interesting than the duties of an Assistant Judge Advocate. He considered exceedingly worthwhile such tasks as arranging transportation for a group of penniless Negro women to a plantation on which they would have secure homes and could earn a living; investigating a murder; obtaining for a blacksmith money due him from a miserly farmer; withholding payments for cotton purchased by the government until the field hands of the grower had been paid wages due them; enforcing the payment of school taxes; supervising the care of the aged and infirm; and seeing that neglected children were placed in institutions where they would receive proper care. He was particularly interested in the indenture of young boys and girls and, to ensure them further protection, instituted new provisions in the regulations which helped to prevent their exploitation.

Marcus Reno's superiors considered him ideally suited for these complicated tasks. He displayed a compassion not found in many officers, and they acknowledged that he was greatly responsible for the successful and efficient functioning of the Bureau during its first months of operation. Employment was found for the freedmen, terms and wages were fixed, and labor contracts were carefully supervised. Homeless Negroes were settled on confiscated lands with the assurance they would receive just treatment. Hospitals, orphanages, and schools were established.

To Reno it was rewarding work, but progress was made only under great difficulties. From the time of the Bureau's founding there had been bitter conflicts between Regular Army officers, whose only interest was to assist the homeless and the impoverished of both races, and the unscrupulous scalawags and carpetbaggers who placed self-aggrandizement before any other consideration. Frequently corruptors driven out of one place by military officials were reinstated in other locations by the Radical Republicans in Washington.*

When the 1st Cavalry Regiment, to which Captain Reno was still attached, was ordered to California, General Baird took steps to retain him in New Orleans. The general wrote Washington that Captain Reno was one of a very few officers who

being entirely free from local interests and local prejudices have been able to inspire confidence in all with whom they have had to do business, and the character of the Bureau has thereby greatly improved.

Captain Reno is now occupying the position of Provost Marshal General, and his duties are very important. His Regiment, however, has just been sent to the Pacific. . . . Could we not have him regularly transferred to the Bureau? I would be greatly embarrassed if I lost him.

General Phil Sheridan approved the suggestion. He called Captain Reno a man of "strong character," adding that he had "noticed a very great improvement in the condition of the Freedmen of this state. The white people have confidence in this gentleman and Freedmen have also, and know that the money received for their benefit is safe, and under his control will be legitimately expended."

The Adjutant General abruptly rejected the request and ordered Captain Reno to report to Carlisle Barracks for reassignment. General Baird and Sheridan arranged an appeal to the Commander in Chief. President Grant directed that Captain Reno continue his good work in New Orleans.

A few weeks later new orders directing Captain Reno to re-

*It was after Reno and other Regular Army officers had been transferred that the Union League, and various groups of spoilsmen, got complete control of the Freedmen's Bureau. The League worked for punishment of southern leaders, confiscation of Confederates' properties, and Negro suffrage. The Bureau, now completely corrupt, supported the League's efforts to organize the blacks into a political party opposed to the whites. Countless millions of dollars' worth of white property was stolen by carpetbaggers. Together the Bureau and the League became a vast political machine dedicated to the spoliation of the white South and the perpetuation in power of the Radical Republicans. The excesses committed comprise an odious and shameful chapter of American history.

port at once to Carlisle Barracks, where assertedly he was needed to supervise pressing cavalry problems, arrived. Baird and Sheridan made no further efforts to hold him.

Late in the summer of 1866, wondering what pressing cavalry problems he would be called upon to solve, Captain Reno took his family back to Harrisburg. There he was promptly given ninety days' leave.

Although she was glad to be home again, Mary Hannah knew she would never understand the mysterious processes of reasoning by which the United States Army functioned. They appeared to be beyond human comprehension. Captain Reno had long before reached the same conclusion.

It was perhaps idleness which prompted him to dwell at length on his own position, and his considerations brought a growing dissatisfaction, especially in regard to his immediate future. Reorganization of the postwar Army under Secretary Stanton had been in progress for more than a year; yet he had received no word regarding a permanent assignment. Even more significant was the fact that the promotion he had so long expected had not materialized. A number of his friends whose combat records were less distinguished than his own had received their majority. Moreover, he continued to hear reports which stirred anger in him of officers of the Volunteer Service with political affiliations who had been commissioned as colonels in the Regular Army.

He determined that the time had come for him to take steps in his own behalf, and late in the fall of 1866 he went down to Washington, where, with no difficulty at all, he demonstrated his remarkable ineptness as a politician.

A conference with his old friend, General Benjamin Brice, Paymaster General of the Army, disclosed there were several high vacancies in that department. He filed an application which Ben Brice gladly endorsed.

Captain Reno promptly returned to Harrisburg, anticipating an early notice of his assignment to the Paymaster General's office, and his promotion to major.

In the belief that he might further strengthen his case, he called on Governor Curtin, and the Governor, well recalling his highly creditable leadership of the 12th Pennsylvania Volunteers, wrote to President Andrew Johnson requesting that he be given the post.

When nothing regarding the matter had been received by December, he made a second trip to the capital. There he also wrote a letter to President Johnson politely requesting the assistance of the White House. He informed the President that his "financial responsibility would be vouched for by Jay Cooke and Company . . . my field service by General Grant, and my fitness for the position . . . by General Brice."

He next appealed to Senator Richard Yates, who had been wartime Governor of Illinois, and the Senator willingly sent a letter to Secretary Stanton in which he declared that Captain Reno's requested appointment and promotion "seems justified by his distinguished service during the war, and will give great satisfaction to a large circle of admiring friends in Illinois, his native State."

Once again he returned to Harrisburg to await the favorable action he believed would soon result.

If he had remained for a longer period in Washington, Captain Reno might have learned sooner than he did that he could hardly have been more unwise in the methods he employed in attempting to improve his position. Ability, experience, and a distinguished combat record were not taken into consideration by Secretary Stanton in appointing an officer to a post or in promoting him. He attached far more importance to political endorsements, and those which Captain Reno presented were totally unsuitable. Senator Yates and Governor Curtin were conservatives whom the Radical Republican Stanton detested. The captain resided in Pennsylvania, yet he had presented no letter from Thad Stevens. In the conniving mind of Secretary Stanton that could only mean that Captain Reno was either a moderate or an opponent of the radical reconstruction program. In either case, Captain Reno was an enemy. Moreover, Captain Reno had ignored him and appealed directly to the White House. It was apparent that Captain Reno was too stupid to understand who was running the War Department. Secretary Stanton rejected

Captain Reno's application, and subsequently the captain was ordered to rejoin his regiment, then stationed on the Northwest Pacific Coast.

Captain Reno, Mary Hannah, and their small son sailed from New York for Panama, en route to Fort Vancouver, Washington Territory, on February 8, 1867. He had in his charge a group of recruits from the 2nd Artillery Regiment who had been assigned to the Presidio of San Francisco.

It was May, 1867, when the Pacific mail ship on which they had traveled from Balboa sailed into the Columbia River. Expecting all manner of discomforts and hardships in a post so distant from civilization, Mary Hannah was delightfully surprised to find their quarters at Fort Vancouver more complete and less shabby than the gloomy rooms to which they had been assigned at West Point.

Since his regiment was in the field and there was a shortage of officers at Fort Vancouver, Captain Reno was detained for temporary duty on a court-martial board. On June 22, 1867, he was named Acting Inspector General for the Department of Columbia, a duty very much to his liking. He would have an opportunity to travel over the area that he had known so well before the war.

On July 9, he left on an inspection trip to Fort Walla Walla, traveling by boat to the lower Cascades, thence by train past the upper Cascades, and by boat to The Dalles. He spent the night at the elegant Umatilla House, which boasted two baths to serve the guests in its 123 rooms, and provided the rare accommodation of an inside toilet in the cellar.

In the few years since he had first seen it the inroads of civilization had wrought great changes in the Columbia River country. From The Dalles he traveled by railroad to Celilo Falls and took a boat to Wallula, where he spent the night. The next day he went by stage to Walla Walla. As he rode along the busy main street he recalled that it had been little more than an Indian trail when he had first seen it. He rode a horse from town out to Fort Walla Walla.

His trips of inspection took him as far east as the present

State of Idaho, into Nevada, and through Washington Territory over a period of more than two years. In June, 1869, he received the word he had so long hoped would come. Promoted to the rank of major, he had been assigned to the 7th Cavalry. His orders directed him to report to Fort Leavenworth, in far-off Kansas.

Traveling by ships, Reno and his wife and son went to New York, thence by train to Harrisburg, where he spent a short leave. In August, 1869, they set out for Fort Leavenworth.

9

Shortly after the major's several months' tour of detached duty in Santa Fe to sit on a General Court-Martial (after which he returned to Fort Leavenworth), he was assigned to command Fort Hays in Kansas. Reno and Mary Hannah still hoped for a transfer to the Adjutant General's Department, and he renewed his request, but it was summarily rejected.

Two hundred and eighty-seven miles west of Fort Leavenworth, Fort Hays had been established to protect the builders of the Kansas Pacific Railroad. It stood like a cluster of warts under the enormous bowl of the prairie sky. On each side of it the high plains reached in smooth, unbroken sweeps to the horizon. Half a mile to the east the shacks and false fronts of Hays City formed a ragged sister island in the otherwise empty immensity of the surrounding grass sea.

There were few settlers in the area—the only cultivated fields lay along adjacent creek bottoms—but ranches were being established, and trail herds were coming north from Texas to the shipping pens along the railroad. The cowboys, ragged, weary, and hungry for both whiskey and women, made a bedlam of the saloons and bawdyhouses in Hays City from June until late fall. The Indians, on hunting and stealing forays, generally bypassed it. Red raiders lurked along the wagon and stage trails, watching for lone travelers, small caravans, or unprotected railroad track workers, to kill and rob, and seldom let themselves be seen by cavalry patrols or strong groups of armed trail herders.

Major Reno's command at Fort Hays was comprised of three companies of the 7th Cavalry. In charge of Company G was First Lieutenant Donald McIntosh, a young officer of whom he knew nothing but who appeared to be diligent and seriously determined to improve both his ability and his own status.

Although he had no personal animosity toward Captain Thomas B. Weir, he was disappointed to find him at the head of Company D. Weir, a veteran of the Civil War, had joined the 7th as a strong partisan of Custer, and had made trouble for several officers who did not share his high opinion of the "boy general." In return for Weir's loyalty, Custer had soon arranged to have him promoted from first lieutenant to captain.

Taking over command of the regiment, Colonel Samuel D. Sturgis did not hesitate to let it be known that Custer's show of favoritism was distasteful to him. Moreover, he had long disliked Weir and considered him an incompetent and undesirable officer. When Congress ordered that the number of commissioned officers be drastically reduced, the War Department established boards designed to carry out the mandate, instructing them to work with regimental commanders in cleaning out of the Army any officers considered unfit for service. The nickname "Benzine boards" quickly came into usage.

Sturgis submitted Weir's name, and Custer, always outwardly responsive to the wishes of his superior, agreed to throw over his old supporter and testify against him. Unknown to Sturgis, however, Custer then had a private conversation about Weir with General John Pope, commander of the Department of Missouri. In his complaint to the trial board, Sturgis charged that Weir was "not only of dissipated and dissolute habits, but is a low, vulgar man, devoid of moral principles and unfit to associate with officers and their families." As witnesses who would substantiate the accusations he named Custer, Major Lewis Merrill, and Lieutenant Myles Moylan.

Sturgis raged and cursed when he learned that the trial board, acting on the recommendation of General Pope, had voted against the dismissal of Weir.

Offsetting Major Reno's disappointment at the presence of the troublemaker Weir at Fort Hays was his pleasure in finding Fred Benteen, the senior captain of the 7th, there as the commander of Company H.

Major Reno was in full accord with the popular opinion that the candid, cantankerous, honest, and intrepid Frederick William Benteen was the ablest officer in the entire 7th Cavalry. He was short, heavy-set, prematurely gray, with distinct lines running from both sides of his nose to the corners of his broad mouth. He was tough-minded and always had a chip on his shoulder.

The son of a wealthy plantation owner, Benteen had been reared in a luxurious and gracious environment. The conviction that slavery was a divine institution, however, was not shared by him. At the start of the Civil War he accepted a commission as a first lieutenant of Volunteers in the Union Army. He was promptly and wrathfully disowned by his family. His father cursed his name and pledged himself to pray each day that his son, who had gone forth in an alien uniform to fight his own people and their principles, would meet death from an avenging bullet fired by one of his own kin.

In more than four years of combat Captain Fred Benteen established a record for bravery and daring that had few equals. It was hardly less than ironical that it should fall to him to capture his own father, who had become a blockade runner on inland rivers. Mustered out a colonel of Volunteers, he held no desire to return to civilian life. His application for a commission in the Regular Army brought him a captaincy and an assignment to the newly created 7th Cavalry.

Benteen's dislike for Custer stemmed from their first meeting at which the "boy general" had attempted to impress him. Benteen was not a man easily impressed, but neither was he a man who would permit personal aversions to influence the performance of his assigned duties. He carried them out with diligence and to the best of his ability, but he did not consider it incumbent upon him to display loyalty to any commanding officer in excess of those limits. If this was a weakness, it was not one that prompted deviousness or a reticence to speak his mind. He made no effort to conceal his opinion that Custer was incompetent, lacking in any sense of responsibility, and an insufferable egotist. After the disaster on the Washita his repugnance became a hatred that at times placed a heavy tax on his civility. This was especially true when he was in his cups, a condition which occurred with some regularity. On such occasions his belligerence made him a dangerous man, yet his record was evidence that whiskey had never interfered with the conduct of his duties.

Admiration and respect for Benteen were not confined to enlisted men. Lieutenant Frank M. Gibson was to express the feelings of many junior officers when he wrote his wife that Captain Benteen "is one of the coolest and bravest men I have ever known." A sergeant, Charles Windolph, went farther, declaring, "He was just about the finest soldier and the greatest gentleman I ever knew." That compliment came after twelve years of service under Benteen, but even higher praise was written by Major General Hugh L. Scott, who called him "my model . . . and the idol of the 7th Cavalry." Captain Benteen, said the general,

governed mainly by suggestion . . . I never once heard him raise his voice to enforce his purpose. He would sit by the open fire at night, his bright, pleasant face framed by his snow white hair [Captain Benteen was prematurely gray] . . . and often I watched to find out the secret of his quiet steady government, that I might go and govern likewise. For example, if he intended to stay a few days in one camp he would say to his adjutant, "Don't you think we had better take up our regular guard mount while in camp?" The Adjutant thought it better, and so did everybody else. If he found this kindly manner misunderstood, then his iron hand would close down quickly, but that was seldom necessary, and then only with newcomers and never twice with the same person.

The blizzards swept down from the north and west, paralyzing life and destroying it, stopping the frail wood-burners that followed the tenuous threads of rail across the endless plains.

Both the buffalo and the longhorn herds drifted ahead of it, keeping their rumps to the biting winds, while the settlers huddled in their sod huts, and the cavalrymen cringed on their sentry posts against the blasts and watched for danger they knew would not come.

Nothing would come, for nothing could live in that barren white world beyond the gates, nothing but the wolves that howled their suffering and their hunger to the cold brilliant nights, trailing a weakened buffalo or a bony steer, savoring the smell of cavalry horses they could not reach, and hating the smell of man that came upon the icy air from the posts and the clapboard shanties of the towns.

The spring brought forgetfulness of winter's death. It brought new life in greening grass and warming skies; it brought new life in the burrows and dens and in the sod shanties; the buffalo and the longhorns moved back, with the new life in the heavens and in the earth, and dropped their calves; and the Indians were stirred by new dreams of conquest and great hunts.

A land was changing, all its living things, man and animal, moving toward a transition that would leave nothing of the old. The Indians saw the smoke and fire and cinders of the woodburners, listened to shrill whistles that were the whistles of death, and saw the buffalo hunters wading in their slaughter and the cattle herds moving in to consume the grass among the whitening bones. And they saw the sod huts and the potato patches and the false fronts spring up, and they watched the cavalry patrols creeping across the vastness.

The Indians stayed at a safe distance. They moved in small bands, committing their depredations, hunting their meat and hides, dancing to their gods, and vanishing into the nothingness. The Indians were ghosts living only in the burning eyes of the weary troopers. Once, after a patrol of more than five hundred miles, Major Reno could report that no more than three or four Indians had been seen together at any time. The troopers might well wonder whether they had seen any at all, and it was difficult for them to understand that they were not pursuing chimeras that lived only in the minds of the armchair strategists in Leavenworth and Washington. The troopers wondered how they could be deterrents when they saw nothing to deter, nothing but a few wraiths that eluded them like distant dust spouts. Headquarters provided no explanations, simply sent out orders, and the patrols went on, along the Smoky Hill and the Saline and Hackberry Creek beyond Round Mountain, and clear out to Kit Carson, Colorado Territory, and the Republican and Beaver creeks, and on and on until they could see the hazy blue wall of the Rockies standing against the West.

Dispatches arrived—always the scouts came in with dispatches if trains and telegraph lines were disrupted—and Major Reno was ordered to report to Fort Leavenworth to sit on a retiring board. It was September, 1870, when he left his command in the field. He was delighted to find Mary Hannah and his son waiting for him at the fort.

Mary Hannah had learned how to move quickly, to make do, living only in the day at hand and giving little thought to the future. Several large crates of fine linens and sterling, all thoughtfully selected by her mother from the great supply of finery in the Ross home, had arrived. Most of the officers' wives welcomed the opportunity to enjoy the lace tablecloths, initialed napery, cut glass, and exquisite imported flatware at afternoon teas and dinners in the Reno quarters, concealing their jealousy behind a sincere appreciation of such luxuries. But gossip had it that Elizabeth Custer had made some caustic remarks about them and complained to the colonel. She had nothing comparable, and Libby Custer was not one to be bested in any display of affluence or the social graces by the wife of an officer who held a lower rank than her husband.

It was late in March of 1871 when they returned to Fort Hays. During the winter, unknown to Major Reno, a new first lieutenant had arrived to join the command. His name was Thomas W. Custer, a handsome, lithe young man of twenty-five with a quiet and pleasant manner. It was Captain Benteen who remarked that the only similarity between Tom Custer and his arrogant, boastful, swaggering brother, George, was their name, and Major Reno had acknowledged the accuracy of the statement. Both the captain and the major had soon found themselves liking Tom Custer, and Tom Custer had indicated a similar feeling for them.

Although he had lived during his brief military career almost constantly in the shadow of his more glamorous brother, Tom Custer had, through his own ability and courage, won for himself everlasting renown. In the Civil War he had been awarded two Congressional Medals of Honor, a distinction achieved by only one other soldier in the history of the nation.

Wishing to make his own way, he had enlisted at the age of sixteen as a private in the 21st Ohio Infantry. This was not a status which either his brother, rising swiftly toward a generalship, or his father, Emanuel, close friend of the Secretary of War, would tolerate. George Armstrong Custer, Major General of Volunteers, supported by Emanuel's letters to Washington, soon had a lieutenant's bars on Tom Custer. He was transferred to General Custer's staff as an aide-de-camp. If this was a plum in one sense, it was not a sinecure. Nor did Lieutenant Custer permit the favoritism to serve as a shield or inhibit him in his actions.

Appomattox brought no desire for peace to Tom Custer, and he announced his intention to join the Regular Army and become a career soldier. His honors and his record would have been more than sufficient to win him a commission, but Emanuel Custer was not one to permit a son to make his way alone. If Emanuel Custer held great pride in Tom's achievements, he had more faith in Secretary of War Edwin M. Stanton. He and Stanton had been close since their youthful days. At one time they had been the only Democrats in Harrisburg County, Ohio. When Stanton was a struggling young attorney, Emanuel gave him his legal business. An unrestrained request for an appointment, interspersed with unabashed praises for Tom Custer's sterling qualities, went off to Washington.

On February 23, 1866, Tom Custer was commissioned a second lieutenant of the 1st Infantry. Emanuel had expected more. George, too, was dissatisfied, and with the formation of the 7th Cavalry he quickly arranged to have his young brother transferred to it, to serve under him as a first lieutenant.

If Tom Custer disliked the role of a satellite, he had no alter-native. His orders assigned him to the 7th Cavalry, and a lieutenant was not permitted the prerogative of objecting to an assignment.

From the day of his arrival, Tom Custer found himself in a difficult position. As a brother of the man whose character and actions had created a sharp conflict between the feelings of the regiment's officers, his every action was noted and studied. At the unmarried officers' mess, where he took his meals when he could not eat with the colonel and Libby, his remarks, opinions, and statements were construed as the official pronouncements of his brother. Being one's self was virtually impossible.

While he had been at Fort Leavenworth with the retirement board during the winter, Major Reno had heard rumors that be-cause of the dire situation in the South the War Department was contemplating sending more troops there. That the rumors were founded on fact was soon confirmed. On May 18, 1871, the 7th Cavalry left Kansas with orders that assigned its companies to several southern stations. Major Reno was placed in command of all troops in the area of Spartanburg, South Carolina.

It was a transfer which greatly pleased Mary Hannah. They were soon settled in a spacious house on Main Street. Around it were large grounds, shaded by great trees and bordered by flow-ering hedges.

Spartanburg, a small but prosperous college town, had been fortunate to feel only the backlash of the war. While all of its able-bodied men and boys had joined the Confederate Army and many had not returned, it had not known the devastation wrought on other areas.

In the spring of 1865 an understrength company of Federal troops was garrisoned in the town. An office was opened in the dusty and long-neglected courthouse where citizens of the late Confederacy might take the oath of allegiance to the Government of the United States.

James H. Carlisle, Jr., in his *Memoirs of Wofford College,* tells of being with his father, who was talking on the street across from the courthouse with Lt. Colonel John H. Evins, a returned veteran with his arm in a sling, who was later to be elected to the United States House of Representatives. The two men discussed the sad plight of the South and of Spartanburg: the "great gravity of the situation"; that "the semblance of authority and majesty of the law appeared nowhere."

Finally Dr. Carlisle turned to Evins and said, "Well, Colonel, I can stand tyranny and even despotism, but I cannot stand anarchy. I propose to step across the street and take the oath of allegiance. If you have no objection, I would like for you to go along with me." The doctor crossed the street and entered the courthouse, followed by the colonel.

The people of South Carolina, robbed and cheated by a carpetbag government and afraid of its ignorant Negro militia on the one side, and beaten, tortured, and menaced by the fanatical, lower-class Klansmen on the other, were grateful for the presence of disciplined Federal troops. They hoped that Major Reno and his men would maintain order, bring about honest government, and drive the night riders to cover.

Originally organized in December, 1865, by six bored young Confederate veterans of Pulaski, Tennessee, the Ku Klux Klan was at first merely a frivolous social organization. Almost by accident the hooded and wild-riding Klansmen became one of the weapons used to cow the Negro and destroy his exploiters.

It was inevitable that, in some areas, the control of such an organization would fall into the hands of violent men and be used as an instrument of personal power. By 1870 the Klan, in many places, had become lawless bands feared equally by their enemies and the conservative whites.

During his stay in Spartanburg, Reno became quite friendly with young Lieutenant Benny Hodgson, who spent considerable time with Reno and Mary Hannah at their quarters.

Hodgson had a strong, well-molded face, dark hair, brown eyes beneath heavy brows, and full lips that were quick to loosen in a smile. He came from a well-to-do family of paint manufacturers in Philadelphia.

Major Reno found no pleasure in his assignment. It was a prolonged headache, a flood of problems that only time and the cooling of blood could solve, and no amount of military force could do more than prevent large-scale destruction, decrease the infliction of brutalities, and halt the perpetration of senseless acts of injustice.

His experience in New Orleans had given him a better understanding of the tasks he faced than most of the other officers had. Obviously, headquarters had taken that into consideration in selecting him to direct operations in the most troublesome area of the South. The difficulties in Louisiana had been small in comparison with those of South Carolina.

South Carolina continued to be the paradise of the carpetbagger and the scalawag. The corruption was virtually indescribable, but it was conceived and carried on not only by intruders from above the Mason and Dixon Line but by men who were Southerners by birth and South Carolina patriots by profession. Thieves, blackmailers, extortionists, and grafters flowed southward in an unbroken polluted stream.

South Carolina's Governor, Robert K. Scott, had come from Ohio, where he had practiced medicine without a license. He held the distinction, of which he liked to boast, of being the most corrupt Northerner to enter southern politics after the war. His cronies, both from Massachusetts, were Nelson G. Parker, a fugitive from justice, and Benjamin Franklin Whittemore, a former Congressman who had sold cadetships to the Military and Naval Academies. With Scott they created a political dictatorship that made a vassalage of the state. They issued millions of dollars' worth of illegal bonds, and divided the money among the faithful. They lived in the manner of potentates, padded the public payrolls with thousands of names of nonexistent employees, and pocketed the salaries. To pay for their corruption they imposed new and higher taxes on a helpless people who had already been made destitute by five years of devastating warfare.

The military was almost as helpless to interfere as were the civilians. It was forced to stand idly aside while Governor Scott, who could hold office only through brute force, distributed seven thousand rifles to Negro militiamen, his personal army, and while his State Constabulary, five hundred men armed with Winchester repeaters, stole ballot boxes, beat and murdered objectors, and trampled on basic civil liberties. When Scott informed President Grant that the orderly conduct of elections was threatened by his opponents, the President sent more Federal troops to insure the peace.

The result was a steady trend toward anarchy and rebellion. If the people were obliged to accept the defeat suffered on the battlefields, they had no intention of becoming serfs to the corruptionists. They rose, by necessity in secret, and the Ku Klux Klan, the Knights of the White Camellia, the White League, the Invisible Circle, and the Pale Faces, were born, all dedicated to white supremacy, a recovery of the way of life they had so long known, and the re-establishment of their once prosperous economy. They were as lawless, as unscrupulous, as brutal, as the carpetbaggers who occupied the State House and ruled the land.

In between these opposing forces stood the Regular Army. Stories of the excesses and the crimes of the secret orders appeared each day in the northern press, public indignation flamed, and it all was meat for the so-called Radical Republicans. It bolstered their program for a devastated and prostrated South. The "bloody shirt" was waved in Congress, and Southerners were called traitors to the Union, gnawing at the pillars of good government.

The Administration cried that orderly government—meaning in this case Radical Republican government—had to be maintained at all costs, and the Klu Klux Klan Act was forced through Congress. President Grant, who had inherited the southern reconstruction turmoil from President Johnson in 1869, next was induced to suspend the right of habeas corpus in nine troublesome areas in which the Klan had become a dominant factor. One of them was Spartanburg County.

The motives of the Administration may have been to maintain political gains rather than to bring peace to the South, but the scheme placed in the hands of Major Reno a powerful weapon. It was not the kind of weapon he would have liked to have—under martial law he could have attacked the northern corruptors as well as the night riders—but it was all he had, and he looked upon it as better than nothing.

Spartanburg had its first taste of Klan violence in the fall of 1870, when some twoscore riders, which the local newspaper described as "fantastically attired," swept down the streets and left town "screeching like wild men."

Said the Spartanburg *Spartan:* "This is the first time our town has been visited by these outlandish gentry and we hope it will be the last."

It was far from the last. Visits of Klansmen continued, and their boldness and viciousness steadily increased. In December, 1870, Anthony Johnson, the only Negro trial justice in the county, was taken from his home and murdered. Stories were circulated that the slaying had been committed by an injured husband and wronged property owner, but northern papers placed the guilt directly on the Klan.

Two weeks later, Governor Scott's heavily armed colored militia killed Nathaniel Stevens, a one-armed Confederate veteran, in adjacent Union County, and the fears of law-abiding and conservative residents that they would suffer reprisals increased.

With the arrival of Federal cavalry and infantry, the citizens of Spartanburg expressed their relief. While they did not extend a gracious welcome to the Union soldiers, as they were termed, they could breathe easier with the hope that law and order would be restored. The *Spartan's* comment perhaps expressed the sentiment of the community:

We have been afflicted with unprincipled men whom we would gladly exchange for any United States soldiers we have ever seen. We do not object to their presence, as they are a gentlemanly and well-disciplined body of men under the command of an accomplished officer [Reno] whose stay among us we hope will be pleasant.

The Klan was not easily intimidated or halted. On the night of March 22, 1871, a group of robed men bearing guns appeared at the country residence of Dr. John Winsmith. A descendant of a distinguished Revolutionary family, Winsmith had represented

Spartanburg in the state legislature for fifteen years. He had outraged public opinion by supporting Governor Scott for re-election. As a reward the governor had made him a brigadier general in the state militia. It was reported that Winsmith had stored in his house several hundred rifles and five thousand rounds of ammunition, sent to him by the state adjutant general. The raiding Klansmen demanded the arms.

Winsmith defied them and ordered them to leave. When they refused, he fired several shots at them, allegedly killing one man and seriously wounding another. The Klansmen returned the fire, and Winsmith suffered seven wounds. The invaders fled. Winsmith recovered.

The months of August and September, 1871, were especially busy periods for Reno's small command. An average of 126 men, in detachments of twenty troopers and a commissioned officer, were in the field each day. However, not only crimes committed by Klansmen occupied their attention. One of their chief duties was to act as process servers for the United States marshal. One of their most troublesome assignments involved the detection of illegal stills and the collection of overdue taxes from residents of mountain areas.

Reno reported: "Nearly every man in the mountains is an illicit distiller. . . . It is almost impossible to get at them. They are a lawless desperate class, like Indians in hiding and avoiding pursuit." He recommended that an infantry company be quartered in the remote mountain sections as the most effective means of countering the illegal traffic.

He, too, rode at night with his patrols. Klan leaders were captured, jailed, and tried. Some of them were sent north to Federal prisons. Major Reno had the power to make arrests, and if the juries who tried the accused were packed with henchmen of the northern politicians, that was an issue he could not resolve. The governor and his State House machine controlled the judiciary.

The whippings, the ear-cuttings, the murders stopped. The jails of Spartanburg County were filled beyond capacity. The trials continued. New hope had arisen in the oppressed, and in that knowledge Major Reno found a profound gratification. Progress toward the fulfillment of his hope had been made. The northern press continued to rage, and a new attitude, based on a modicum of sincerity, was beginning to be seen in Washington, in Congress.

The Klan was not dead, but it was crippled by wounds, and Spartanburg County knew a quiet it had not enjoyed for years. The corruption was not halted, but it was a suffering wasting disease, and the State House gang was deeply concerned. The Southerners of quality continued in their refusal to welcome the invaders, but not a few of them crossed the barrier far enough to express their respect for Major Reno.

He accepted his exclusion without complaint, assuring the civilians that his greatest wish was to see them resume the normal courses of life. He ordered the 7th Cavalry Band to give concerts in the public square. The troopers tooted to empty seats at first, but in time the square was overflowing with people, young and old, who thoroughly enjoyed the music. "A fascinating and soul capturing band," one man wrote, "playing marvelous waltzes and old love tunes." He liked especially "The Captain with the Whiskers," and "Kate Darling."

Relationships between the townspeople and the soldiers continued to improve until, even though the invaders were not yet welcomed into Spartanburg's homes, the *Banner* could report editorially:

They are not so bad after all. If the Legislature thinks it discomforts this part of the country by asking Grant to retain his troops here, it is very much mistaken. They are remarkably well-behaved, and their officers gentlemen of culture and refinement.

Spartanburg was quiet. The fact was noticed in Washington. Most of the Regulars were removed and sent to less peaceful areas. Major Reno was left with only one company of the 7th and a company of the 2nd Infantry.

In July, 1872, he received his own orders to leave. He had been selected to sit on an ordnance board in New York City which would pass judgment on new firearms and ammunition. It was not only an assignment which carried great prestige, but it would give him several months of per diem in a fine New York hotel.

"Spartanburg County," reported its Grand Jury, shortly after the Renos had left, "is entirely free of any unlawful bands of raiders or clans or disguised men. We know of no unlawful combination of men who refuse to obey or who resent the laws of the country."

10

*M*ary Hannah's joyful expectation of spending several months in a great metropolis was made impossible by the illness of her mother. She and the major and eight-year-old Ross went directly to Harrisburg from South Carolina. Dr. Wilson, showing his age but no lack of attentiveness, informed them that the nature of Mary Haldeman Ross' sickness indicated to him a decline that would end in her death.

Major Reno went to New York alone on the second of September, 1872, taking quarters in the Army and Navy Club. During the next few months, while the members of the board were studying the merits of bayonets, rifles, carbines, and other military weapons, he managed to spend a few weekends in Harrisburg, and twice Mary Hannah was able to leave for a few days in New York, but otherwise it was, in the largest city of America, a lonesome assignment for him. It was the middle of May, 1873, before the work was completed and the board adjourned.

He had only a short stay in Harrisburg before he was ordered to report to St. Paul, Minnesota. Mrs. Ross had weakened, and the responsibility of the big house and caring for her younger brother had fallen on Mary Hannah. Although he agreed that by all means she should remain behind—he did not yet know what assignment awaited him—he left not a little dispirited by the thought that she would be obliged to face a time of great sorrow without him.

At St. Paul he was directed to Fort Snelling, and there he was informed that he was to be commanding officer of a military contingent that would accompany a new International Commission on a survey of the Canadian–United States border from the Lake of the Woods to the summit of the Rocky Mountains. It would mean that throughout the summer and fall he would move westward across the great plains of the Dakota and Montana Territories, and he was glad that Mary Hannah had not come with him, only to be left alone to worry about her mother in St. Paul or Bismarck.

The escort of which Major Reno had command was comprised of two companies of the 7th Cavalry. The officers, if not his close friends, were well known to him. Myles Keogh and Thomas B. Weir, who had previously served under him, were the captains. The lieutenants were James M. Bell, the quartermaster, Winfield S. Edgerly and Richard H. L. Alexander.

Keogh was a soldier of fortune who came from a prominent Irish family. At the age of seventeen he had been a lieutenant in the Papal Army, and as leader of the St. Patrick's Battalion had fought with great distinction against the Piedmontese at Spoleto. Migrating to America in 1862, he was commissioned a captain of Volunteers in the Union Army. His bravery and able service in the battles of that year brought a request from General McClellan for his assignment as an aide. He remained on Little Mac's staff until after Antietam. Thereafter he served with honor in Tennessee, Virginia, and Georgia. Mustered out of the Volunteers, he promptly secured a commission in the Regular Army. He inherited wealth, but continued the career he loved, that of a cavalryman in the West.

Captain Keogh was suave and gentlemanly and was an especial favorite of Colonel and Libby Custer. He had an abundance of dark curly hair, a muscular face adorned with a trim mustache and a goatee, and a gay manner. He kept the officers of the 7th

85

and their ladies continuously entertained with his droll stories and Irish wit. He was a heavy drinker, and it made him brutal, with the result that he was detested by the enlisted troopers. He never married, but more than one story of his affairs with unattached ladies was told about cavalry campfires.

It was for Major Reno a difficult, troublesome, and discouraging summer and fall. The civilian surveyors thought themselves entitled to give orders to individual soldiers at will, and disputes over authority frequently occurred. Dr. F. O. Nash, the surgeon assigned to the escort by General Alfred H. Terry, commander of the Department of Dakota, was a drunkard, stole merchandise from the commissary, and sought to give chloroform to officers who were afflicted with a hangover. Major Reno eventually was obliged to dismiss him and send him back to Fort Snelling.

At Fort Pembina the contingent was joined by Dr. Elliott Coues, an Army medical officer on loan to the Border Commission as surgeon and naturalist and far more interested in studying botany and zoology than the ailments of human beings. Dr. Coues had induced the commanding officer at Fort Pembina to issue an order stating he was engaged

in preparing a report on the ornithology of the Northwest, and he is desirous of obtaining specimens of all wild animals, birds, fishes, reptiles, and insects, and any enlisted man who desires to be absent from the garrison, when not required for duty on the Post, may have a pass for the purpose of killing birds of all kinds, catching fish, collecting insects, beetles and bugs, obtaining snake specimens as well as turtles, frogs, toads, reptiles and snail shells.

If Dr. Coues' activities brought pleasures to the enlisted men who aided him, they did not amuse his superiors in the Surgeon General's Department, and he was severely reprimanded for his refusal to treat ailing soldiers after Nash was dismissed.

Difficulties increased as the detachment pushed farther into the Great Plains. Major Reno was unable to obtain Indian scouts, although he had been promised that a number would be assigned to him. The drunken Dr. Nash sobered up long enough to make out a good case for himself at headquarters. Major Reno received a rebuke.

Dr. Nash was assigned by order of the Department Commander . . . the effectiveness of your order requires peculiar and extraordinary circumstances to justify. You will again place him on duty and submit reasons governing his relief by you.

Major Reno's report that Dr. Nash was intoxicated on duty obviously had not been sufficient reason to dismiss him. Dr. Nash returned, and the escort moved on into the Indian country, but Major Reno watched for an opportunity to dismiss him once more for cause. It soon came when Dr. Nash admitted that he did not know how to compound simple prescriptions. Fearing that some patient might be poisoned, Major Reno defied headquarters and once more sent the inebriated medical man packing for Fort Snelling.

While awaiting the arrival of a replacement, Major Reno sought the aid of Dr. Coues. Dr. Coues refused to minister to the sick, declaring that he was a naturalist. Moreover, he maintained that he was not technically a member of Major Reno's command; therefore he did not have to take orders from him. Dr. Charles A. Hart at last arrived, and the controversy ended.

The civilians abused the cavalry horses. Frequently they were not relieved of the saddle at night until it was too late for them to fill themselves with grass before they were resaddled in the morning. Major Reno, possessing the true cavalryman's love of horses, frequently clashed bitterly with the offenders. When two surveyors rode their horses to death, after being warned by a corporal that they were traveling too fast and too far—some sixty-five miles in a single day—Major Reno later reported to headquarters that two fine horses had been driven by the surveyors until their hearts burst, but he received little satisfaction from his superiors.

Major Reno brought his escort back to Fort Totten on Devil's Lake, Dakota Territory, through bitter cold and snow in October, 1873. A letter was waiting for him from Mary Hannah telling of her mother's death. Mary Haldeman Ross had passed away in September, but the letter had not been forwarded to him. He left immediately for Harrisburg. Special requests because of personal problems and accumulated leave made it possible for him to spend the winter with his family in the old mansion on Front Street.

In the spring he was back once more alone at Fort Totten. The plans for the second expedition of the Border Commission progressed on schedule. This time Major Reno was not faced with a medical problem, for the efficient Dr. George E. Lord, a dedicated medical officer who could treat horses as well as the troopers, and seemed to like both equally well, was on hand. His command was considerably larger, the Department of Dakota taking advantage of an opportunity to make a show of force in the Indian country under the flag of scientific observation. Four hundred and twenty infantry, 119 seasoned troopers, 109 civilians attached to surveying parties, and 543 horses and pack mules moved in an impressive array across the immensity of the northern plains.

Major Reno had established camp fifty miles above Fort Benton, on the Missouri River in Montana Territory, on July 13, 1874. There a courier reached him with a telegram.

Mary Hannah had died suddenly three days before. As his trembling hand held the message, as the tears streamed down his face, services were being held beside her grave in the Harrisburg cemetery.

Major Reno turned over his command to the senior captain of the expedition, Thomas B. Weir, and rode hard through the night to Fort Benton. It was dawn when he routed out a telegraph operator.

He paced the parade ground and the dusty roads, waiting for a reply from St. Paul. It came within the hour. "While fully sympathizing with your affliction," it said, "the Department Commander feels it is imperative to decline to grant you leave. You must return to your command."

In time letters came which told him that his son was well and was being cared for by Mary Hannah's sister, Bertie Orth. All was well in Harrisburg, all that is except his not being there himself. The Orths and the Haldemans were no more than polite in the letters, and the words were stiff with reserve as they inquired when he intended to return. Major Reno understood. Neither the Rosses, the Orths, nor the Haldemans were military people. His wife had died, and they could not understand his absence. The excuse that he was unable to obtain permission to leave was insufficient. When a man's wife died, a man went home, no matter where he was, no matter what he was doing.

It was the end of September, 1874, when Major Reno stepped from the train at Harrisburg. Ross leaped into his arms, but the joy of his son was countered by the coldness of Bertie Orth and her husband.

Mary Hannah had died intestate. Her large estate had been put into trust for her only child, and would be inherited by him at the age of twenty-one. Inasmuch as Major Reno had not seen fit to return for nearly two months after his wife's death, Bertie and Wilson Orth had taken things into their own hands.

Major Reno made no objection. On October 3 he crossed the river to the New Cumberland Depot. There he sent a message to the Adjutant General in Washington requesting permission to take a leave of eight months from the Army. He obtained it, and a few days later he and Ross sailed from New York for Europe. In Paris, three additional months' leave were granted him. He was not yet ready to face life on the western plains without Mary Hannah, while also knowing that his son would be reared by people who would never forgive him for not returning home when she died.

11

*T*he Major Reno who crossed the Missouri River from Bismarck to Fort Abraham Lincoln, in Dakota Territory, late in October, 1875, was not the man the officers of the 7th Cavalry had once known. The changes were not so much in his appearance as in his manner, yet there was a brittleness in his eyes which reflected a cold light, and it seemed to give to his entire face a fixed expression of sternness. He was not unfriendly when he reported to the headquarters of Colonel George Armstrong Custer, but neither did he display warmth or enthusiasm as he shook hands with members of the regimental staff. His calm detachment and almost exacting formality had an instantaneous effect on others, prompting a sudden cautiousness and reserve in their attitude toward him.

All the time Reno had been in Europe with his son he had been torn with indecision. The urge to give up his military career, enter some kind of business, and establish a home for Ross had been strong in him. Factors he considered significant had weighed heavily against such a program. He had no training in any kind of commercial enterprise or industry, and he feared his possible earnings as a civilian would not provide the advantages he wanted Ross to enjoy. In the home of the wealthy, cultured Haldemans, the boy would not only receive loving care, but he would know an unquestionable security, an atmosphere of refinement, and the many opportunities which normally were corollaries of long association with affluent and influential persons. The suggestion that he might keep Ross with him in the Army was unthinkable. In this respect he was adamant. Ross was willing, even eager to remain with him—his first memories were of the posts in the Northwest and of Forts Leavenworth and Hays —yet he had no intention of exposing an 11-year-old, motherless youth to the hardships, brutalities, and crudities of an Indian country fort.

He left Ross in Harrisburg with a feeling that he would never again be close to him, that the affection of his only son would gradually diminish until the memory of him as a loving father would be destroyed, and in the end he would be no more than a name, meaningless and almost completely forgotten. He felt the weight of a greater loneliness than he had ever known as he took the train for the West.

It might have been quite possible for him to obtain an assignment to the headquarters of the Department of Dakota in St. Paul. General Alfred Howe Terry, in command there, had detained him several days so that he might familiarize himself with general departmental problems, and obviously would not have been averse to attaching such an experienced and capable officer to his personal staff. Major Reno did not raise the subject. To the contrary, he expressed satisfaction with his assignment to Fort Abraham Lincoln. He wanted to be once again on the western plains. He wanted to be in the saddle, riding at the head of a cavalry column. He wanted hardship, danger, the crack of carbines, the sound of Indian drums, the wild howls of naked warriors, and the triumphant yells of charging troopers. He wanted action and combat and duty that would give him few moments to dwell on the sorrows of the past year.

12

In the late fall of 1875, when Major Reno rejoined the 7th Cavalry, Fort Abraham Lincoln had been built only three years. Originally established under the name of Fort McKeen, to protect crews constructing the Northern Pacific Railroad, it soon was rechristened, and its activities and responsibilities had been swiftly increased until it had become the largest and most vital post on the entire frontier.

Strategically located on high bluffs across the Missouri from Bismarck, and slightly below the little group of shacks called Mandan, it boasted facilities and accommodations greatly superior to those to be found in most western military establishments. It had its own telegraph office, linking it directly with General Terry's headquarters in St. Paul. Thus it was no more distant from the War Department in Washington than the click of a key. Except for the occasions when blizzards and subzero cold hampered rail transportation, the daily delivery of mail was maintained. Outlined against the western sky, the stockades and buildings and blockhouses created an impressive sight, symbolizing a formidable barrier against the dangers lurking in the plains that swept away to the horizon on every side.

The dangers sometimes were felt at close hand, brutally real. Half-starved raiders attacked railroad contruction crews and carried off supplies. Three mail carriers were ambushed and slain. The cows of the officers' mess were killed. Colonel Custer's home was burned by an invader who slipped past sentries.

Rain-in-the-Face, the noted Hunkpapa Sioux warrior and chief, escaped from the guardhouse. He had been accused of killing a white trader, and had been captured by Captain Tom Custer. He was ordered held at Fort Abraham Lincoln, but the guards had been careless and he had slipped away. A report came back that he had gone west and had joined Sitting Bull, declaring that he would cut the heart out of Tom Custer and eat it.*

Custer led two companies into Bismarck to recover a stolen shipment of government grain, and captured the thieves. Three times in the summer of 1873, once during Sunday morning church services, strong bands of Sioux had boldly raided the Fort Abraham Lincoln Reservation and stubbornly engaged the troops.

A railroad engineering party escorted by twenty troopers under the command of Lieutenant Carlos Camilio De Rudio was attacked by a hundred warriors on the Heart River. De Rudio conducted an orderly retreat under constant fire, until the attackers were repulsed by a relief contingent from the fort.

A band of Hunkpapa stampeded and drove off ninety mules. Custer pursued them with three companies, recovering the animals, but the Sioux escaped in timber along the Heart River. Night raiders wiped out the families of settlers who had sought to establish farms adjacent to the protective garrison, and even in broad daylight pickets and outer guards were shot down by red snipers in the prairie grass.

The Sioux were an ever-present threat, but their depredations, as well as those of white thieves, were less of a nuisance and feared less than the mosquitoes. Netting and smoke fires were necessary to human survival, and even on blistering days windows and doors had to be closed. Some cattle and horses, unable

*He would have a chance to make good his boast on the Little Big Horn, but he would fail to carry it out.

to endure the torture, were driven mad and died of exhaustion from fighting the pests which attacked them in shadowy clouds. Whimpering dogs sought relief in holes they dug into the sides of prairie swells. Fort Abraham Lincoln, said veteran cavalrymen, was the worst place on all the western plains for mosquitoes.

The buildings in which the infantry companies lived, both officers' quarters and the barracks of enlisted men, had ceilings and partitions of thick paper. They had been thrown together with a minimum of materials, and they were cold and bleak.

Although the quarters of the favored cavalry were roughly plastered and somewhat sheltered by bluffs, keeping warm in them during the long, bitterly cold Dakota winters was impossible. The unseasoned timber with which they had been constructed warped and opened cracks in the walls, and the wood provided for fuel was green and moist. There were no wells on the post, and water had to be transported in tank wagons from the river, but when the river was frozen it was delivered to the officers' quarters and barracks in chunks of ice and had to be melted in barrels. Bath-taking in the winter was an ordeal most persons avoided until driven by their own odors to endure it.

Colonel Custer permitted each company to be host at an annual winter ball, and there were dances on Thanksgiving, Christmas, New Year's, and St. Patrick's Days. He approved the building of a small theater in which amateur plays and musicals were given. These were presented to noisy capacity audiences, but the saloons and whorehouses of Bismarck drew greater patronage from the soldiers. In them a man could get into a good drunken argument which often led to violence that had to be halted by fort police, and, if he had a dollar, he could enjoy briefly the attractions of a half-breed slut or a chippy from the East. No extra charge was made for gonorrhea or syphilis.

With General Sturgis off most of the time on detached duty, Colonel Custer was in supreme command. Following the destruction of his home by arson, more spacious quarters were built for him and Libby. Having no children, Libby maintained what she termed with maudlin sentiment "my little family." It was comprised of Lieutenant Tom Custer; the colonel's younger brother,

Boston; his nephew, Armstrong Reed; and his sister and brother-in-law, Lieutenant and Mrs. James Calhoun. Frequently at Libby's table were other fanatical supporters of "Autie" (her favorite nickname for the colonel), prominent among them Captain William Winer Cooke, Captain Myles Moylan, Captain George W. Yates, Captain James M. Bell, and Lieutenant De Rudio.

They were a gay group, and their widely diverse backgrounds and personalities provided an unending fund of entertainment. "Cooky" Cooke, a Canadian whom Libby called "Lord Dundreary," because of his handsome mustache, was a favorite in the Custer household. A second lieutenant of Volunteers in the Civil War, he had, upon being mustered out, decided to make a career of the Army, and he had written the New York political boss, Thurlow Weed, an old friend of the Cooke family, for assistance in securing a commission as a first lieutenant. Weed wrote to Stanton, and the Secretary of War responded with a second lieutenant's commission and an assignment to the newly formed 7th Cavalry.

Custer immediately liked young Cooke, urged him to apply for a captaincy, and sent an endorsement of him to the War Department. Although General Grant expressed the view that "other officers have stronger claims to promotions than Lieutenant Cooke," he was made a first lieutenant. Custer appointed him regimental adjutant.

Cooky Cooke and Carlos De Rudio were the only veterans of the war in the 7th who had not been cited for gallantry or meritorious service. Home on leave from Fort Abraham Lincoln, Cooke had revealed his disappointment at not having a single brevet to display, and his mother had determined to rectify what she felt was a decidedly unfair situation. Augusta Cooke was a woman of action, and she set out for Washington, where, after some arguments with lesser officials, she won an audience with President Johnson. The President listened patiently to her, then asked that she put her request in writing, after which he would see what could be done. In a letter written that night in her hotel room, Augusta Cooke told the President that her son was entitled to three brevets, and she cited the instances in which he had shown great bravery and courage. She concluded her letter with an emotional statement that Lieutenant Cooke, being

possessed of no great political influence, and depending wholly upon his meritorious service, and that sense of justice and honor which I feel assured controls your Excellency's public conduct, I place the matter in your hands with the utmost confidence that my prayers will be successful and that you will nominate my son for the brevet rank his service and good conduct entitles him to.

President Johnson, perhaps hoping that Augusta Cooke would not come pounding again at the White House doors, scrawled on the back of the letters, "Let the brevets be made as requested." Lieutenant Cooke became brevet lieutenant colonel.

Carlos De Rudio appeared unperturbed by his lack of Civil War brevets. He had numerous other types of honors to display, not the least of them his record as a graduate of the Royal Austrian Military Academy and his commission in the army of Emperor Franz Josef. He did not reveal that he had deserted in 1848 —he spoke of it as resigning under the pressure of conscience —to fight for Italy, his native land, as an aide to Garibaldi.

Short and stocky and with an imperial, De Rudio bore a striking resemblance to Louis Napoleon. He was witty, a good actor, an accomplished raconteur, and was noted for his charming manner.

For a time after the end of the Italian Civil War he served as a French officer in Algeria.

Falling in with a group led by a fellow Italian, Count Felix Orsini, De Rudio joined in a conspiracy to assassinate Louis Napoleon and Empress Eugénie. The plan was put into execution on the evening of January 18, 1858. Driving home from the opera, Napoleon and Eugénie had reached the Rue Lepelletier when three bombs were thrown beneath their carriage. More than a hundred persons, pedestrians who had paused to watch the Emperor pass, lancers, and footmen, met death or were wounded. The royal carriage was demolished, the horses pulling it were killed, but both Napoleon and Eugénie escaped without serious injury.

The assassins were quickly captured, one of them De Rudio. He had thrown the second of the three bombs. Sentenced with his co-conspirators to death on the guillotine, he was rewarded for testifying against them by banishment to Devil's Island for life. Newspapers reported that De Rudio escaped from prison at Toulon, but he maintained that he had spent several months at Cayenne when he fled with twelve other convicts in an open boat and after extreme suffering at sea reached freedom in Dutch Guiana.

Continuing his flight to the United States, he enlisted as a private in the Union forces, but after being for so long an officer of high rank in foreign armies, the rugged life of the barracks was not for him.

If he preferred officers with the proper political affiliations, Secretary Stanton seemed to possess an almost equally strong affection for European adventurers, and he had no hesitancy in commissioning De Rudio a second lieutenant in the 2nd United States Colored Infantry, an assignment for which there were few requests from white officers.

De Rudio saw little, if any, combat in the war, and on January 5, 1866, was mustered out of service. He applied soon thereafter for a commission in the Regular Army, and for the second time Secretary Stanton awarded him a lieutenancy. After considerable difficulty in passing the required physical examinations, De Rudio was sworn in and sent to the 7th Cavalry.

De Rudio was in great demand by Libby Custer, who was quite partial to anything European, human being or manufactured goods. Moreover, she considered Lieutenant De Rudio's manner simply charming, and his knowledge of good wines really astounding. In the eyes of Libby Custer, Carlos De Rudio was a Count of Monte Cristo.

Although Captain Myles Moylan had neither the *savoir-faire* nor the acting ability which Libby Custer so much admired, she had no alternative but to accord him every benefit and service of her household, and to accept him virtually as a permanent guest. This situation was not brought about by his incomparable and unqualified devotion to Autie, but by the refusal of the bachelor officers to admit him to their mess.

Captain Moylan, without benefit of any formal education, had accomplished the incredible feat of rising three times from the ranks to a commission. A clerk in a Massachusetts grocery, he had enlisted the first time in 1857. By the time the Civil War began he was a sergeant, and after two years in the ranks was appointed a second lieutenant of the 5th Cavalry. Nine months later he was stripped of his bars and dismissed from service for visiting the city of Washington without permission. Undaunted in his determination to pursue a military career, he changed his name to Charles E. Thomas and enlisted as a private in the 4th Massachusetts Cavalry. In less than a month he had once more risen to a sergeancy. In less than two months he was First Lieutenant Thomas. In less than a year he had been promoted to a captaincy. His gallantry in combat brought him a brevet majority. He was honorably discharged in March, 1866.

Still determined to be a soldier, he shed his alias, and before the summer ended he had re-enlisted under his own name as a private in the 7th Cavalry. In ten days he had become a sergeant. More important, he had attracted the attention of George A. Custer.

From the first time he met him, Custer liked Moylan. He called him his kind of man—that is, brave, rough, and tough— and he urged Moylan to seek a commission, volunteering to write a strong endorsement for him. On Custer's recommendation, Moylan was given an examination, but he failed to pass it. Moylan's knowledge of geography was limited to the parts of the United States he had seen. He had no idea of the location of the Mediterranean Sea, nor could he bound England. Custer took it upon himself to tutor Sergeant Moylan, and when he thought him prepared, arranged for a second examination. Moylan obtained a passing grade, and for the third time became a lieutenant.

The refusal of the bachelor officers to share their mess table with Moylan was not based on the manner in which he had obtained his commission, for a number of them had themselves risen from the ranks. If not aristocrats—although some of them were sons of refined and prominent families—George Wallace, Charlie Varnum, Ed Mathey, Luther Hare, Benny Hodgson, Win Edgerly, and Tom French considered themselves gentlemen. If they were not prudes, neither were they dissolute, and the coarseness, lewdness, and vulgarity which Moylan appeared to take pleasure displaying in masculine company were greater than they were willing to endure.

The exclusion of Moylan was an affront to Custer, but inasmuch as he had sponsored him and aided him to obtain a commission, he had no alternative but to invite him to take his meals at the Custer table. In time Custer gained a large measure of revenge by having Moylan advanced to a captaincy over the other first lieutenants who were eligible for promotion. The annoying situation was greatly relieved when Moylan married the sister of Lieutenant Calhoun, the husband of Colonel Custer's sister, Maggie. It was a match of which the colonel and Libby not only heartily approved, but which they went to some lengths to bring about.

Tall, blond, and handsome Jimmy Calhoun had long been a close Army friend of Custer, for whom he held unstinted admiration. In 1869, when he was an assistant quartermaster at Fort Grant, Arizona Territory, an inspector general had discovered that a shipment of hay ordered for the post had not arrived. Investigations cast suspicions on Lieutenant Calhoun, and he was directed to stand trial before a Benzine board. Calhoun's commanding officer, Colonel George Stoneman, wrote the board:

This officer, while acting quartermaster, was guilty of evident rascality. . . . I would recommend that he be discharged and the allowance of one year's pay be not allowed until the above property is accounted for.

George Custer's political affiliations and influence were never better tested than when he sprang to the assistance of his good friend, Jimmy Calhoun. Custer sent telegrams and wrote letters to his supporters and sponsors in Washington, and appeared before the Benzine board to testify in Calhoun's behalf. The trial resulted in Calhoun's being permitted to remain on duty under an agreement to reimburse the government for the missing hay. Custer thereupon induced General Sherman to transfer Calhoun to the 7th Cavalry. Nine days after Lieutenant Calhoun reported for duty, Custer secured for him a promotion to captain. Maggie Custer Calhoun was Libby's most intimate friend. They traveled together when the regiment moved, and when their husbands were away in the field, Maggie lived in the Custer home.

Of all the officers of the 7th Cavalry who were members of Libby Custer's little family, none had received more favors from Colonel Custer than Captain George W. Yates. When Custer took command of Fort Abraham Lincoln, he and Yates had been close friends for more than ten years. They had first met in 1862 when they both were attached to the staff of Major General Alfred Pleasanton.

Yates also had entered the Army as a private, had soon become a quartermaster sergeant, and within a year was commissioned a second lieutenant. He was mustered out of the Volunteer Service as a captain. Wishing to continue his military career, he appealed to his friend, Colonel Custer, for help in obtaining a commission in the Regular Army. Custer had only to write a letter to Secretary Stanton to secure a second lieutenancy for Yates. Within another year Custer had arranged to have Yates promoted to a captaincy and assigned to the 7th Cavalry.

As if he were not satisfied with the assistance he had given Yates, Custer somewhat reprovingly informed the War Department that Yates, an officer who had served with gallantry at First Bull Run, Fredericksburg, Antietam, Chancellorsville, and Gettsyburg, had received not a single brevet. The War Department corrected the oversight by breveting Captain Yates a lieutenant colonel of Volunteers.

Libby Custer did not conceal her disappointment that neither the senior captain of the 7th Cavalry, Fred Benteen, nor the regiment's second-in-command, Major Marcus Reno, was a partisan of her husband. She had never forgiven Captain Benteen for the letter he had sent to the newspapers about the Washita massacre, and never spoke to him unless forced by circumstances to acknowledge his presence. As for Major Reno, she treated him with cool politeness. She had never liked Mary Hannah, accusing her of putting on airs and making shows of her silver and china, but even with Mary Hannah in a Harrisburg grave she showed neither sympathy nor consideration for the lonely major. She had no more liking for him as a widower than she had had when Mary Hannah was alive. If she could find no grounds for accusing the major of being an enemy of her husband—as she could in the case of Captain Benteen—she could see no reason for looking upon him as a friend. An officer who did not repeatedly proclaim his admiration of Autie and swear undying allegiance to him was, in her often-voiced opinion, not to be trusted.

It was incredible to Elizabeth Bacon Custer that anyone could dislike or think ill of her beloved Autie. She had an almost obsessive need to injure those who criticized him. Many officers who had known her would have subscribed to the words of the eminent historian, Fred Dustin:

> She was blind, deaf, and dumb to any shortcomings of her husband. . . . To her Custer was a God, an immaculate hero, a knight without stain . . . he could do no wrong . . . he was a victim of subordinates who envied or hated him . . . all were wrong except Custer.

This idolatry had not developed in Elizabeth Bacon Custer after years of life on the western plains. It had existed from the time a young officer, tanned, extremely handsome, dashing, gracious, and fresh from battles of the Civil War, had walked into her life in Monroe, Michigan.

Elizabeth was the only child born to Daniel Stanton and Eleanor Page Bacon. He mother died when she was twelve, and her father, a probate judge and well-to-do businessman, placed her in a seminary of which he was a trustee. Because of Judge Bacon's prominence, she lived in privileged opulence at the school, having her own bedroom and parlor with a fine view, while other students were obliged to share quarters with roommates. Libby Custer appeared to enjoy telling friends of later years how she had, without reticence or shame, taken advantage of her position as "that poor motherless Libby Bacon." "What an excuse I made of it for not doing anything I didn't want to do," she would say. "And what excuses were made for me on that score!"

Judge Bacon remarried when Libby was seventeen. His bride was the widow of a Congregational minister, and Libby considered her "not objectionably intellectual." She went home to live, and she and her stepmother became fast friends.

Judge Bacon was above all else a materialist. He maintained that one should first determine the intrinsic value of an object, after which thought might be given to spiritual or sentimental considerations. He had striven to instill in his only child this philosophy, and his efforts had not been entirely futile. Libby was sincerely appreciative of good music. However, at the age of ten, when she was given a piano and stool, she promptly recorded in her dairy, not her pleasure, not the thought that the instrument would provide music for herself and others, but the practical information: "It cost $275 and the stool $10.00."

Judge Bacon was deeply distressed to learn that Libby had fallen in love with a professional soldier. He had selected for her a young man of a good Monroe family who had bought a substitute to serve for him in the war, and who had remained at home to continue making money in the real estate business. The judge was himself extremely patriotic, he favored the Union, he was opposed to slavery, he gave ringing speeches for the northern cause and made generous contributions to it, but his opinion of professional soldiers—in fact, any kind of soldiers—was that, though in their colorful uniforms they might appear very charming to an inexperienced young lady, they could not possibly be taken seriously. Why, he exclaimed in alarm, a man who went to war might be disabled, thrown back on one's hands, physically or mentally crippled, a permanent charge, even a derelict! He would not hear of Libby facing the possibility of taking on such a burden—which would, of course, be as much a burden to himself. If she had any sense or appreciation of the true values of life, she would marry a young man who left the fighting to mercenaries and remained at home to establish himself with good property.

When neither George Armstrong Custer, whose family was not in the social category of the Bacons, nor Libby appeared to show much judgment in the matter, she was bundled off to Toledo, and made to promise that she would not see or correspond with the brash young lieutenant. Months passed during which Libby kept her promise. She did not see George Custer, but she kept informing a friend what she would say to him if she could see him, and the friend promptly relayed her words to the lovesick lieutenant. His replies were similarly delivered to Libby.

When George Custer became a brigadier general, Judge Bacon's attitude underwent a transformation, and he finally withdrew his objections to the marriage and welcomed General Custer into the family. The General and Libby were married in a brilliant church ceremony on February 9, 1864.

Her love for Autie as a general was no less qualified than it had been for him as a lieutenant. She was never known to complain about the hardships or disappointments of Army life. She followed him from post to post like the loyal and devoted worshiper she was, endlessly striving to give him every comfort she could devise, strenuously defending him, untiringly making every effort of which she was capable to publicize him, increase his prominence, and spread his renown by word of mouth and letters to newspapers and periodicals. Having no child upon whom she might bestow part of her affection, she poured all of it on Autie.

Libby Custer understood that her husband's principal motivation was a craving for glory and fame, and, looking upon it as the noblest of ambitions, she stood ready to make any sacrifice to help him achieve it. When he revealed his greatest ambition, to be the President of the United States, her answer was: "Why not?"

George Custer had come out of the Civil War breveted a major general and a national hero. He had taken time from his military career to barnstorm with Andrew Johnson, and he had heard countless audiences cheer him instead of the President he was supporting. He had condemned the corruption of Grant's Administration and that had brought him into strong favor with leading northern newspapers.

The New York publisher, James Gordon Bennett, was already proposing him as the Democratic candidate. Both were convinced that a great victory against the Indians in the West could seal the nomination for him. Custer's supporters in Congress, encouraged by a press which was inflaming the public with cries for peace on the frontier, demanded that he lead a campaign to crush once and for all time the red menace.

It all was music to Custer's ears, and he envisioned himself as the great conqueror of the West, the military genius who succeeded where all others had failed. After that incomparable feat the road to the White House would surely be open to him.

Loyalty to his commander, a common attribute of the West Point graduate, was conspicuously lacking in George Armstrong Custer. Fealty simply did not exist in him, except in relation to himself. Not even Libby, for whom he professed great love, not even the members of his family and his relatives, to whom he avowed devotion, were beyond the reach of his infidelity. He wanted them with him, he demanded their attention and offered inducements to secure it, for their presence and their praises were vital nourishment to him. Without constant adulation he would have sickened.

The defiance he had shown to his superiors would have brought disgrace and ruin to officers with less political support. No man under whose command Custer had served was without admiration for his courage, but none was unaware of the necessity of keeping him under tight controls. As a junior officer he was extremely valuable, but only when he was used with a checkrein. If he could escape from the watchful eyes of a commander, he disregarded orders, often with results that verged on disaster. General Sheridan had understood that Custer was a dangerously insubordinate young officer, and he had made a point of keeping him well in hand, thereby making successful use of his many talents. Other commanders, who had not been so wise, found themselves faced with predicaments that placed them at a distinct disadvantage. Custer always found means of circumventing them, of going over their heads surreptitiously, and keeping himself in the limelight.

The Washita massacre, in which Custer had abandoned nineteen of his men, leaving them to fight to their deaths only two miles from his camp, had forcefully illustrated to commanders in the West both his ineptness and his insensitivity. He thought of himself as supreme among men, not subject to the common rules and principles by which others were governed.

George Custer had reached great heights as a very young man, and there his mental growth stopped. He was essentially an adolescent, his love of horseplay, his romping, his vanity, his cruelty, all indicating an arrested development. A spoiled child of fortune, a critic called him. He never tired of racing out on the plains on one of the fine hunters from his private stable—always with a contingent of troopers following to insure his safety—and shooting down any game he came across. Particularly did he enjoy chasing and slaughtering buffalo, leaving their carcasses to rot on the grass.

As a fully grown man, he had the vitality of a youth. In camp he was the first to arise in the morning, and often, after a grueling day in the saddle, he would spend hours writing or reading by yellow candlelight while other officers were asleep. But his nocturnal activities did not involve efforts to improve himself. He cared little for military tactics, and he made no attempt to understand and master them. To him all situations were the same and called for only one maneuver: advance, maintain the offensive. Defensive tactics he considered unworthy of his attention. He was supremely confident that given a well-trained and experienced regiment he could soon end the Indian Wars without other assistance.

If Libby Custer made clear her dislike for Major Reno, her husband gave no indication that he harbored a similar feeling. She saw the major as stolid and dull, and she resented his failure to appear impressed by her presence. Major Reno was polite, well mannered, and reserved at all times, and she recognized these traits not as qualities to be admired but as indications that he cared not at all whether he received attention from her or favors from Autie. The colonel looked upon Major Reno in quite another way, seeing him as an officer whose dependability and capability were assets for which he could be thankful. Colonel Custer understood that he need have no concern about the efficient operation of Fort Abraham Lincoln so long as Mark Reno was on duty there under him.

Major Reno appeared not in the least perturbed by Libby Custer's opinion of him. He believed that when he had joined the 7th Cavalry he had in large measure achieved the middle course he had so greatly desired. If the members of the Custer clique did not care for him as a person and resented his neutrality, he felt that they respected him as an officer. He asked nothing more.

He gave dinners which he thought his position demanded. However, he found himself strangely ill at ease in the presence of the officers' wives, although they—especially Maggie Calhoun, Emiline Bell, and Mary Godfrey, who were particularly charming and professed a great admiration for him—appeared to enjoy themselves thoroughly as his guests.

If Lieutenant Godfrey had had his way, he would not have attended any social function in the quarters of Major Reno. He appeared there with his wife only when protocol, if not good manners, demanded his presence. Her husband's personal animosity toward the major appeared to have no influence upon Mary Godfrey, however, and when her husband was absent from the post she gladly accepted Reno's invitations to join his other guests at a dinner or for an evening of whist.

Mary Godfrey and Emiline Bell were very close—although Lieutenant Godfrey thought very little of Captain Bell—and one might be certain that where one of them was to be seen the other was not far away. It was a rather odd companionship, for Mary Godfrey was generally reserved and retiring, whereas Emiline Bell was an extrovert and overfamiliar in manner.

For several years stories had been circulated about poker tables and field campfires of the 7th that did nothing to enhance Emiline Bell's reputation. She had engaged in flirtations, and escapades of a more serious nature, which on several occasions had been the subject of quiet official inquiries. The burden had weighed heavily on Captain Bell, but his forbearance, if not his profound affection for his wife, had caused him to refuse to file charges against the officers involved. An open scandal, which would have brought action by a military board, was avoided, but the memory of the affairs remained alive.

James Montgomery Bell was the son of a prominent Pennsylvania contractor who had built the "Crooked Dam" on the Juniata River. He had served as a captain in the 13th Pennsylvania Cavalry during the Civil War and married Emily Hones, thirteen years his junior, in 1872, while he was on recruiting duty in Pittsburgh. He served as quartermaster with Reno on the First Border Survey.

The stories about Emiline Bell grew more vivid with retelling and were greatly embellished for the edification of newcomers to the regiment or for the officers of other contingents who had not heard them.

The conviviality and apparent success of his social functions brought little real pleasure or satisfaction to Major Reno. He had not yet adjusted himself to life without Mary Hannah, and the presence of the women stirred thoughts of her that left him depressed. He found more enjoyment, greater escape, in entertaining the unattached officers or those whose wives were not with them at the post.

There were many pleasant evenings when two, three, perhaps half a dozen of them sat with him by his hearth, a bottle before them, and swapped stories and recounted experiences far into the night. His close friendship with Benny Hodgson, which had begun in South Carolina, continued, and he developed a sincere liking for Win Edgerly, Tom McDougall, Charlie Varnum, and George Wallace.

Hodgson's family had wanted him to follow in the footsteps of his forebears and become a naval officer. His excuse for attending West Point instead of Annapolis had been that he didn't get as sick on a horse as he did on a ship. Actually, he was deeply attached to the cavalry, and his fondness and profound respect for Major Reno had existed from the time they had first met.

The major had no less regard for the affable, gentlemanly, and brilliant lieutenant.

Troopers said that Winfield Scott Edgerly deserved his illustrious military name, for he not only acted like a cavalry officer but looked like one. Major Reno was not alone in pronouncing him one of the ablest of the young officers of the 7th. He was particularly attached to Captain Benteen, but he refused to join the anti-Custer group. Like Major Reno, he sought to hold himself aloof from any partisanship. "The Army can't get too many like him," a fellow officer said of Edgerly.

Thomas M. McDougall was the son of a distinguished Army surgeon who had tried to keep him from enlisting. With the realization that his efforts would be futile, he sought to have him commissioned in the 19th Infantry whose colonel was his cousin. Young McDougall, in keeping with traditional Army perversity, was made a second lieutenant in a regiment of Negro troops. Following the Civil War, both General George Meade and General U. S. Grant recommended Tom McDougall for a commission in the Regular Army. In 1870 he was appointed to a first lieutenancy in the 7th Cavalry, much to his pleasure. Shortly before Major Reno arrived at Fort Abraham Lincoln, McDougall had become a captain.

When he assumed command of the 7th Cavalry, the choleric Colonel Sturgis took a personal dislike to Second Lieutenant Edward Gustave Mathey, apparently for no better reason than that he had been born in France and was the son of poor French immigrants. He sought to have Mathey dismissed by a Benzine board as undesirable officer material.

Mathey had served gallantly through the Civil War, rising from the ranks. Asking no help from Custer or any other officer of the 7th, he had carried on his own defense before the board and convinced its members that the charges of Colonel Sturgis were without foundation. He was returned to duty.

Luther Rector Hare, the son of a Texas lawyer, had been sent directly from West Point to the 7th Cavalry. Major Reno thought of him as "daring, courageous, reserved, conscientious, an ideal soldier," and the words were echoed in military annals.

Charles Albert Varnum went from the Navy to West Point, was a classmate and companion of George D. Wallace. Wallace was the son of a South Carolinian who had turned against his own state to support the Union. Varnum and Wallace, graduating from West Point in the Class of 1872, had both been sent to the 7th.

When he reported for his first Army assignment, to Troop G of the 7th Cavalry at Spartanburg, South Carolina, Second Lieutenant Wallace was only a few miles from his home. He could look back on sorrowful years in the area. Because of his father's loyalty to the Union, the Wallace family had been shunned by neighbors they had known all their lives, their farm had been destroyed, and they had been driven from their home. Staunchly continuing to stand by his convictions, the elder Wallace had by hard work restored his property, and following the war been elected to Congress from the state which had disowned him. He was overjoyed to have his son appointed to the 7th Cavalry, and he wrote Secretary of War Belknap that his personal acquaintance with the 7th's officers stationed in South Carolina "shows me they are gentlemen whose tastes and habits are such that I would be glad to have my son under their influence and instruction when just entering the service, as he is."

Major Reno understandably had wondered whether Second Lieutenant Wallace's southern background would influence his conduct as an officer in the troublesome sector, but he had soon learned that it would not. A strong friendship, bolstered by mutual respect, quickly developed between the veteran major and the green young lieutenant. It was a friendship that grew steadily stronger.

If at the time he became second-in-command at Fort Abraham Lincoln, Major Reno had an enemy in the 7th Cavalry, it was none of the men who disliked him because of his failure to show partiality for Custer. It was Lieutenant Edward Settle Godfrey.

Godfrey's hatred, which had been born with their first meeting at Fort Leavenworth, presented an enigma which Major Reno was unable to solve. The situation was complicated by two significant factors. Godfrey appeared to harbor grudges against other officers who had made sincere efforts to be friendly and cooperative, and he despised Custer. One might have supposed that his attitude toward the colonel sprang from the tragic events of the Washita massacre, for Godfrey was the officer who had several times suggested to Custer that Major Elliott and his men might be in trouble, only to be ignored. Yet Godfrey had consistently declined to join the anti-Custer group, even refusing to discuss either the Washita massacre or Custer's shortcomings, and he had never disclosed the reasons for his detestation of his commanding officer.

Godfrey was a small man, and a walrus mustache did nothing to improve his generally unattractive appearance. Self-righteous, prim, precise, and finicky, he in reality had nothing in common with the frank, generous, easygoing Major Reno.

Reno probably admitted that, in spite of his peculiarities, Lieutenant Godfrey was a conscientious and able field officer. His career with the 7th had been marked with difficulties which might have defeated a man of less tenacity. Newspaper accounts of his actions at the time of the Washita massacre had placed him in an unfavorable public light. A year later, Colonel Sturgis had sought to have him dismissed from the service "as unfit for the proper discharge of duties." Lieutenant Godfrey, Sturgis told the Benzine board, is "indifferent, complains that Cavalry service interferes with his domestic comfort and convenience and is distasteful to him. With these notions it is not probable that he will ever add to the efficiency of the service." Sturgis had taken seriously the immature grumblings of a young and lonely lieutenant.

General John Pope was not to be rushed into making a decision that might well ruin the career, if not the life, of an inexperienced West Pointer of twenty-seven. An investigation showed that Sturgis' accusations and opinion were supported by poor evidence. A young officer who did not gripe at all would have been more suspect than one who went about mumbling that he was inconvenienced.

Confronted with a stiff letter from Pope, Colonel Sturgis quickly withdrew the charges and replied:

In presenting the name of this officer I was influenced solely by the reasons set forth by himself in a conversation to me asking for a transfer to the Artillery, in which said communication he said the Cavalry Service discommoded his domestic affairs, all of which led me to believe that he was not a suitable person to remain in the Cavalry arm. I am satisfied from personal observation that he did himself an injustice in that conversation and really possesses the elements of a good officer.

Only a short time had passed after his return to Fort Abraham Lincoln before Major Reno was informed by Colonel Custer that he and Mrs. Custer soon would leave to spend the winter in the East. If this came as a surprise, in view of the plans for extensive campaigns then being formulated, it was not a disappointment. Custer seldom discussed his personal affairs with Major Reno, but the major had no trouble learning from others the chief reasons for the colonel's desire to visit New York and Washington at the time.

Custer's political ambitions were not a military secret, and 1876 would be a campaign year. He was fired by grandiose dreams, not alone that of taking the oath of office as the nineteenth President of the United States. If that great honor should for some unaccountable reason be denied him, there were others which he would be willing to accept, which might well serve as steppingstones to greater future glory. Not the least of the acceptable alternatives were the office of Secretary of War or appointment as Commanding General of the Army of the United States.

Colonel Sturgis had some months previously been detached from his command of the 7th Cavalry for a long tour of administrative duty, and with Colonel Custer's departure from Fort Abraham Lincoln, Major Reno became the senior officer of the post. It was for reasons other than pride that Major Reno welcomed the situation. The burden of his loneliness, while gradually becoming lighter, still weighed heavily on him. Command of a thousand soldiers, Indian scouts and civilian employees, and responsibility for the efficient operation of the biggest fort on the frontier—including the procurement of supplies, ammunition, and equipment, the maintenance of good order, the physical welfare of all military personnel and several score wives and children, guarding against depredations and thefts by both Indians and renegade whites, a thousand and one administrative duties, and the training and preparation of expeditions that were to start with the advent of spring—would leave him little, if any, time to dwell on his own sorrows.

Major Reno plunged into the heavy work with renewed spirit and an increasing determination to be successful, and he swore that he cared not at all what the future held in store for him.

13

I n the eighteen-seventies any American, and especially officers of the Army stationed in the West, would have been hard put to explain the Indian policy of the United States. Indeed, there was no defined official policy. Each Administration and various Federal departments had what were called Indian policies, but they were based in each case on personal beliefs, conceptions, and prejudices. The people of the West had a policy of their own, as did the organized churches, the commercial and financial interests, and the Army. No single one conformed with any of the others.

Even if reconciliation had been possible—which it was not—it would have brought little progress toward a solution of the troubles. In any case, direction—honest, forceful, competent direction—was mandatory. Without it nothing could be achieved. But it required an overriding power that was not attainable by any group, bureau, or even the Administration itself. The confused, vacillating, naïve man in the White House, Ulysses Simpson Grant, was incapable of enforcing a definitive program even if he had been capable of formulating it, and no one else possessed the necessary authority to try.

The Indian Bureau was composed of two camps, but both advocated a policy of peace and goodwill to the "noble Red Man," and this won it the support of most Easteners.

The Indian Bureau camp of starry-eyed idealists was the largest, but it was not the strongest. By comparison, the contingent of grafters, swindlers, and venal adventurers—the hard-minded, the practical, the unconscionable—although few in number wielded far more power, and thus were far more effective.

Practicality seldom disturbed the dreamers, reality never. They wanted decent treatment for the Indians, they wanted justice, but most of all they wanted peace, and in the hope of obtaining it they argued that it was cheaper to furnish the hostiles with the necessities of life, which included arms and ammunition, than to engage them in warfare. Peace at any price was the doctrine they preached, and they dressed it in noble phrases which were difficult for any honest person to question.

As for the thieves in the Indian Bureau, they had every reason to give such a policy their support. It was made to order for them, for peace on the plains meant a larger pork barrel. You couldn't furnish Indians with the necessities of life if you couldn't find them, or if you had to fight them. No one had devised a scheme for supplying dead Indians with anything but graves. As it was, even a mildly enterprising agent could save ten to twenty thousand dollars a year on an annual salary of twelve hundred, and comparable thriftiness could bring a clever manufacturer or wholesaler even greater returns on an investment. These were not insignificant rewards, but they would be inconsequential before those to be gained if all Indians could be induced to abandon their historic way of life and take residence in permanent establishments. Under such circumstances the number of wards to whom the government was obligated to furnish the necessities of life would be immeasurably increased.

For entirely different reasons both groups in the Indian Bureau advocated a cessation of hostilities, but actually the wide separation of their goals had little significance. The theories of the intellectual idealists were fatuous and illusory. The proposals of the corruptors were born of dishonesty and conniving schemes. Complete domination by either faction would not have helped to eliminate the evils of the situation. Theoretical blankets and beef would have been of no more benefit to the Indian than the bacon and beans stolen from him.

The religious groups who concerned themselves with the great problem believed that the Lord would make everything right if only they could build missions and spread the Word among the heathens. It appeared to be inconceivable to them that a man whose means of living had been taken from him, whose wife and children were ragged, cold, and starving, whose own belly was empty, would not display eager interest in the Christian Gospel.

A great many of the so-called frontiersmen, pioneers, and conquerors of the wilderness, so highly lauded and eulogized for a courage that did not exist in them, were distinguished by instincts and moral principles generally attributed to coyotes. They proposed a method of putting the Indians in touch with Heaven that was far less complicated and much easier to carry out than that of any religious organization. It was ruthless extermination.

In the center of all groups, pressured from all sides, stood the United States Army. Assigned the task of maintaining order on the frontier, it was given inadequate forces, harassed by Washington politicians, exploited by corruptors, and frequently made helpless by conflicting orders.

If it caught and punished murderers, either red or white, it was castigated for its cruelty. If commanding officers showed compassion and attempted to carry on with an understanding of Indian problems, they were branded weaklings and charged with betraying their own people to bloody savages. If it shot raiders in the act of carrying off white women and children, it was a ruthless force determined to destroy the poor redskins.

Some settlers and merchants of the little western towns had a good word for the Army because it protected them, but more often than not the praise was qualified with the criticism that the Army was too stringent in the enforcement of laws and tried to rule the populace. Members of Congress frothed in fury at reports reaching it through the War Department—prepared from the testimony of responsible, intelligent, and fair-minded officers —that most of the troubles and tragedies of the West were brought about by the greed and lawlessness of the farmers, storekeepers, and businessmen who coveted the land and the resources of the Indians. In every conceivable way the Indian was cheated, robbed, beaten, maimed, and murdered by white persons who attended services in little clapboard churches on Sunday morning.

As if it did not have enough with which to contend in launching its post-Civil War campaigns to bring peace to the West, the Army's burdens were greatly increased by the insane act of a sadistic, Methodist preacher named John Chivington. It did the Army little good to protest that Chivington was not a Regular, but only a political colonel of the Colorado Militia. As far as the public and Congress were concerned, the identification was of no import. It did not alter the fact that Colonel Chivington had directed one of the most terrible and savage massacres in modern history.

In the autumn of 1864 the Governor of Colorado sent out an invitation through traders and scouts to all friendly Indians to come "into the neighborhood of the forts, and be protected by the United States troops." Three large bands of Cheyennes, led by the dependable and intelligent chiefs, Black Kettle, White Antelope, and War Bonnet, came into Fort Lyon, on the Arkansas River in southeastern Colorado. They were given supplies by the commandant, Major Scott Anthony (the brother of suffragette Susan B. Anthony), and instructed to go to Sand Creek, thirty miles to the northeast (near La Junta), and establish a winter camp. Told they could be assured of complete safety, they obeyed.

On November 28 Colonel Chivington led his troop of Colorado Militia and renegade frontiersmen out of Fort Lyon fully intent upon violating the promise of protection given to the Cheyennes. At dawn on November 29 he quietly approached the sleeping camp, but a squaw heard the sound of the horses' hooves on the frozen earth and called out that a herd of buffalo was passing.

Indians ran from the lodges, hoping for a chance to hunt. They saw not buffalo but a wave of blue uniforms sweeping down on them.

Between 450 and 500 Cheyenne men, women, and children were slaughtered in the next hour.

A long and exhaustive government inquiry into the massacre disclosed that White Antelope was shot to death as he stood with folded arms before the advancing troops. The American flag floated over the lodge of Black Kettle, and below it was tied a small white flag as a symbol of surrender—a precaution Black Kettle had been advised to take at Fort Lyon. Beneath these emblems of country and peace Chivington and his men carried on their butchering.

Scores of witnesses, troopers and civilian whites who had participated in the massacre and others who had visited the scene, were called by the investigating committees. Their testimony contained these statements:

Women and children were killed and scalped, children shot at their mothers' breasts, and all the bodies mutilated in the most horrible manner. . . .

The dead bodies of females profaned in such a manner is sickening, the Colonel all the time inciting his troops to their diabolical outrages. . . .

I saw a man dismount from his horse and cut the ear from the body of an Indian, and the scalp from the head of another. I saw a number of children killed; they had bullet holes in them; one child had been cut with some sharp instrument across its side. I saw another that both ears had been cut off. . . .

I saw several of the Third Regiment cut off fingers to get the rings off them. . . .

I saw one squaw lying on the bank, whose leg had been broken. A soldier came up to her with a drawn saber. She raised her arm to protect herself; he struck, breaking her arm. She rolled over and raised her other arm; he struck, breaking that, and then left her without killing her. . . .

I saw one squaw cut open, with an unborn child lying by her side. . . .

There was one little child, probably three years old, just big enough to walk through the sand. The Indians had gone ahead, and this little child was behind, following after them. The little fellow was perfectly naked travelling in the sand. I saw one man get off his horse at a distance of about seventy-five yards and draw up his rifle and fire. He missed the child. Another man came up and said, "Let me try the son of a b——. I can hit him." He got down off his horse, kneeled down, and fired at the little child, but he missed him. A third man came up, and made a similar remark, and fired, and the little fellow dropped.

Cried a Denver newspaper:

All acquitted themselves well! Colorado soldiers have again covered themselves with glory!*

Proudly the colonel proclaimed that he had "defeated" the Cheyennes, and declared his belief that it was "right and honorable to use any means under God's heaven to kill Indians."

He shouted: "Kill and scalp all, big and little. Nits make lice."

High-ranking Army officers held a different view. The opinion of the famous General Nelson A. Miles was: "The Sand Creek massacre is perhaps the foulest and most unjustifiable crime in the annals of America." His feeling was shared by the members of the investigating committee, whose report said: "It is difficult to believe that beings in the form of men . . . could commit or countenance the commission of such acts of cruelty and barbarity."**

These were noble words, but of little consolation to Black Kettle and the few survivors of the Cheyenne bands.

Chivington resumed his preaching after the Civil War and eventually moved to Ohio, where he started a newspaper and ran for Congress. His opponent labeled him "Sand Creek John," and he was defeated. The stigma was more than he could bear, and he vanished into the western mountains.

Following the massacre, a great hue and cry arose from an

*Denver *Rocky Mountains News*, Dec. 17, 1864.
**Three distinguished military men were committee members: General William Tecumseh Sherman, who would become head of the Army, and Generals Alfred H. Terry and C. C. Augur, both of whom were friends and colleagues of Reno.

outraged public for a new approach to the Indian problem, and Congress responded by appointing a joint committee to formulate a definitive policy. This, of course, was an impossibility, but the work of the committee made it clear with incontrovertible evidence that it was the white man, not the Indian, who was in the main responsible for the troubles in the West.

This had no more influence on the political corruptors than official expressions of regret had on the thinking of the Indians. If they had suspected it before, the Indian people now held the unshakable conviction that their Great White Father had only one course in mind, and that was their complete annihilation. They vowed to fight to the death, until the last member of their race had been destroyed.

When Congress in 1867 finally appointed a committee to treat with the hostile tribes of the West, the corruptors were on hand to protect their own futures. They succeeded in securing the appointment of at least two members who would not be inimical to their best interests. The majority of the committee, however, were men of high principle and honor, with every intention of giving their undivided efforts to achieving success in the mission to which they had been assigned. Holding the chairmanship was Lieutenant General William Tecumseh Sherman, well acquainted with the hardships and vicissitudes of war. Three other Regular Army generals held seats. They were Alfred Terry, Civil War hero; Christopher C. Augur, whose military record was highly commendable; and William S. Harney, a forthright officer who knew more about Indians than any of his eight colleagues on the commission.

Neither the general public nor the Indians had reason to feel comfortable about the civilian members. They were Senator John B. Henderson of Missouri, chairman of the Senate Committee on Indian Affairs, but whose main interests were with eastern industrialists and had nothing in common with the government wards he had been delegated to assist; N. G. Taylor, the Commissioner of Indian Affairs, a former Methodist minister to whom, as one committeeman observed, sanctity still clung like a well-fitted coat; General (political) J. B. Sanborn, a Minnesota lawyer, party hack, and self-appointed court jester; and Colonel (political) S. F. Tappan, who rarely spoke and maintained a position in Taylor's shadow.

It was hardly surprising that when the commission arrived to conduct negotiations at Fort Laramie, located on the North Platte at the mouth of the Laramie River in Wyoming Territory, on September 13, 1867, representatives of the hostile Dakota and Montana Indians were nowhere in sight. A conference with them was finally arranged for November 1, but when that date was reached, Red Cloud, the most influential of the Sioux chieftains and the man the commissioners were most anxious to meet, did not appear. Word was received through an emissary that Red Cloud would not negotiate a treaty of peace until the garrisons at Forts Phil Kearney and F. C. Smith had been withdrawn. (Fort Phil Kearney, in Nebraska Territory, had been built to protect travelers on the Oregon Trail. Fort F. C. Smith was located on the Big Horn River in south central Montana.) The commission adjourned until April 1, 1868, to consider the matter.

It was not until some months later that the military members of the commission were able to convince Congress that Red Cloud's demands were reasonable. The forts were abandoned. On February 24, 1869, Red Cloud put his thumbprint on a treaty.

It was in many respects a sensible and just document. Article II reserved the absolute and undisturbed use and occupation for the Indians of all the land within the limits of the Territory of Dakota, west of the Missouri River. The area included virtually all of the Black Hills country. Article XI stipulated that the tribes "reserved the right to hunt on any land north of the North Platte River and on the Fork of Smoky Hill River, as long as the buffalo may range thereon in such manner as to justify the chase." Article XII declared that "The United States hereby agrees and stipulates that the country north of the North Platte River and East of the Summit of the Big Horn Mountains shall be held and considered to be unceded Indian Territory, and stipulates and agrees that no white person or persons shall be permitted to settle upon or occupy any portion of the same, without first obtaining the Indians' consent."

Unfortunately, the value of the immense territory so generously awarded to a few thousand Indians was not known, and no attempt was made to classify it. There was little or no information as to the timber and mineral resources within it. Rumors had been strong for some time that the Black Hills contained gold deposits, but the matter was not taken into consideration. The commission opined that the Black Hills country was unfit for any use except the grazing of buffalo. Railroads had been planned—indeed were being built—through the country assigned to the tribes, but this fact was ignored.

Nor did the commission take the trouble to secure the approval of numerous Indian leaders who were politically powerful among their people. The ink had no more than dried on the parchment before a number of Sioux chieftains let it be known that they felt themselves free of any obligation the treaty imposed. They had not signed it, and they did not admit its validity. Rising young Indian statesmen allied themselves against Red Cloud, and his prestige began to wane. Sitting Bull, whose hatred for all white men was unexcelled, quickly took advantage of the situation. Surrounding himself with his own Hunkpapas and numerous groups of malcontents from other tribes, he organized a strong opposition party. It was Sitting Bull's contention that no piece of paper was needed to show that the territory specified in the treaty was the homeland of the northern tribes, especially the Sioux. He would sign no agreement giving him the right to live in his own country.

Land grabbers, cattle barons, mining companies, railroad corporations, industrialists, bankers, and every form of businessman joined in a unified assault on the treaty. They presented insuperable strength, and the Administration capitulated.

On the ground that it was impeding the orderly expansion and development of the nation—that is, the construction of the Northern Pacific Railroad and the throwing open of valuable agricultural lands to settlement—the treaty was torn up.

The first major violation of the treaty occurred in the summer of 1871 when a Northern Pacific Railroad engineering party was escorted to the Yellowstone by a force of 450 soldiers. No Indians were encountered. Colonel D. S. Stanley commanded a similar expedition the following summer. A few skirmishes occurred, but the desultoriness of the attacks suggested that at the moment the Indians were interested more in annoying the railroad surveyors than in a serious attempt to stop them. The Indians had their own private plans.

In 1873 Colonel Stanley once again was ordered to escort the railroad builders to the Yellowstone for more surveys. In addition to thirteen infantry companies, his force included ten companies of the 7th Cavalry under the leadership of Colonel George A. Custer, a total strength of 1,540 soldiers, 275 wagons, 2 field pieces, 353 civilians, and 20 Indian scouts.

It was the most formidable and powerful American military force ever seen on the northern plains. Custer was in his glory, and usually rode far ahead of the troops, followed by a pack of hunting dogs and armed with an array of sporting rifles, but he was angered and disappointed by orders which directed that combat with Indians was to be avoided. More than anything else he wanted to fight the dirty redskins, acquire a few more feathers for both his military and political caps, and he was delighted when, on three occasions, he found himself unable to escape from engaging small bands of Sioux who were bold enough to attack.

Colonel Stanley had been forewarned about Custer's character, his impetuosity, and his way of usurping the prerogatives of his commanding officer. He was prepared to meet him head on when the expedition left Fort Rice.

Eight days out on the plains, Stanley wrote his wife:

I have had no trouble with Custer and will try to avoid having any, but I have seen enough of him to convince me that he is a coldblooded, untruthful, and unprincipled man. He is universally despised by all the officers of his regiment, except his relatives and one or two sycophants. He brought a trader [one Baliran] in the field without permission, carried an old Negro woman and a cast iron cooking stove and delays the march often by his extensive packing up in the morning. As I said, I will try but am not sure I can avoid trouble with him.

Stanley, far from being a teetotaler himself, objected to Custer's trader, Baliran, selling whiskey to the troops. When an order to desist was disregarded, Stanley decided to raid the trader's wagons and confiscate the liquor in them. Baliran was warned of the impending action by Custer, and the whiskey was removed and secreted before Stanley's men could strike. Stanley wrote his wife again in July:

I had a little flurry with Custer, as I told you I probably would. We were separated four miles and I intended him to assist in getting the train [of wagons] over the Muddy River. Without consulting me, he marched off fifteen miles, coolly sending me a note to send him forage and rations. I sent after him, ordered him to halt where he was, to unload his wagons and send for his own rations and forage and never presume to make another movement without orders.

I knew from the start it would have to be done and I am glad to have had so good a chance when there could be no doubt who was right. He was just gradually assuming command and now he knows he has a commanding officer who will not tolerate his arrogance.

Custer appeared to be contrite, and Stanley later could tell his wife that "he behaves very well." In reality, Custer had recognized the unprofitableness in defying Stanley so far from headquarters and without the means of taking their differences secretly to his friends of higher rank.

There were few white men living who knew the Black Hills, but the Indians knew them. The heart of the treaty country was their cathedral, the holy land. In these hills dwelt their gods, and in them their ancestors lived in the happy hunting ground of eternity protected by the Great Spirit.

It was Colonel George A. Custer, the man who worshiped only himself, who was ordered to explore the land of the tribal gods. At the head of ten companies of the 7th Cavalry, two companies from the 17th and 20th Infantry Regiments, sixty Arikara and Santee scouts, and a long wagon train, he left Fort Abraham Lincoln on July 1, 1874. It was a reconnaissance expedition assigned to examine the Black Hills and report on their natural resources, but Custer made of it a gala parade across the plains, his chief purpose to add renown to his own name. He could leave the military problems to a competent staff, the senior officers of which were Colonel William Ludlow, an engineer; Colonel George A. Forsyth, an aide to General Sherman; and Colonel Fred D. Grant, a son of the President. Custer took with him the 7th Cavalry Band, and morning, noon, and evening the selections he requested rolled across the plains to audiences of startled prairie dogs, astonished antelope, and buffalo, mocked by the howling of lobos and the wails of coyotes. Custer took with him civilian naturalists, artists, newspaper correspondents, photographers, and mineralogists.

It was a great disappointment to him that, as the long column wended its way across the grass sea and into the beautiful valleys of the Black Hills, no Indians were seen. But if the correspondents were denied the opportunity to describe his gallantry in a fight with the savages, Custer saw to it that they were constantly supplied with colorful quotes from him for their dispatches, and material for descriptive stories of the "unknown" country into which he was so courageously leading his men. He also assumed the role of a journalist, sending a steady stream of letters to eastern newspapers, the better to be certain that thoughtfully contrived statements pointing up his own capabilities and his accomplishments as a conqueror of the Sioux heartland reached the public.

Custer's reports painted glowing pictures of the beauties and richness of the Black Hills. Gold was to be found there, as well as other precious minerals, copper, silver, and lead, and there were lovely valleys for farms and ranches, unlimited water and grass and timber, not to mention a most salubrious and healthful climate.

Although a few mounted Indians and some smoke signals had been sighted in the distance almost every day, there had been no fighting. Between July 1 and August 31 scarcely a shot had been fired, but the expedition had sealed the doom of the northern Indian nation. It had no more than returned to Fort Abraham Lincoln before the first group of prospectors had broken through to the Black Hills. By the following spring a stampede of miners, settlers, gamblers, road agents, prostitutes, storekeepers, and preachers was in full progress. Long wagon trains moved out from the steamboat landings on the Missouri. Stage lines were established, and men and women fought for seats in the coaches.

This was an invasion of the treaty territory, but the politicians only shrugged, an attitude the Army was not privileged to adopt. Legally the treaty still existed, and morally the Administration, the government, was obligated to abide by its provisions. The weight of the duty fell upon the Army. Until it received orders to the contrary, it was obliged to halt the violations.

The troops rode again into the Black Hills in the spring of 1875, Custer commanding one of the contingents, and began removing miners and settlers. The Sioux aided in the work of raiding settlements, ranches, and mines, and scalping their occupants. Still the long wagon trains crept westward, still the stages were filled beyond capacity. It was doubtful if ten times the number of troops in the field could have stopped the human flood. Recognizing the futility of the task, Congress ordered negotiations with the Sioux for the surrender of 600,000 square miles of the Black Hills country.

Surrender was a word the Sioux no longer understood. They responded to the appeal with pillage, torture, and murder.

Those who had signed the treaty and had agreed to live on reservations had long since learned what their rewards were to be under the wing of the Great White Father. Food consigned to them was often inedible, flour was wormy, beef was rotten, or more often it never reached them, but was stolen by Indian Bureau agents. They were forced to flee the agencies to survive, forced to hunt. The alternative was slow starvation. Out on the great buffalo plains the Indians who had been willing to live in peace were drawn into the camps of those who had rejected it.

The Administration, with an election year swiftly approaching, dispatched Senator William B. Allison of Iowa and a commission to buy the Black Hills. The Sioux refused to appear at a council fire. On November 3, 1875, President Grant issued a confidential directive that the Army was not to "hinder whites" entering the Black Hills country.

The Indian Bureau, under heavy political pressure and frantically trying to cover up its own corruption, abandoned its vaunted policy of "peace at any price." On November 9, only six days after Grant's directive had been received, United States Indian Inspector E. C. Watkins recommended that the War Department be given control of all hostile tribes who refused to remain on reservations. Secretary of the Interior Zachariah Chandler promptly issued an order to Indian agents to notify all tribes, especially the Cheyenne and Sioux, to present themselves at their respective agencies before January 31, 1876. Any absent after that date would be declared hostile, and would be hunted down by the Army.

The best that could be said in Chandler's defense was that he was ignorant of true conditions in the West, but that was hardly acceptable under the circumstances. He was Secretary of the Interior, and he was acting with the advice of men who presumably were experts in Indian affairs. The order was issued at a time when the western plains were locked in the grip of winter, when transportation was all but halted. Weeks passed before it was received at remote forts and agencies. Some dispatch carriers sent out with it were not heard from until the following March. Indian camps in that vast snowbound territory could not be reached, even if their locations were known. It was manifestly impossible for the Indians who had left the reservations to return by January 31. The burden of the evidence was against not only Chandler but President Grant and his political advisers, who had approved the order. They understood very well that it could not be obeyed.

On February 1, 1876, the Indian Bureau transferred control of all Indians in the West who were not at their assigned agencies to the War Department. A week later, General Sheridan had received orders to proceed against the hostile tribes.

14

*I*n February, 1876, General Sheridan presented his plans for an immediate winter campaign. Three columns would march against the hostiles. Indians defeated in winter usually starved to death, for they had no reserve resources.

A southern column under the command of General George Crook would advance north from Fort Fetterman, Wyoming Territory, through the Powder and Tongue River areas. A Montana column commanded by Colonel John Gibbon, would advance eastward from Fort Ellis (located at the eastern end of the Gallatin Valley in Montana) along the north bank of the Yellowstone River. Colonel Custer would lead a Dakota column westward from Fort Abraham Lincoln to the Yellowstone. The three spearheads would rendezvous on the Big Horn River. Military intelligence submitted a finding that the strength of the renegade Indians was estimated at between five hundred and a thousand fighting men, a force that could easily be defeated by any one of the expeditions. The most difficult problem to be faced was locating the hostile camps.

In the absence of Colonel Custer, Major Reno concentrated on training the troopers and obtaining supplies and equipment for the Dakota column, which he might command.

Colonel and Elizabeth Custer were enjoying a daily round of gay social affairs in New York City, and the colonel was busily laying the groundwork for the presidential campaign he would conduct following the Democratic Convention. The White House seemed nearer than it ever had before, and his publicity was steadily increasing his stature as a hero.

Orders that he would head the Dakota column in the three-pronged drive to smash the hostile Indians were gleefully received by Custer. The great victory against the Indians that his political advisers had declared he should achieve was now virtually within his grasp. By late summer he would be back in the East to receive the plaudits of his party leaders, the great peacemaker of the West, and to go on to the presidency.

General Crook was the first to move. In March, 1876, he set out in deep snow from Fort Fetterman with ten companies of the 2nd and 3rd Cavalry Regiments, two companies of the 4th Infantry, eighty-six wagons drawn by mules, and four hundred pack animals.

General Sherman spoke of George Crook as the "greatest Indian fighter" in the Army. After graduating from West Point in the Class of 1848, Crook had served as a lieutenant in the Rogue River War of the Northwest. Shortly after the start of the Civil War he was appointed to a colonelcy in the 36th Ohio Infantry. He rose to command a brigade, a division, and finally a corps, and was breveted to major general.

Back on the frontier following the war, he brought peace to the Snake River country, and was rewarded with the command of the Department of Columbia. In May, 1871, President Grant, over the protests of Secretary of War Belknap and General Sherman, appointed Crook to command the Department of Arizona in which the Apaches were conducting a reign of terror.

In spite of interference from the Quaker Indian Peace Commissioner, Vincent Colyer, from Bible-spouting General O. O. Howard, and from corrupt Indian agents, Crook, displaying rare energy, ruthlessness, and uncommon organizational ability, brought a relative calm to the desert territory by October, 1873. It was at this time that he was promoted to the rank of brigadier general. The following spring he was sent to the Department of the Platte, and he was in command of that district when General Sheridan's orders to proceed against the northern tribes were received.

General Crook had no love for military uniform and military splendor, but preferred civilian clothes, which he often wore in odd combinations in both office and field. He was spare and lithe, always appearing to be in good physical trim. At the time of the Rosebud campaign, he was described by a correspondent as having "fair hair, clipped close, and a blond beard. His nose was long and aquiline, and his blue-gray eyes were bright and piercing." Crook did not possess the dash and showiness of such men as Custer. Indeed, he had no liking for it, but he was not lacking in courage, conscientiousness, and good manners.

General Crook led his troops northward through ice and snow. At one time the temperature dropped to thirty-nine degrees below zero. Striking the Tongue River, he followed it to within a hundred miles of its mouth. When he saw no sign of Indians, he turned eastward toward the Powder. At the mouth of Otter Creek pony tracks were found, and General Crook halted the column and sent Colonel Joseph Jones Reynolds with six companies of cavalry and one day's rations to trail the Indians to their village and capture or destroy them.

For the first time it was learned how incorrect had been the military intelligence furnished General Sheridan. After an all-night ride, Reynolds came in sight of a village. It was an encampment of the important chief, Crazy Horse, and contained seven hundred Indians, three hundred of whom were well-armed warriors.

Crazy Horse, one of the most capable, fearless, and determined warriors, was an Oglala Sioux chief. Legend said that he received his name because a wild pony dashed by the lodge in which he was being born. His bold, adventurous disposition made him a leader of the southern Sioux. He scorned reservation life and delighted in conducting raiding expeditions against the Crows. With the invasion of the Black Hills by white miners and settlers, in violation of treaties, he resolved to wreak vengeance upon the intruders, and he led his powerful warrior forces into an alliance with Sitting Bull.

The attack launched by Reynolds' forces caught the Indians by surprise, and their pony herd was quickly captured. Reynolds, intent on destroying the lodges and food supplies of the camp, neglected to occupy some nearby bluffs. It was to this high ground that the warriors fled on foot. From their new vantage point the Indians hit the troopers with a withering volley of rifle fire.

Reynolds quickly realized that the village could not be held, and ordered a retreat. In the hasty withdrawal, not only the bodies of slain troopers were abandoned, but a wounded man, Private Lorenzo Ayres of Company M, 3rd Cavalry, was left to a terrible death by torture. The pony herd was abandoned and soon retaken by the warriors. Reynolds, meanwhile, led his defeated contingent back to the main forces at the mouth of Otter Creek.

General Crook's rage was terrible to behold. The Indians had been alerted. Runners would race to every village in all the immense territory to spread an alarm. With his rations running low, he had no alternative but to turn back to Fort Fetterman, his expedition a failure.

Crazy Horse's scouts did not let Crook's column out of their sight, and generally not beyond the range of their guns, as it retreated through the bitter cold. The troopers were harassed by random shots and false night alarms, and the rear guard was forced to maintain a constant lookout for Indian sorties.

At Fort Fetterman Crook filed charges of disobedience and dereliction of duty against Reynolds, Captain Alexander Moore, and Lieutenant Henry E. Noyes. A court-martial found all three guilty. Reynolds was suspended for a year, Moore for six months, and Noyes was reprimanded. Not until late in May, two months after the Reynolds debacle, would Crook start north again over the same trail.

Colonel John Gibbon, leader of the Montana column, was lean, hard, and deeply bronzed by his years in the open. His features were strongly carved, with a large, slightly arched nose, big ears, clear blue-green eyes set deeply under a high brow. His mustache was shaggy and massive, his beard like a rough short pony tail, and there was a bright black sheen to his thick hair. A graduate of West Point in 1849, he was a veteran of the Civil War, and he had seen considerable combat with Indians.

On March 22 he moved his Montana column eastward from Fort Ellis. Fighting blizzards and below-zero temperatures, Gibbon pushed toward his assignment with six companies of the 7th

Infantry, four companies of the 2nd Cavalry, twenty-five Indian scouts, one surgeon, two interpreters, twenty civilian packers, two Gatling guns, and a Napoleon cannon.

Meanwhile, the train on which Colonel and Elizabeth Custer, their servants and pack of blue-blooded dogs traveled westward from St. Paul was stalled by snowdrifts forty miles east of Bismarck. Telegraph lines, however, were still in operation, and a message was sent to Fort Abraham Lincoln by the colonel. Major Reno dispatched a rescue platoon under Lieutenant Tom Custer. The Colonel, Mrs. Custer, their servants, and the dogs were removed from the helpless train and taken by sleigh to the post. The other passengers, including a woman, were left on the train, and there they remained for ten days in the freezing cold.

In Washington a subcommittee of which Representative Heister Clymer of Pennsylvania was chairman had begun an investigation of corruption in the War Department under Secretary William W. Belknap. Belknap had submitted his resignation to President Grant, and had been arrested and charged with accepting bribes.

Custer saw an opportunity to gain publicity for himself in the role of striking a blow for honesty in government. Moreover, he had long despised Belknap, and had charged him with conniving with dishonest traders in the West. While fully aware that he had nothing but hearsay evidence to present, Custer wrote to chairman Clymer offering to appear as a witness before the committee.

General Alfred H. Terry planned to start the Dakota column from Fort Abraham Lincoln about April 1, and he had looked to Custer to assist him in formulating strategy for the campaign. He was understandably aggravated when, only a few days after returning from the East, Custer was served with a summons by a Sergeant-at-Arms of the House of Representatives to appear before the Clymer Subcommittee. The missive, which could not be ignored, was more of a blow to Custer than to Terry. Although he very much wanted Custer to lead the column, Terry understood that he could, if necessary, give the command to Major Reno with full confidence. Custer, however, saw his great opportunity to win new glory for himself in danger of being denied him.

At Terry's suggestion, Custer wired Chairman Clymer on March 16:

I am engaged upon an important expedition, intend to operate against the hostile Indians and I expect to take the field early in April. My presence here is deemed very necessary. In view of this, would it not be satisfactory for you to forward me such questions as may be necessary, allowing me to return my replies by mail?

Chairman Clymer informed Custer that such an arrangement would not be satisfactory. Custer would kindly respond to the summons in the proper manner. He departed sadly for Washington on March 23. Libby had wanted to accompany him, but he had thought it best for her to remain behind. He wished to travel fast, and she would be an encumbrance. Also, their friend, the Rev. Richard Wainwright, an Episcopal missionary in Fargo, had been invited as a house guest.

Custer was called before the committee on March 29, and it was quickly evident that he had no contribution of value to make. "It was apparent," wrote General George A. Forsyth, "that he did not know anything. His evidence was all hearsay, and not worth a tinker's damn."

But Custer was not to be stopped. He continued to spew forth his worthless accusations. Recklessly he involved President Grant in Belknap's dishonest operations. He charged, without having any proof to support it, that the President's brother, Orvil, had been linked with Belknap in illegitimate trading deals.

Members of the committee were somewhat appalled by Custer's rashness, but they could not see into his mind. His name was being blazoned in all the papers, under the guise of a champion of honest government. Both he and his political advisers knew what they were doing.

In April, 1876, in the first days of a cold spring, General Gibbon's column patrolled the north bank of the Yellowstone River in Montana Territory. They were waiting for the Dakota column to start, and for Crook to march once more north from Fort Fetterman, so that the pincers might be closed against the Sioux.

At Fort Abraham Lincoln Major Reno had the Dakota column in readiness, awaiting orders to start.

In St. Paul General Terry was fuming over the absence of Custer.

In Washington, believing that he had completed his testimony before the Clymer Subcommittee, Custer was on the verge of leaving for the West when he received orders to remain in the capital and hold himself in readiness for another appearance on the witness stand.

Newspapers hinted that Custer was in serious difficulty with his unsupported accusations of President Grant, Orvil Grant, and Ex-Secretary Belknap, and that his military future might be adversely affected. Custer expressed astonishment at the suggestion, and arrogantly made two attempts to confer with the President. The White House doors were closed to him.

On April 4 Custer again appeared before the subcommittee, no less defiant, no less fearless or reckless than he had been previously. He lashed out without restraint at Belknap, declaring that if the former Secretary of War had "been a man of integrity and honesty, these frauds could not have occurred."

Once again he prepared to take the train west, and once again a summons commanded him to remain. Sixteen days passed during which he paced the Washington streets and sat in his hotel room in idleness. On April 20 he was served with a subpoena to be a witness at the impeachment trial of Belknap.

Frantic, caught in the trap he had set himself, Custer appealed to his friend, William Tecumseh Sherman, General of the Army, to intercede in his behalf. General Sherman refused to talk to Chairman Clymer, but he mentioned the matter to the new Secretary of War, Alphonso Taft. Taft made the mistake of speaking about Custer to the President. Promptly President Grant directed that the Dakota column should proceed immediately without Custer. General Sherman spread his hands in helplessness. "See the President," he told Custer.

In May General Gibbon's troops were patrolling the valley of the Yellowstone.

On May 2 Custer left Washington without permission for New York. There he attempted to confer with General Sherman, but his request was refused. He took a night train for Chicago.

On May 4 the anti-Administration New York *World,* attributing their information to an "inside source," launched a vicious attack on President Grant for his ill-treatment of the great Indian fighter, "General" Custer. President Grant demanded an explanation from General Sherman. General Sherman's patience with Custer had reached an end. Disclaiming all responsibility for the attack, he informed the President that Custer "had not been authorized to leave Washington." Moreover, declared Sherman, Custer was not the only man "fit to lead" the Dakota column, and he suggested to the President that "General Custer is now subject to any means of discipline which the Chief Executive may require."

When Custer stepped from the train in Chicago, he was met by General Forsyth, who advised him that he had not been authorized to leave Washington, and was, accordingly, under arrest and would remain in Chicago until receiving further orders.

Three telegrams in which he groveled in pleas for permission to proceed were sent during the day by Custer to General Sherman. No replies came. Beside himself with fear that he would be too late to command the Dakota column, Custer disobeyed General Forsyth and took a night train for St. Paul. There he was amazed to receive a telegram from General Sherman permitting him to proceed to Fort Abraham Lincoln, but informing him that "The President adheres to his conclusion that you are not to go on the expedition."

Moved by Custer's pleadings, and still hoping that Custer would lead the Dakota column, General Terry injected himself into the issue and advised a course of action. Terry was a lawyer as well as an able military man, and, even more important, he understood very well the qualities which comprised President Grant's character.

He immediately aided Custer in composing a telegram to

Chairman Clymer in which Custer withdrew his accusations of Belknap. By inference, if not by direct statement, this served to absolve as well both the President and his brother from the corrupt practices of which Custer had implied they were guilty. Next, Terry composed a telegram to be sent to the President. It appealed to him as a fellow soldier under whom Custer had served with distinction and gallantry to rescind his order.

The strategy was successful. On May 8 Terry received a message from General Sherman which stated that "if you want General Custer along, the President withdraws his objections."

Terry and Custer left at once for Bismarck. The extent of Custer's gratitude to his commanding officer was revealed when he met an old friend, Captain William Ludlow. To Ludlow, Custer declared that once the campaign was underway he would "cut loose" and "swing clear of Terry," and he would conduct operations as he, and he alone, saw fit.

It was the tenth of May when Custer arrived at Fort Abraham Lincoln. He immediately relieved Major Reno of command of the 7th Cavalry.

Seven days later the Dakota column moved out for the Yellowstone.

General Crook left Fort Fetterman for the second time on May 29. His force was comprised of 1,300 troops, 120 wagons, and 1,000 pack mules.

The great three-pronged campaign against the Sioux at last was under way.

15

*T*he 7th United States Cavalry band played "Garry Owen." It was seven o'clock on the morning of May 17, 1876. A brilliant sun reached its golden streamers across the greening plains of Dakota Territory, over the valley of the Missouri, over the stockades and wooden buildings of Fort Abraham Lincoln, and bright darts were struck from insignia and the instruments of the musicians. The Stars and Stripes, the regimental standard, the forked guidons, snapped in the cool spring breeze. Women and children, tears brimming their eyes, watched from the porches of their quarters as the regiment passed in review before General Terry and moved out the post gate.

The right wing was commanded by Major Reno, the left by Senior Captain Benteen. One battalion served as an advance guard, one as a rear guard, and one marched on each flank of the train. Custer, with one troop of the advance guard, rode ahead to select the route and the resting and camping places. He hunted assiduously, racing with his stag hounds after antelope, deer, and buffalo. The meat of the kill was not wasted as it often had been on previous occasions, but was used to supplement regular rations. An order had been received from General Sherman that no newspapermen were to accompany the expedition, but Custer had ignored it and had invited Mark Kellogg, a correspondent of the New York *Herald*, to travel with him as his guest. He did not propose to march entirely unheralded in the press on his great quest for glory.

In the wagons were thirty days' supplies of forage and rations and two hundred rounds of ammunition for every man of the force. Each trooper, armed with a carbine and a revolver, carried fifty rounds in his belt and a similar amount in his saddlebags. The two-horse wagons, hired by contract, were loaded with fifteen hundred to two thousand pounds of material. The six-mule Army wagons carried from three to five thousand pounds. The Gatling guns were drawn by condemned cavalry horses, and moved in advance of the main train. Two light wagons were loaded with axes, shovels, pickaxes, pine boards and scantling for short bridges. Spring snows and rains had made a quagmire of much of the country, and the advance was often delayed hours at stream crossings.

During this time, [Ed Godfrey wrote] the Cavalry horses were unbitted and grazed, the men holding the reins. Those men not on duty at

134

the crossing slept, or collected in groups to spin yarns and take a whiff at their dingy dudeens. The officers usually collected near the crossing to watch the progress, and passed the time in conversation and playing practical jokes. About noon the strikers, who carried the haversacks, were called, and the different messes had their luncheon, sometimes separately, sometimes clubbing together.

When the haversacks were open the horses usually stopped grazing and put their noses near their riders' faces and asked very plainly to share their hardtack. If the polite request did not receive attention they would paw the ground, or even strike their riders. The old soldier was generally willing to share with his beast.

The length of the day's march, ranging from ten to forty miles, was determined by the obstacles encountered, by the existence of wood, water, and grass, and by the distance to be traveled to reach such necessities. The night camp was established in the form of a parallelogram. On the longer sides the wings camped, facing each other, and headquarters and the guard were located at the end nearest the creek. At the opposite end was the wagon train. After supper, pipes were lighted. The troopers grouped about the fires and sang and spun yarns. Taps brought a silence broken only by the measured tread of sentries, the munching of grass and fodder by the picketed horses, and the howls of lobos and coyotes savoring the smell of the closely guarded beef herd.

Reveille was sounded with the first gray light of the morning. Breakfast consisted of hard bread, bacon, and coffee. Within two hours the wagons were crawling onward across the endless grass, the Indian scouts were out, and the troops were moving forward in their assigned positions.

They saw no red horsemen, and only an occasional smoke signal, but always they knew they were being watched. The scouts found pony tracks and the ashes of old campfires, but neither the animals nor the men who had left the signs. Glasses roved the distant swells throughout the daylight hours, quickly settling on anything that moved, anything with shape or outline that was not immediately recognized, and at night the eyes of the guards stared into the shadows under the stars that fumed up from the invisible rims of the earth, and ears strained at sounds and whispers that came from the cottonwood trees and the grasses and the running waters, and fearful thoughts dwelt on them.

The nights were cold and the days were hot in the transition from spring to summer. One afternoon the slanting sun burned across the plain in a consuming fire, and no air stirred, and the closeness dried sweat on faces and burned about narrowed eyes, and there was no twilight. Suddenly the sun was gone and great thunderheads stood up against the onsweeping darkness, crimson on their bold faces and purple in their vast canyons. The stifling air gave way under the pressure and began to move, spinning up dust clouds.

Flash winds came first and then a driving gale that forced the troopers to bend almost double as they plodded forward. When the march was halted, they had to throw up earthen mounds to shield their campfires. No tents could stand. Lightning slashed the heavens. In the premature darkness they heard the violent approach of a hailstorm. Sweeping toward them, it echoed the thunder. Horses broke their tethers and stampeded. The troopers took refuge under canvas or wagons.

The hail struck, and stones the size of apples battered men and animals, and left the camp covered in a sheet of melting ice. Then, as suddenly as it had come, the gale dwindled to a whisper, the clouds broke apart, and stars glittered in the dark vault of the sky.

On the twenty-seventh of May the command reached the Bad Lands of the Little Missouri River. Working their way along the route followed by General Sully in 1864, they followed the rambling course of Davis Creek. The latter stream had high, brush-clad banks, and the country was so rough and impenetrable that the command found it necessary to ford the creek ten times during the day's march.

By the morning of the thirtieth they had reached the confluence of Davis Creek and the Little Missouri. Camp was made on the east bank of the river. Special parapets for the defense of the camp were erected since they expected to find hostiles in the area.

Custer, accompanied by Troops C, D, F, and M and a dozen scouts, explored the region without, however, finding any recent signs of the Sioux. General Terry was forced to conclude that the Indians would be found farther west, and came to realize that the campaign would be much longer than had been originally anticipated.

The month of June began with a blinding snowstorm that completely immobilized the regiment. Snow fell to a depth of two feet on the plain and drifted halfway to the top of some of the tents. The Arikara scouts were disturbed by the storm, believing that it was another portent of the disaster they were convinced awaited the troopers.

After the storm broke, the weather turned milder and the snow began to melt quickly so that on the afternoon of June 2 the forage and supply wagons were readied for an early departure. On June 3 the crossing of the Little Missouri was accomplished, and the command pushed into the Bad Lands, a country of rugged red buttes, saffron and topaz washes, rusty ridges, distant tablelands bathed in violet mists, emerald clusters of cottonwoods along the banks of small creeks, and the olive sweep of sage and ground cedar.

There were dwarfed sunflowers patching the bottom lands, red thistles, Indian tobacco, nodding arrowheads, wild roses. Magpies flitted through the brilliant sunlight, cowbirds watched for moving buffalo to stir up insects, snipe ran about the water holes, while killdeer screeched, sage hens flushed from under the hooves of the horses and whirred away. High overhead eagles, riding the air currents, watched the invaders, now and then plunging earthward to sweep up a careless ground squirrel, a sleeping badger or woodchuck. There were days when alkali dust whitened faces and burned eyes and mouths, when the sun ran in red fire over the buttes. On other days they rode through pleasant valleys on thick grass carpets fringing a clear stream in which trout leaped for flies.

It was the seventh of June when they came to the Powder, the river which was said to be four hundred miles long, a mile wide and an inch deep. Game had always been plentiful in the valley of the Powder, the timber was thick, and it had been since time immemorial a favorite winter camping place of the Indians. General Terry had sent Scouts north. They brought word that the steamer, *Far West,* was at the confluence of the Powder and the Yellowstone, and he left with his staff to make his headquarters on the boat and to open communications with General Gibbon and the column from Fort Ellis.

The captain of the *Far West* was Grant Marsh, a colorful individual, whose reputation for navigating the shifting channels of the Missouri was known throughout the Territory. It was said of him that he could navigate a river steamboat on a light dew. The *Far West,* built in Pittsburgh in 1870, had been especially designed to operate on the shallow and treacherous rivers of the West. One hundred and ninety feet in length and with a beam of thirty-three feet, she had two engines, as well as two capstans on the bow, to drive and pull her through the rapids. In her cabins were accommodations for thirty passengers, and she could carry more than two hundred tons of freight. General Terry and his aides were quickly ensconced in comfortable quarters aboard.

General Gibbon soon arrived. It was his opinion that the hostiles were west of the Powder and south of the Yellowstone. On the basis of this intelligence, General Terry returned to the regiment's camp, and issued orders for Major Reno to leave as soon as possible on a scouting expedition.

The orders which Acting Assistant Adjutant General Edwin Smith prepared, and which were approved by General Terry, said:

Major M. A. Reno, Seventh Cavalry, with six companies (right wing) of his regiment and one gun from the Gatling battery, will proceed at the earliest practicable moment to make a reconnaissance of the Powder River from the present camp to the mouth of the Little Powder. From the last named point he will cross to the headwaters of Mizpah Creek, and descend that creek to its junction with the Powder River. Thence he will cross the Pumpkin Creek and Tongue River, and descend the Tongue to its junction with the Yellowstone, where he may expect to meet the remaining companies of the Seventh Cavalry and supplies of subsistence and forage.

Major Reno's command will be supplied with subsistence for twelve days, and with forage for the same period at the rate of two pounds of grain the day for each animal.

The guide Mitch Bouyer and eight Indian Scouts, to be detailed by Lieutenant-Colonel Custer, will report to Major Reno, for duty with this column.

Acting Assistant Surgeon H. R. Porter is detailed for duty with Major Reno.

The orders brought a vigorous protest from Custer. He had taken it for granted that he would lead any major scouting expedition to be sent out. Terry refused to accede to Custer's demands, and Major Reno departed with six troops of cavalry, a group of Indian scouts, a Gatling gun, and a train of sixty-six pack mules loaded with rations and forage for a march of twelve days.

Custer was ordered by Terry to lead the remaining six troops down the Powder to the Yellowstone and establish a base camp at that point. Terry and his staff returned to the *Far West,* and Captain Marsh was directed to move it to the mouth of the Tongue, where the general would await a report from Major Reno.

Disgruntled at being left in the rear, Custer was delighted when orders came from Terry for him to move up the Yellowstone to the Tongue. He broke camp on the Powder on June 15, leaving the band, all equipment he concluded was unnecessary, and a number of the newer recruits as guards. The Tongue was reached the following day, and a camp was established on the bank near the anchorage of the *Far West.* Adjacent to the camp was a large Indian burial ground. Custer permitted the troopers to tear down the scaffolds on which the corpses rested, and rob them. "Several persons," said Ed Godfrey, "rode about exhibiting their trinkets with as much gusto as if they were trophies of their valor, and showed no more concern for their desecration than if they had won them at a raffle."

16

As June began, General Crook was pushing northward through the magnificent country upon which the afternoon shadows of the Big Horn Mountains fell. The weather was unseasonably cold, and the same snowstorms that delayed the Dakota column slowed his progress.

He was aware that his force was under constant surveillance. Smoke signals etched the skies each day, and frequently his scouts and outriders caught sight of distant horsemen. On the evening of June 9 two troopers were wounded in a skirmish with a small band of Cheyennes.

He had advanced for the first fortnight in a widely open formation, his troops at times being spread out over a distance of four miles. On June 15 he had reached Goose Creek near the base of the Big Horn Range. There he reorganized his command. Taking his cavalry and mounting two hundred infantrymen on horseback, he started across the divide between the Tongue River and Rosebud Creek. The balance of the troops and the civilian packers were left behind to guard the supplies and wagons.

Unknown to Crook, several thousand Sioux and Cheyennes were encamped in the valley of the Little Big Horn, only a few miles to the west. When scouts reported his position to them, fifteen hundred warriors under the leadership of Crazy Horse set out on a night ride, reaching the Rosebud at dawn.

Crook left his camp on the Rosebud at three o'clock on the morning of June 17. Five hours later his scouts sighted their Indian counterparts. Shots were exchanged. The Battle of the Rosebud began.

Reports of his Crow and Shoshone scouts, and the presence of numbers of Indians on surrounding hills and ridges, convinced Crook that he had met Crazy Horse's main force, and that the chief intended to carry out his warning not to let them cross the Rosebud. He ordered two charges. Captain Anson Mills' battalion was sent toward a bluff across the Rosebud Valley, where a large number of Sioux had gathered. Major W. B. Royall led his men toward high ground in the opposite direction. A center line was established and fought the Indians advancing toward it.

Both charges were well executed. Mills drove the Sioux off the bluff, moving forward in the face of heavy fire. Royall swept through the Indians ahead of him. Then the advances of both columns were slowed by large numbers of Sioux moving upon them from every side. Mills asked for assistance, and Crook rushed a battalion to him, but the reinforcements did not improve the situation. There were simply too many Indians, and they continued to increase.

Royall found himself in serious danger. On his left was Captain Guy V. Henry's command, but there was no opportunity to unite with them. Crazy Horse obviously recognized the weakness of the cavalry positions, and launched a strong offensive. Only one troop held as waves of Sioux rolled forward. The others were driven back, and hand-to-hand fighting took place under clouds of dust as the soldiers went back down the hills Royall had taken. Crook's line was temporarily stabilized, and a countercharge was launched to reach the troop which had held its ground ahead. It was successful, and the surrounded men were brought back.

Now Crook ordered a general retreat to find a stronger position. It was executed under continuous fire.

Crook mistakenly surmised that Crazy Horse's village was located up a canyon running northeast from the valley. He sent Mills with seven companies to destroy it and capture the women, children, and horses.

Strangely, Mills and his men were not opposed as they rode up the canyon between precipitous walls. The Sioux continued to press against Crook's main front.

Suddenly Crook changed his mind, and sent a courier after Mills with an order for him to return. It had been brought to Crook's attention that some of the Sioux seemed to be withdrawing from the line, and he had shrewdly concluded that they had been attracted by the diversion of Mills.

Mills had not gone far when the courier caught up to him. He promptly turned about. Had he not done so, he and his men undoubtedly would have been wiped out. He was riding into a dead-end canyon—a fact later learned—and Crazy Horse was waiting to trap him.

As the sun vanished behind the great purple wall of the Big Horns, the Sioux vanished into the shadows, taking their wounded with them, but leaving their scattered dead where they had fallen.

Twelve troopers had been killed and twenty-three were seriously wounded. Throughout the night, camping on the battlefield, Crook considered his situation. It was obvious that he was badly outnumbered, and the Sioux were well armed. He concluded that with limited supplies of ammunition, with twenty-three wounded to care for, it would be advisable to withdraw to the base camp he had left on Goose Creek two days before. He moved slowly back, reaching the camp on June 19.

If Crook was not willing to concede the fact, his scouts and some of his experienced officers understood he had suffered a serious defeat. Not only had Crazy Horse made good his threat to attack on the Rosebud, but he had sent a powerful force of twelve hundred superbly equipped troopers reeling back, badly mauled.*

Crook's next moves made it apparent that he knew he was beaten. At least, he was convinced that he might meet with complete disaster if he attempted to pursue Crazy Horse. He ordered a wagon train, guarded by most of his infantry, a scouting force, and the packers and muleteers, to take the wounded to Fort Fetterman and return with supplies. It also was his opinion that before any resumption of the campaign against the Sioux he should be strongly reinforced, and he requested more infantry, which he knew was available at the forts to the south.

Crook then settled down to rest, doing no more than sending

*The twelve hundred did not include mule packers and wagon drivers.

142

out scouts to reconnoiter. Tedious days followed. He and some of his officers went fishing and hunting for elk and bighorn sheep in the mountains—a pleasant vacation in a delightful land of warm days and cool nights.

Crazy Horse's checking of Crook, and the general's dallying in his base camp, destroyed irreparably the plan for a three-pronged assault against the Sioux, which had been so long in the making. His scheduled juncture with Gibbon and Terry was prevented. He had more than a thousand able-bodied troopers, and neither his ammunition nor his supplies were so low that he could not have marched on to the Yellowstone, in a dash if necessary.

The tragic events which followed might well have taken a different course had he not sojourned, licking his pride and awaiting the arrival of supplies and reinforcements, while the troopers of Custer, Reno, and Benteen were dying, only a few miles away from him.

The scouts of Crazy Horse kept an eye on Crook. When it became apparent that he did not intend to advance at once after the Rosebud fight, Crazy Horse led his warriors back to the valley of the Little Big Horn. There was wild dancing to celebrate his victory. The soldiers of Crook had been driven away! No, they had run away! The confidence of the Sioux and their allies soared to new heights. Sitting Bull announced he had a vision of an even greater victory to come. Great days lay ahead!

17

*M*enton Mitch Bouyer was Major Reno's chief scout. A retiring, slow half-breed, he spoke Crow, Sioux, and English, but always with a paucity of words and always in a voice so soft that at times it was scarcely audible. He knew well the country through which the major had been ordered to make a reconnaissance, for he had spent years among the Indians.

Carrying out his instructions, Major Reno moved up the Powder to the mouth of the Little Powder, crossed to Mizpah Creek, thence to Pumpkin Creek, proceeding down it to the Tongue. No recent Indian signs were found. Observations along the Tongue produced no tracks or abandoned village sites, and after a conference with Bouyer Reno decided to extend his reconnaissance westward to the Rosebud, before starting back to the Yellowstone.

Major Reno had had enough experience with men like Mitch Bouyer to understand that their actions and pronouncements were not always impelled by reason. Frequently they were the result of a strange sensitiveness. Bouyer could give no explanation for his feeling that new Indian trails would be picked up along the Rosebud. Something was in the wind. He could sense it.

Bouyer broke a trail which brought the troops to the Rosebud at a point twenty-five miles from its mouth. They rode down into the little valley directly to an Indian camp site. Bouyer and the other scouts carefully studied the scene. A large village had stood there no more than three days before. It had contained no less than 380 lodges, perhaps three thousand Indians, of whom at least a thousand might have been warriors. The arrangement in which the tepees had stood indicated that their occupants had been Sioux, but Bouyer had reasons—discarded clothing, a segment of a belt, some feathers—to believe that Cheyennes also had been there.

Bouyer and his sharp-eyed aides quickly ascertained the direction the Indians had taken. Horse tracks and travois marks were clear in places, and so recently had the village moved that the course could be followed by broken grasses and other vegetation which had not had time to recover from its wounds. The trail went slightly south of west.

For forty miles they followed it, and then Mitch Bouyer told Major Reno: "Greasy Grasses."

Greasy Grasses was the Indians' name for the valley of the Little Big Horn.

It was the seventeenth of June. Only forty miles away, General Crook was being defeated.

Brevet Brigadier-General Marcus A. Reno, U.S.V.,
Harrisburg, Pennsylvania, 1865

The United States Military Academy, West Point, N.Y., 1860

U.S. Signal Corps Photo, National Archives

General Alfred Archimedes Torbert and Staff, Virginia, 1864.
(Reno fourth from left top row under flag)

The Rebels shelling the New York Militia on the Main Street of
Carlisle, Pennsylvania, 1863, Sketched by Mr. Thomas Nast

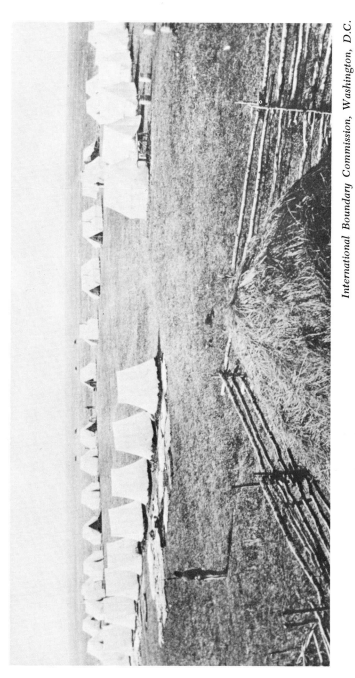

International Boundary Commission, Washington, D.C.

Major Reno's camp while escorting the
International Boundary Commission, 1873

Major-General George Armstrong Custer U.S.V.,
Captain Tom Custer, and Elizabeth Bacon Custer

Cadet Benjamin H. Hodgson of Philadelphia, Pa., U.S.M.A., 1870

Brigadier-General Alfred Terry, North Carolina, 1846

U.S. Signal Corps Photo, National Archives

A Seventh Cavalry group prior to the Battle of the Little Big Horn, taken at Fort Abraham Lincoln, 1876

The grave of Lieutenant James G. Sturgis, Seventh Cavalry,
Battle of the Little Big Horn, June 25, 1876

The Steamer, *Far West*, 1876

Colonel James Montgomery Bell, 1900

U.S. Signal Corps Photo (Brady Collection), National Archives

Brigadier-General Samuel D. Sturgis, U.S.V., 1864

Fort Snelling, St. Paul, Minnesota, 1880

Photo from a newspaper cut by Copelin

THE RENO COURT OF INQUIRY, PALMER HOUSE, CHICAGO, ILL., 1879

Reading from left to right: Col. Wesley Merritt; Col. John H. King (President of the Court); Lt. Col. Royall. Seated at center table: Mr. H. C. Hollister, the official reporter; Major Reno, in front of right window; Lyman Gilbert on Reno's left. Lieutenant DeRudio, the witness, is facing Lt. Jesse M. Lee, the recorder, seated at table in the foreground. The figure at bottom right is Frederick Whittaker

Providence Hospital, Washington, D.C., 1889
Under the Charge of the Sisters of Charity

Deep concern filled Mitch Bouyer's intense black eyes. Major Reno saw it, and wondered at its source. The answer came. Mitch Bouyer gazed into distance, as if he might be looking far beyond the surrounding hills and benchlands. "Many," he murmured.

That night the major sat in his tent in profound thought. Both his rations and grain were running low. Horses and men were extremely tired. They had ridden more than 240 miles on the reconnaissance. The word "many" repeated itself in his mind. Hardly more than a day's ride to the north was the Yellowstone, and the waiting Terry, Gibbon, and Custer. His allotted time would be almost exhausted before he could reach it.

He made his decision. To rush in against an unknown number of Sioux and Cheyenne—he had no doubts as to the soundness of Bouyer's estimate—with weary troopers, tired horses, and few supplies was poor military strategy, if not the height of folly. He saw danger, as well, in an attempt to determine the strength of the hostiles. The delay might bring them down upon him with disastrous results. His proper and his most strategic move, with the Yellowstone so close, was to report.

At dawn he and his troopers were on their way down the Rosebud.

Major Reno reached the mouth of the Rosebud on June 19 to find Gibbon encamped on the opposite bank of the Yellowstone. He immediately sent dispatches down-river to General Terry on the *Far West*, anchored at Tongue River, reporting his discoveries and asking for orders. Terry replied with instructions for him to remain where he was and await Custer and the remaining companies of the 7th. The *Far West* would be moved upstream to the Rosebud, and thus both the Western and Dakota columns would be reunited in full strength.

On June 21 the steamer hove into sight, valiantly fighting the strong June currents. General Terry at once instructed Gibbon to march upstream to the mouth of the Big Horn. Custer's anger at being left behind while Reno conducted a scout had not abated, and he feared that Major Reno would be commended for the accomplishment. To forestall such an event, he wrote two letters, one to Libby and one to the New York *Herald*.

In the letter to his wife he criticized Major Reno not so much for disobeying orders as for failing to pursue the Indians and destroy them on the battlefield. He understood that Libby would see that the letter received wide circulation.

Custer's letter to the *Herald* was anonymous, written in the third person, inaccurate, and intentionally dishonest. It castigated Major Reno while referring in glowing terms to the great Custer, who, at last, had been called upon to save the day:

> In the opinion of the most experienced officers, it was not believed that any considerable, if any, force of Indians would be found on the Powder River; still there were a few, including Major Reno, who were convinced that the main body of Sitting Bull's warriors would be encountered on Powder River. The general impression, however, is and has been, that on the headwaters of the Rosebud and Little Big Horn Rivers the "hostiles" would be found.

This was an unmitigated falsehood. Major Reno had found the Indians on the Rosebud. Ergo, Custer had known they were there all the time.

> It was under this impression [Custer continued] that General Terry, in framing the orders which were to govern Major Reno's movements, explicitly and positively directed that officer to confine himself to his orders and instructions, and particularly not to move in the direction of the Rosebud River, as it was feared that such a movement, if prematurely made, might "flush the covey," it being the intention to employ the entire cavalry force of the expedition, when the time arrived, to operate in the valleys of the Rosebud and Big Horn Rivers.

Criticism of General Terry by strong inferences followed. This was in keeping with Custer's long-standing habit. His loyalty to a commanding officer had never been greater than the small amount of consideration he displayed for a subordinate.

> Custer and most of his officers looked with little favor on the movement up the Powder River, as, among other objections, it required the entire remaining portion of the expedition to lie in idleness within two

marches of the locality where it was generally believed the hostile villages would be discovered on the Rosebud, the danger being that the Indians, ever on the alert, would discover the presence of the troops as yet undiscovered—and take advantage of their opportunity to make their escape.

This was sheer nonsense. Ever since they had left Fort Abraham Lincoln the Dakota column had been observed by the Indians. It was observed on the Yellowstone and on the Powder, and Custer was fully apprised of the fact. Every move Major Reno made on his reconnaissance was watched by Sioux scouts and duly reported to the chiefs who were assembling their fighting men in the valley of the Little Big Horn, and if Custer did not know of this, he had not listened to the words of his own scouts. Custer continued:

Reno, after an absence of ten days, returned, when it was found, to the disgust and disappointment of every member of the expedition, from the commanding general down to the lowest private, that Reno, instead of simply failing to accomplish any good results, had so misconducted his force as to embarrass, if not seriously and permanently mar, all hopes of future success of the expedition. He had not only deliberately, and without a shadow of an excuse failed to obey his written instructions issued by General Terry's personal directions, but he had acted in positive disobedience to the strict injunctions of the department commander. Instead of conforming his line of march to the valleys and water courses laid down in his written orders he moved his command to the mouth of the Little Powder River, then across to Tongue River, and instead of following the latter stream down to its mouth, there to unite with the main command, he, for some unaccountable and thus far unexplained reason, switched off from his prescribed course and marched across the country to the Rosebud, the stream he had been particularly cautioned not to approach.*

He struck the Rosebud about twenty-five miles above its mouth, and there—*as Custer had predicted from the first*—signs indicating the presence of a large force of Indians were discovered, an abandoned camp-

*One cannot refrain from remarking that if Reno had not taken Bouyer's suggestion and looked in on the Rosebud Valley, he would have returned without finding any Indian camps. In view of what happened, that result might have been very beneficial to Custer.

ground of the Indians was found, on which 380 lodges had been pitched. The trail led up the valley of the Rosebud. Reno took up the trail and followed it about twenty miles, but faint heart never won fair lady, neither did it ever pursue and overtake an Indian village. Had Reno, after first violating his orders, pursued and overtaken the Indians, his original disobedience of orders would have been overlooked, but his determination forsook him at this point, and instead of continuing the pursuit and at least bringing the Indians to bay, he gave the order to counter-march and faced his command to the rear, from which point he made his way back to the mouth of the Tongue River, and reported the details of his gross and inexcusable blunder to General Terry, his commanding officer, who informed Reno in unmistakable language that the latter's conduct amounted to positive disobedience of orders, the sad consequences of which could not yet be fully determined. The details of this affair will bear investigation.

A court-martial is strongly hinted at, and if one is not ordered it will not be because it is not richly deserved.

Poor Terry. He had no alternative but to call upon Custer to pick up the pieces, or, as Custer himself put it for the elucidation of the *Herald*'s readers:

Of course there was but one thing to do and that was to remedy as soon as possible the effects of Reno's blunder. . . .

Yesterday Terry, Gibbon and Custer got together, and, with unanimity of opinion, decided that Custer should start with his command up the Rosebud Valley to the point where Reno had abandoned the trail, take up the latter and follow the Indians as long and as far as horseflesh and human endurance could carry his command.

General Terry had no thought of ordering a court-martial for Reno, or even reprimanding him. In the first place, Reno had not been forbidden to look into the Rosebud Valley. It hadn't been mentioned in his written orders, and it would be rather a waste of time to court-martial a man for doing something he had not been forbidden to do. In Terry's opinion Reno had used his head (and perhaps Mitch Bouyer's head) and had demonstrated his good sense by not attacking a force the size of which he had not ascertained. Moreover, it was not Terry's way to punish an officer who had succeeded in an assigned mission, and Reno had done that. If he had gone a few miles beyond the limits as set down in the orders, he had picked up the trail of the hostiles. After all, that was what he was sent out to do. Terry had more than one reason to be thankful that Custer had not been in Reno's place on the reconnaissance.

The strategy General Terry proposed was remarkable in its simplicity. Gibbon's troops were already en route to the mouth of the Big Horn. There they would be ferried across the Yellowstone by the steamer. Gibbon would lead them southward up the Big Horn, planning to arrive in the valley of the Little Big Horn on June 26. Custer, with the entire 7th Cavalry, would advance up the valley of the Rosebud until he came upon the Indian trail discovered by Major Reno. At this point, Terry's verbal orders to Custer were clear, precise, and specific. Custer was not to follow the Indian trail, but simply determine that it did lead into the valley of the Little Big Horn. That done, he should proceed southward to the headwaters of the Tongue. At a suitable point in that area he should swing west, feeling constantly to his left, so as to preclude the possibility of the escape of the Indians to the south. Custer was to time his marches to coincide with Gibbon's entry into the Big Horn Valley. Terry knew well Custer's propensity for dashing through a country, and in a further effort to keep the advance to the proper pace, he directed that Custer should examine the upper end of Tullock's Creek, and from there endeavor to send a scout through to Gibbon with a report of his reconnaissance. Terry had hopes of catching the Indians in a pincer movement. Several times he stressed to both Custer and Gibbon the importance of timing.

Terry offered to give Custer four companies of Gibbon's cavalry, but Custer expressed the opinion that he had no need of them, that the 7th could do the job alone. He also declined an offer of a battery of Gatling guns brought from Fort Abraham Lincoln. Questions and further discussions convinced Terry that all officers in the conference fully understood the plan of the campaign. The orders he dictated for Custer to carry with him were, therefore, not as detailed as those delivered at the conference table.

The written orders were prepared by Captain E. W. Smith, Acting Assistant Adjutant General. They read:

Camp at Mouth of Rosebud River,
Montana Territory, June 22nd, 1876

LIEUT.-COL. CUSTER, 7TH CAVALRY.

COLONEL:

The Brigadier-General Commanding directs that, as soon as your regiment can be made ready for the march, you will proceed up the Rosebud in pursuit of the Indians whose trail was discovered by Major Reno a few days since. It is, of course, impossible to give you any definite instructions in regard to this movement, and were it not impossible to do so the Department Commander places too much confidence in your zeal, energy, and ability to wish to impose upon you precise orders which might hamper your action when nearly in contact with the enemy. He will, however, indicate to you his own views of what your actions should be, and he desires that you should conform to them unless you shall see sufficient reasons for departing from them. He thinks that you should proceed up the Rosebud until you ascertain definitely the direction in which the trail above spoken of leads. Should it be found (as it appears almost certain that it will be found) to turn towards the Little Horn, he thinks that you should still proceed southward, perhaps as far as the headwaters of the Tongue, and then turn towards the Little Horn, feeling constantly, however, to your left, so as to preclude the possibility of the escape of the Indians to the south or southeast by passing around your left flank. The column of Colonel Gibbon is now in motion for the mouth of the Big Horn. As soon as it reaches that point it will cross the Yellowstone and move up at least as far as the forks of the Big and Little Horns. Of course its future movements must be controlled by circumstances as they arise, but it is hoped that the Indians, if upon the Little Horn, may be so nearly inclosed by the two columns that their escape will be impossible.

The Department Commander desires that on your way up the Rosebud you should thoroughly examine the upper part of Tulloch's Creek, and that you should endeavor to send a scout through to Colonel Gibbon's column, with information of the result of your examination. The lower part of the creek will be examined by a detachment from Colonel Gibbon's command. The supply steamer will be pushed up the Big Horn as far as the forks if the river is found to be navigable for that distance, and the Department Commander, who will accompany the column of

Colonel Gibbon, desires you to report to him there not later than the expiration of the time for which your troops are rationed, unless in the meantime you receive further orders.

Immediately following his conference with Terry, Custer issued orders to his company commanders. They were to transport on pack mules fifteen days' rations of hard bread, coffee, and sugar; twelve days' rations of bacon; and fifty rounds of carbine ammunition per man. In addition, each trooper was to carry on his person and in his saddlebags a hundred rounds of carbine and twenty-four rounds of pistol ammunition and twelve pounds of oats. The pack mules also were to be loaded with extra forage. When Captain Moylan and Lieutenant Godfrey protested that the mules, especially those which had been used by Major Reno on the long reconnaissance, were in poor shape and many of them probably would break down under the excessive loads, Custer replied in irritation:

"Well, gentlemen, you may carry what supplies you please. You'll be held responsible for your companies. The extra forage was only a suggestion, but bear this fact in mind: We will follow the trail for fifteen days unless we catch them before that, no matter how far it may take us from our base of supplies. We may not see the steamer again."

Custer turned away, hesitated, and added:

"You had better carry along an extra supply of salt, too," he said in a tone of sarcasm. "We may have to live on horse meat before we get through."

Once the nature of Custer's orders had been made known throughout the ranks, nearly all the troopers busied themselves with writing letters. The Adjutant was entrusted with a number of newly drawn wills, and countless instructions, both verbal and written, for the disposition of personal property.

At noon on the twenty-second of June, 1876, the 7th United States Cavalry, battle-ready, with guidons flying in a breeze that brought the sweet smells of curing prairie grass and the pungent odors of pine and sage, rode in review before General Terry. As the last of the troopers passed, Custer saluted, and was turning away when Colonel Gibbon called out:

"Now, Custer, don't be too greedy. Leave a few Indians for us."

"No, I won't,"* Custer replied and, with a wild wave of his arm, galloped after his men.

18

*T*he 7th Cavalry had hardly ridden out of sight of the camp, when Custer called a halt. He relieved Captain Benteen and Major Reno of their usual commands of the left and right wings, ordering that henceforth all officers would report directly to him.

The Rosebud, a small shallow creek, derived its name from the profusion of wild rosebushes growing along its banks. Custer held close to the stream through the afternoon. When he stopped for the night's camp, a distance of twelve miles had been traversed.

At sundown the officers were surprised to receive an oral message to report at once to a staff conference. It was an entirely new procedure for the General.** While he frequently talked with a small group of his subordinates, particularly his favorites, it was not his way to discuss his plans, to explain his motives,

*The meaning of Custer's answer to Gibbon has always been a matter of debate. It is believed by some historians that he had a premonition of death. They point to his nervousness, peculiar moods, and unusual joviality on occasions just before the Battle of the Little Big Horn as evidence indicating this feeling. Others maintain that it would not have been in keeping with his character to promise not to be greedy, for he wanted nothing more than to wipe out the hostiles and to enjoy the glory which he believed would come to him from such a triumph. Probably no one will ever know what was in his mind as he spoke to Gibbon.

**In formal orders, Custer was generally addressed by his Regular Army rank of Lieutenant Colonel. His men called him "General," the rank to which he had been breveted.

or in any way to take into his confidence all officers of the regiment.

Answering the summons, which had been delivered by a trumpeter, the officers found Custer lying on his bed. They gathered around it. Within a few moments it was clear they were confronting a Custer they had never known. His usual arrogance and self-assurance seemed to have left him. In their places had appeared a conciliatory manner and an attitude of depression.

Almost in the manner of an apology, Custer announced that, in keeping with an effort to prevent the Indians from knowing their whereabouts as long as possible, no more bugle calls would be sounded. A silent reveille would come at three o'clock each morning. The march would begin at five, and they would advance no less than twenty-five nor more than thirty miles before halting for the night. He would select the camp sites, but the details of watering and resting companies would be left to their respective commanders.

During the first day's march considerable troubles had occurred with the mules. They were trained to drawing wagons and were unused to packs. Many of them had straggled badly, and packers had difficulty in keeping them up with the column. Custer ordered Lieutenant Mathey to take command of the 70 troopers and 175 mules which comprised the supply train, and to correct the unsatisfactory condition.

The colonel then broached the matter of cooperation with him in the strenuous days to come. His words came almost in the manner of a plea rather than as a request. There had been, he declared, a good deal of grumbling, and some of the junior officers had openly criticized his decisions and his actions. He expressed the hope that he would hear of no more dissension.

Anger shone in the eyes of Captain Benteen. "General, it seems to me you're lashing the shoulders of all of us," he said. "Wouldn't it be better to specify the officers you're accusing?"

Custer stared at the captain, as if he might be going to reply with harshness, but his words were no more than firm. "Captain, I'm not here to be catechized by you, but for your own information, I'll state that none of my remarks have been directed toward you."

The slight clash seemed to fade immediately from Custer's thoughts. He launched into an explanation of reasons for rejecting additional troops and the Gatling guns. It was his opinion from the number of old lodge fires discovered by Major Reno that they would be faced by no more than a thousand warriors. While in Washington in March he had taken the opportunity to consult with officials of the Indian Bureau as to the probable number of hostiles in Montana Territory—that is, those Indians who persistently refused to return to the reservations—and had been informed that the number might have been increased to fifteen hundred by young men known to have disappeared from various agencies. Certainly, the 7th Cavalry could defeat such a force. If not, then no other regiment could.

Watches were synchronized, and the meeting ended.

Lieutenants Godfrey, McIntosh, and Wallace walked away together. They had gone some distance in silence, their faces pensive, when Wallace said in a quiet voice, "I think Custer is going to be killed, and knows it."

"Why?" Godfrey asked.

"I never heard him talk that way before."

In the evening, Major Reno strolled to the bivouac of the regiment's Indian scouts. He found Lieutenant Godfrey sitting about a fire with Mitch Bouyer, Half-Yellow-Face, and Bloody Knife. Half-Yellow-Face was talking and Bouyer was acting as interpreter.

"Have you ever fought against the Sioux?" Half-Yellow-Face asked Godfrey.

The lieutenant said he had.

"How many you expect to meet?"

"General Custer thinks about fifteen hundred," Major Reno said.

Half-Yellow-Face's lips twisted, as if he were attempting to suppress laughter. "You think you can whip that many?'

"General Custer thinks so," Godfrey said.

Mitch Bouyer and Half-Yellow-Face engaged in a private

conversation in the Crow tongue. When he spoke again, Bouyer's eyes were lighted, as if reflecting the flame and the heat of the fire before them. "General Custer blind," he said in a thick voice. He gestured toward Half-Yellow-Face and Bloody Knife. "They and me can tell you we will have one damn big fight." He spat, arose, and disappeared into the night.

At five o'clock on the morning of the twenty-third of June, 1876, Custer rode out of the camp on the Rosebud. Directly behind him two mounted sergeants carried the regimental standard and his personal flag, a red and blue forked pennant with naked crossed sabers in white. It was the same pennant he had displayed while commanding his cavalry regiment during the Civil War. The troops, commanded by arm signals, filed for more than three miles behind him.

The camp site which Major Reno had discovered was reached after a march of eight miles. Horse droppings, tracks, and lodge marks were studied by the scouts, and their consensus was that perhaps as many as three thousand Indians had recently paused there. Going on up the valley of the Rosebud, three more camp sites, all less than a fortnight old, were found.

"Not all together," Mitch Bouyer said, and other scouts nodded their agreement. "Not all here at same time, but all going same way. All friends."

Half-Yellow-Face pointed to the west, and spoke one word. Bouyer repeated it in English. The word was "Many."

On the morning of June 24 Major Reno's wisdom in turning back was made clearly apparent to the officers of the 7th. A score of Indian camp sites recently used were passed. Custer appeared to be unimpressed by the pronouncement of his scouts that the camps were almost all of the same age, but had not belonged to any single village. Numerous bands had used them over a period of several days.

Little rain had fallen in the valley of the Rosebud during the past month, and the ground was extremely dry. Custer ordered that the regiment proceed in three columns along separate routes to prevent stirring up large dust clouds. On each side of the little stream, the ground was profusely marked by lodge pole scars and hoofprints which a rain would have obliterated, but which remained as indisputable proof of the heavy Indian traffic that had recently passed over it.

In the afternoon the scouts, keeping well ahead of the troops, came upon an exceptionally large camp site. The grass for half a mile on each side of it had been closely cropped. Near the center stood the framework of a Sun Dance lodge. Hanging from a pole was the scalp of a white man.

Discovery of the site of the Sun Dance excited the Indian scouts. It was an annual ceremony of great significance, directed by a self-perpetuating priesthood, but always under the control of some great war chief. It was performed for a number of reasons: the overcoming of certain cosmic elements, such as to avert lightning; to gain new strength, health, and courage; to purify the heart; to win rebirth.

The rituals and dramas of the Sun Dance continued for eight days and nights. The lodge in which it was held was a roofless enclosure some hundred feet in length, with a tall center pole erected to represent the sun. Voluntary self-laceration or torture was practiced, the most common form being to insert in the breast a skewer attached to a thong, then fasten the thong to a buffalo skull and drag it around the lodge. Vomiting and sweating were employed as purification rites.

Sometimes an enemy captured in war was suspended from the pole, to die a lingering death, while the painted dancers performed about him. The finding of the white man's scalp in the Sun Dance lodge indicated that some unidentified trooper, trader, or scout had been sacrificed there.

The scouts carefully inspected the area, then squatted beside the Sun Dance lodge to confer. In the circle were Mitch Bouyer, Curley, White Man Runs Him, Half-Yellow-Face, Goes Ahead, Hairy Moccasin, Stab, Bloody Knife, and Bobtailed Bull. There were many new and some strange signs in the big camp. Bouyer listened thoughtfully to the statements and opinions of each man. Then he went back to report to Custer.

The troops were halted, and a silent officers' call was sent out. Bouyer's remarks were repeated to the assembly. The big camp had been a point of concentration for many diverse bands, and a large number of the Indians who had stopped there had come great distances. They were warriors from territories as far away as the Missouri, the Belle Fourche, the Cheyenne, and the Platte rivers.

When an officer inquired the reason for their assemblage in the valley of the Rosebud, Mitch Bouyer replied that the Crow members of the scouting force had given him the answer to that question. They were reservation Indians who had responded to an appeal from Sitting Bull, the great medicine man, for help in defeating the soldiers. Sitting Bull was not a chief, said Bouyer, but his medicine was very strong. It made the blood of young men race.

Custer's eyes were filled with delight. He added to Bouyer's statements the information that the scouts also had come upon fresh pony tracks near the big camp. As he spoke a stiff breeze suddenly rose, swirling dust into the sober faces of the men about him. His headquarters flag was toppled and fell. An officer stepped forward quickly, lifted it, and stuck the staff into the ground. The flag fell again, and once more the officer picked it up. He secured it by supporting the staff with sagebrush.

As they left the meeting, Lieutenant Wallace spoke to Lieutenant Godfrey in a voice which reflected profound concern. "It was a bad sign."

"What?" Godfrey asked.

"The falling flag."

"Why?"

"It fell twice to the rear."

At sundown the regiment camped in the shadow of a high bluff. Twenty-eight miles had been traveled during the day. Custer ordered that all fires were to be extinguished immediately after the evening meal had been prepared. No lights were to show in the camp during the night.

The scouts who had followed the fresh pony tracks returned at nine o'clock. The Indian trails, both old and new, passed over the divide west of the Rosebud and into the valley of the Little Big Horn.

Once more Custer summoned his officers. They stumbled toward his cot, being guided only by the flame of a single candle he had lighted. Curtly he ordered them to have their companies ready to ride at eleven P.M. The scouts, declared Custer, had told him of a high hill known to Indians as the Crow's Nest. From it the entire valley of the Little Big Horn could be seen. Lieutenant Varnum would leave at once for the observation point. He would take with him eleven Indian scouts and the white scout, Charlie Reynolds.

The intelligence Custer had received—most of which he had ignored—on the march up the Rosebud had been sound and significant. He had thought the various estimates of the strength of the Indians apparently gathering along the Little Big Horn as gross exaggerations, and in some instances ridiculous. The opinions of the Crow scouts that as many as three to five thousand Sioux and Cheyenne warriors had joined forces he viewed as nonsense.

Repeatedly Custer assured the Indian scouts, numbering more than fifty, that they would be richly rewarded after he had defeated the hostile tribes. They would be permitted to plunder, to take home with them all the spoils of war they desired. They would receive great honors and be hailed as heroes among both their own people and the white men. In talking with the scouts who were to go with Lieutenant Varnum to the Crow's Nest, Custer appeared to be exuberant. His eyes glistened in the candlelight. He revealed the conviction that he was on the verge of achieving a great victory, after which he would protect all loyal Indians, see that they were well fed and well housed and never cheated. All this would be possible, because after he had returned triumphant from the West he would become the Great White Father, he would live in the big lodge in Washington, and his word would be law.

As Custer waited in the darkness for the hour of eleven o'clock, on the evening of June 24, 1876, he was far ahead of the schedule General Terry had set for him. He had pressed with all possible speed up the Rosebud. The night march he contemplated would bring his command into the valley of the Little Big Horn at least twenty-four hours before Gibbon's column was due to reach the junction of the Big and Little Big Horn rivers.

If Custer's reasoning that evening was not disclosed by him to the other officers, there were few if any of them who did not understand it. The Sioux, led by the laughing Crazy Horse, and the powerful politician and maker of strong medicine, Sitting Bull, were in the valley of the Little Big Horn, only a few miles from him. The orders given him by Terry were clear:

> He [General Terry] thinks that you should proceed up the Rosebud until you ascertain definitely the direction in which the trail above spoken of leads. Should it be found (as it appears almost certain that it will be found) to turn towards the Little Horn, he thinks that you should still proceed southward, perhaps as far as the headwaters of the Tongue, and then turn towards the Little Horn, feeling constantly, however, to your left, so as to preclude the possibility of the escape of the Indians. . . .

Compliance with those orders would mean sharing the victory with Gibbon. Even Terry might reach the field in time to direct the fight, and as commanding general he would receive all credit for the triumph. In either case, Custer could see himself being denied the undivided glory he had so long dreamed of attaining, and which his political advisers had assured him would open the doors of the White House for him and Libby.

It was a loss, a sacrifice, a tragedy which he did not propose to suffer. As if there had been no orders from Terry at all, he formulated his plans. The regiment would get as close to the divide between the two valleys as possible with the night march. Throughout the twenty-fifth it would remain concealed in the vicinity of the Crow's Nest. At dawn on the twenty-sixth he would sweep down into the valley of the Little Big Horn, and before the sun of that day had set the Sioux Nation would be broken, its great chiefs annihilated. Gibbon (and Crook, who must be closing in from the south) could carry on whatever mopping up was required. But there would be very little of that to be done, if he had his way. There would be nothing to be mopped up.

Wise and shrewd and as learned in the ways of the Indian world as they were, Custer's scouts had no way of knowing that Crook had been defeated—not by the Sioux and Cheyennes they had trailed along the Rosebud—but by different and larger bands which, after gaining their unexpected victory over the southern column, had set out to join their brother warriors in the valley of the Little Big Horn.

They could not know that the cunning old Hunkpapa, Sitting Bull, had performed a feat incomparable in all Indian history, almost miraculous in its aspects—that of uniting the Sioux Nation in a last desperate defense of their homeland. Sitting Bull had done more than that. He had created an unprecedented alliance with many former enemies of his people. Around a small nucleus of Hunkpapa dissidents he had gathered fighting men from the Sans Arcs, the Blackfoot, the Santees, the Assiniboins, the Brulé, the Oglalas, the Miniconjous, the Cheyennes, the Arapahoes, and an uncounted number of malcontents from other smaller prairie tribes. In little groups, lusting for the blood of the white men, they had journeyed hundreds of miles to the rendezvous in the shadow of the western mountains.

On the night of June 24, 1876, the campfires of more than ten thousand Indians smoldered and blazed for four miles along the banks of the Little Big Horn. Probably four thousand of those encamped there were armed warriors, ready and eager for battle with the troops of Yellow Hair, which their scouts had told them were only a few miles away.*

It was almost midnight, on June 24, 1876, when the 7th Cavalry left the camp on the Rosebud. The night was black, and thick dust stirred up by the horses and mules choked the troopers and hid the few stars showing through scudding clouds. Only eight miles had been traversed by two o'clock. Custer's Indian guides informed him that under the conditions the ridge of the divide could not be reached before dawn. He ordered a halt, and the exhausted troopers fell to the ground beside their weary

*The 7th Cavalry contained twelve companies, about six hundred troopers. Thus on the Little Big Horn they were outnumbered by fighting men by a ratio of almost seven to one.

mounts. Men and animals were suffering from thirst. Some trickles of water were discovered nearby as the first pale light of the coming day rose above the horizon. It was heavy with alkali, and the horses rejected it, although Major Reno, Captain Benteen, and Lieutenant Hodgson managed to use some for bitter coffee in which to soak their hardtack.

At seven-thirty a message was received from Lieutenant Varnum. He and his contingent of scouts had reached the Crow's Nest at two-thirty. As the first streamers of light gave them a view of the Little Big Horn Valley, they had been astonished by the sight that met their eyes. The smoke of hundreds, perhaps thousands, of lodge fires rose to form a gray pall over the surrounding country. Some of the scouts declared they could see an immense pony herd.

Custer did not finish his scant breakfast of alkaline coffee. He shouted orders for the companies to be prepared to move out at eight o'clock, only a few minutes away, and held a brief conference with Major Reno, Lieutenant Godfrey, and several other officers who had come up for any further instructions he might wish to give.

Bloody Knife joined the group and spoke, and Custer asked sharply what the scout had said. A Ree (Arikara) repeated the words in English. "He say you find enough Sioux so must maybe keep fighting two, three days."

Custer's face had been grave, and he had appeared to be occupied by consuming thoughts, but suddenly he laughed. "I guess we'll get through with them in one day," he said, and turned abruptly, mounted his horse, and rode away.

He went to the Crow's Nest. After looking through field glasses into the Little Big Horn Valley, he protested in a tone of disappointment that he could see no Indians. Mitch Bouyer told him quietly that whether he could see Indians or not, he was looking at thousands of them. In thirty years' experience as a scout, Bouyer declared, he had never seen a larger village.

Custer only nodded and started back. He met the regiment at rest in a deep ravine. Outriders had reported that several mounted Indians had been observing the troops. Custer had officers' call sounded, remarking that further concealment would be unnecessary. Obviously his whereabouts was known.

Custer related to the assembled officers that at the Crow's Nest he had been told that the largest Indian village ever known in the West had been established along the Little Big Horn, but as he had been unable to see it, he did not believe it existed. However, there was no question that hostiles in some number were in the valley, and that he was therefore moving forward to attack. He instructed each company commmander to detail one noncommissioned officer and six privates to accompany and protect the pack train.

Shortly after eight A.M. the 7th Cavalry began a descent along Sun Dance Creek toward the valley of the Little Big Horn. Custer ordered a division into battalions. To Major Reno were assigned Captain French's Company M, Captain Moylan's Company A, Lieutenant McIntosh's Company G, the Indian scouts under command of Lieutenants Varnum and Hare, and two medical officers.

Custer assigned to himself Captain Keogh and Company I, Captain Yates and Company F, Captain Tom Custer and Company C, Lieutenant Smith and Company E, Lieutenant Calhoun and Company L, Lieutenant Cooke as adjutant, and the surgeon, Dr. G. E. Lord.

The battalion commanded by Captain Benteen consisted of Lieutenant Gibson's Company H, Captain Weir's Company D, and Lieutenant Godfrey's Company K. The pack train, under the command of Lieutenant Mathey, was to be escorted by Captain McDougall's Company B.

Benteen, moving in the vanguard, was ordered to proceed "to the left of a line of bluffs" about two miles distant. Directing that Benteen was to send out an officer and a squad in advance of him, Custer told him to "pitch in to anything you come across." Thereupon, Benteen broke off from the main column at the head of his men. It was not yet nine A.M.

As Benteen began to move away, Major Reno called to him and asked what orders he had received. Benteen replied that he was being sent to the left "to pitch into any Indians he might find."

Before Benteen's companies were lost to sight in the rugged terrain, Custer twice more sent orders to him. The first were carried by Chief Trumpeter Henry Voss and instructed Benteen that if he should find nothing at the first line of bluffs he was to "go on to the second line of bluffs," clearly visible, and "pitch in." Sergeant Major William H. Sharrow brought a second message to Benteen. If nothing could be seen from the second line of bluffs, he was to "go on until you come to a valley." "Pitch in," Custer said for the third time. Benteen was to report at once if he came upon any hostiles.

Custer advanced along the creek on the right bank, sending Major Reno along the left. The heads of the two columns were nearly on a line with each other.

At eleven A.M., Custer signaled to Major Reno to recross the creek. That done, the columns advanced beside each other until nearly twelve-thirty P.M. A brief halt was made at a long tepee. Inside was the body of a warrior.* Several scouts, led by F. F. Girard, had climbed nearby knolls. They reported to Custer that a band of fifty Sioux had been seen a short distance ahead. Farther on, in the big village along the Little Big Horn, the Indians appeared to be running away.

Custer ordered the scouts to attack the small band nearby. They refused, and he angrily ordered that they be dismounted and their horses taken away from them. He then summoned his adjutant, Lieutenant Cooke, and gave him orders for Major Reno.

Cooke saluted and rode rapidly away. He found Major Reno at the head of his troops and told him "the village was only two miles ahead and running away." Major Reno was to move forward "at as rapid a gait as prudent." After crossing the Little Big Horn, he was to charge, and he would be supported by the "whole outfit."

Major Reno started forward at once, moving at a trot.

*The dead Indian was a brother of the Sioux chief, Circling Bear. He had been killed in the fight with General Crook.

19

*T*he valley of the Little Big Horn, running from east to west, is mostly flat and varies in width from one to two miles. The area along the river, particularly as it bends, is heavily timbered with cottonwoods; on the south, the bottomland gradually rises in flats toward the foothills beyond.

Reno and his battalion, accompanied by Captain Keogh and the adjutant, Lieutenant Cooke, covered the distance to the river at a fast trot. There Reno called a halt to water the jaded and tired horses. Most of the Indian scouts were with Reno, and during the delay at the river they observed that the Sioux had sighted the troops and were coming up the valley to meet them. They called this to the attention of Girard, the interpreter, who started back to advise Custer. Keogh and Cooke were returning to Custer's command and were overtaken by Girard. Cooke promised to deliver Girard's message to Custer—that the Indians were not withdrawing but were advancing to engage the troops.

Crossing the river, Major Reno re-formed his command with Company A and Company M on the line, Hare's Indian scouts on the left flank, and Company G in reserve. He himself assumed a position twenty yards in advance of the troops, and slightly to the right of center. Sending his orderly, Trooper McIlhargey, to Custer with the information "that he [Reno] had the enemy in force on his front," Reno ordered the column forward at a trot. It was now 2:30 o'clock in the afternoon of June 25, 1876.

As the troopers advanced, the hostiles gradually withdrew. Some of Hare's scouts on the battalion's left were initially engaged in drawing off the Sioux's ponies that were grazing toward the flats. Ahead of the command was a vast cloud of dust. Indians mounted and on foot were entering and leaving the haze. Finding himself halfway down the valley without any sign of the promised support, Reno sent a second message of Custer by Trooper Mitchell, a company cook.

Calling up his reserve, McIntosh's Company G, into line, Reno continued the charge at a gallop. The troopers began to cheer, but the major signaled for silence, knowing that in the din, orders would be difficult to hear.

Reno was forty paces ahead of the advancing battalion and could now see the Indian village through the dust screen. He could also see hundreds of charging hostiles. He glanced to the rear; there was still no sign of Custer. A large body of hostiles emerged from a ravine five hundred yards to his front. On his left he saw his Ree Indian scouts give way, and in less than a minute they were in full retreat.

Knowing that his command of one hundred and twelve men was outnumbered at least five to one, that the attacker was in turn being assaulted on both his front and left flank, and suspecting that he might be entering a trap, Reno called a halt to the mounted charge. Several troopers who could not curb their horses' forward movement, dashed into the hostile ranks and were never seen again. It was three o'clock when Reno gave the order to dismount and fight on foot.

The Little Big Horn River at the point where the mounted charge was halted makes one of its many bends, and the area to the battalion's right was heavily wooded. It was here that the horses were led. Without the necessary horse-holders, the ninety remaining troopers stretched in a thin line halfway across the valley. With the Indian scouts gone, the left flank was hanging in mid-air. In spite of all this, the troopers advanced on foot another hundred yards and had almost reached the first of the village tepees.

The enemy's strength on the battalion's front had been steadily increasing and now probably numbered a thousand hostiles. The firing was deafening and heavy. Again Reno glanced back, hoping to see the balance of the regiment. He saw instead that the savages had penetrated around his exposed left flank and were behind the troops. Gunfire and arrows were also coming from the east bank of the river.

Fearing the horses would be stampeded or captured, Reno ordered Company G into the timber. Realizing that his position was now untenable, and since there was still no sign of Custer, Reno pivoted his line to the edge of the timber so that his right was now to the village and his rear was toward the river, whose bend gave some protection to the right and left flanks.

The troopers fought from the timber for about a half-hour. Casualties were comparatively light, although Sergeant Heyn of Company A had been killed. In addition, a number of men had suffered wounds, and several horses had been hit. Reno's command was now completely surrounded, and ammunition was running low. After a brief consultation with his officers, Reno concluded that it was imperative to abandon the timber.

There was a small clearing of about ten acres within the wooded area, and it was here Reno re-formed his column, the men "standing to horse." Company A was in front, M in the rear, and G in the center. Reno gave the command to mount, but before he could order the column forward a group of hostiles gained the timber and killed a trooper and "Bloody Knife," a Ree scout. The major promptly ordered his men to dismount and face this new threat. When it became apparent that this penetration had not been in force, orders were again issued to mount, and Reno led his command on a wild charge out of the timber.

In the confusion, some troopers did not hear the order to leave the timber, some had unmanageable horses, and others were reluctant to abandon the apparent security of the woods for a wild dash through the Sioux.

The men of Company G appeared to be the most scattered and disorganized. Captain McIntosh, their company commander, tried to get them together. In leaving the woods, his horse was killed. One of his men gave him his mount, but he was now behind the column and was immediately killed by the hostiles. The scout "Lonesome Charlie" Reynolds was also late in leaving and became a victim of the Indians. Finally there remained in the woods Lieutenant De Rudio, the interpreter Girard, the half-breed scout Jackson, and fifteen troopers, one of whom was seriously wounded. De Rudio, Girard, and eleven of the men rejoined the command later that evening.

In a column of four, the battalion left the timber at a trot in fairly good order. Hundreds of Indians on the plain between the timber and the river gradually withdrew to the right as the troopers advanced. Reno, leading the column, realized that with the pressure on his right he would not be able to make the ford where he had entered the valley earlier in the afternoon. He led his troops toward what appeared to be the most desirable river crossing, which was about three-quarters of a mile away, over fairly level terrain.

The charge—or retreat, as you may wish to call it—had started at a trot, but was soon moving at a gallop. The Sioux followed the troopers at a distance of about fifty yards on all flanks, particularly on the right and rear, firing their Winchester rifles as fast as they could be loaded.

For the men in the rear and on the right flank it was almost a continuous hand-to-hand combat all the way to the river. About halfway across the plain, Captain Moylan halted Company A and tried to regroup his men to protect Company G in the rear, but his efforts had little effect. Many troopers whose horses were shot from under them were able to catch others whose riders had been killed.

The river at the point Reno had elected to cross was thirty or forty feet wide. The west side had a drop of six feet, while on the east the bank rose even higher. The advance troops reached it in good order, but the six-foot drop was a greater hazard than Reno had realized. Many horses refused to jump and were forced from the bank by others coming up behind them. Into the milling jam of men and horses in the stream the hostiles poured a murderous fire. The river crossing soon became an undisciplined rout with survival every man's sole objective.

Among the many who were killed at the crossing was Lieutenant Benny Hodgson, Reno's adjutant and close friend. Hodgson's Philadelphia family had finally prevailed upon him to resign from the Army, but Benny had desired just one more campaign against the Indians. Shot in the thigh and his horse killed, he had managed to grab a trooper's stirrup, but as he gained the far bank he received a final fatal bullet. Dr. J. M. DeWolf, the regimental surgeon, after crossing the river with his orderly took the wrong ravine. Both were killed and scalped by the Indians.

At a signal from Reno the remnants of the battalion climbed the steep hill that rose abruptly from the east bank of the river. As the troopers, some still mounted and others leading their horses, reached the crest of the bluff, they were hastily posted into positions to meet the expected continuing attack of the Indians.

Three officers and twenty-nine men had been killed, and seven of eighteen wounded were in serious condition. One officer and seventeen scouts were missing. Of the battalion's original strength of one hundred and twelve men, Reno had a casualty rate of more than fifty percent.

While some of the Sioux followed the troops across the river, the bulk remained on the far bank, and large bands began to move back toward the village. As Reno and his officers crouched in their hastily prepared hill position awaiting the expected attack, their thoughts must have bitterly turned to Major Joel Elliott, abandoned by Custer at the Battle of Washita. Where was Custer? Where was his promised support? Reno glanced toward the rear. He saw a large group of horsemen galloping toward his position. It was now after four o'clock in the afternoon of June 25.

20

*F*or twelve miles after separating from the regiment, Captain Benteen led Companies H, D, and K northward through rough country. Seven times in that distance he sent Lieutenant Frank M. Gibson with six troopers to the top of high hills, in the hope of sighting the enemy, and each time they returned to report: "No Indians, only more hills and mountains."

Benteen considered his orders: ". . . if nothing can be seen from the second line of bluffs, then go on until you come to a valley. Pitch in." He had passed several lines of bluffs. His outriders had reported nothing but more hills ahead.

Benteen signaled a right turn and started back.

It was three o'clock on the afternoon of June 25, 1876, when Benteen crossed the regiment's trail. He caught sight of the pack train a mile off. It came up while the battalion's horses were being watered. Crazed by thirst, many of the mules plunged into a morass along the stream and became bogged in mud.

The battalion had gone on only a short distance when Sergeant Daniel Kanipe appeared with a verbal message from Custer for Captain McDougall to "hurry up the packs." Informed the pack train was farther back, the sergeant galloped away.

For another mile Benteen followed the trail, unaware that the forces of Custer and Reno had been separated. Soon a lone rider on a wounded horse dashed up to him. The man was Private Giovanni Martini, whose Army name was John Martin. He handed Benteen a piece of paper. It said:

BENTEEN. COME ON. BIG VILLAGE. BE QUICK. BRING
PACKS.   W. W. COOKE   P.S. BRING PACKS

Being some distance ahead of the troops, Benteen signaled to Captain Weir and Lieutenant Edgerly to join him. As he waited for them he questioned the messenger. Martin, an Italian imigrant who spoke little English, informed Benteen that the Indians Custer had encountered were "skeedaddling." Custer had ordered Cooke to send the message for the packs.

After Benteen had informed Weir and Edgerly of Custer's message, he gave orders to move ahead at a faster gait. The packs were then on the way, and traveling as fast as they could. One messenger, Sergeant Kanipe, already had been sent to urge them on. Benteen felt it more important that he advance and give whatever support was needed.

The three companies moved at a fast trot. Within a few minutes gunfire could be heard ahead. The ford where Reno had crossed the river was reached, and for the first time Benteen knew that Custer and Reno had separated.

The great dust cloud stirred up by the Indians attacking Reno could be seen. Benteen led his men on at a gallop. Sweeping around a bend, he could see a small group of troopers valiantly standing before an onrushing horde of Indians on the bank of the river. The troopers were the rear guard of Reno's retreating battalion.

Benteen started to cross the river, but when he caught sight of troopers ascending a hill ahead of him on the right bank, he raced toward them.

As Benteen's troops swept up to the crest, Reno's men waved hats, and tears marked the grime of their faces. Benteen found Reno wearing a red bandanna, having lost his hat.

"For God's sake, Benteen, halt and help me. I've lost half my men!" Reno called out.

Hare ran up to Lieutenant Godfrey, who was just behind Benteen, grasped his hand and cried: "We've had a big fight in the valley. Got whipped like hell."

Reno was moving about among his entrenched men. "We've got assistance now," he told them. "We'll get revenge. We can hold them now."

Benteen ordered his men forward to the crest. The fire from across the river was growing heavy once more. Lieutenant Hare was sent back to advise the pack train of the situation and to proceed with all possible speed to the scene.

Major Reno and four men moved cautiously down the hill toward the river, concealing themselves as much as possible in the brush. He wanted to make certain that his good friend Benny Hodgson was not lying on the bank suffering from serious wounds.

When they did come upon Hodgson, he was already dead. He had received three wounds, any one of which would have ended his life. Tears touched Reno's cheeks as he bent down and took a ring and some keys from Hodgson's body.

Shots striking nearby told Reno he and his men had been discovered. They quickly filled their canteens and crawled back up the hill.

At this time, Major Reno's command at hand consisted of Companies (or the surviving members of them) A, B, D, G, H, K, and M, and the following officers: Captains Benteen, Weir, French, and McDougall; First Lieutenant Godfrey, Mathey, and Gibson; Second Lieutenants Edgerly, Wallace, Varnum, and Hare and Surgeon Porter.*

Still hoping desperately to hear something from Custer, but greatly relieved by the support of Benteen's men, Reno gave serious consideration to moving. Several troopers had reported hearing firing in the distance, and, as Reno was later to state, he "knew it could only be Custer." He and several others walked cautiously to the highest adjacent bluff, but could make out no troops except his own, nor did he hear firing in the direction Custer had taken.

Captain Weir advocated a general advance to give Custer support, but Reno rejected the proposal. Would Captain Weir advise, he inquired, that they take the wounded along or abandon them? Did Captain Weir realize they were surrounded by five times, perhaps ten times, their number? In any event, if an advance was to be made, it could not be done until their ammunition had been replenished.

Reno and Benteen, carefully observing their surroundings in the late afternoon sunlight, reached the conclusion that their position could be strengthened by several adjustments on the crest. These changes could be undertaken as soon as the pack train with ammunition and equipment reached them.

They were unaware that Captain Weir, frightened and excited, had decided to take matters into his own hands. If he could not advance with his company, he could at least go north and make an attempt to observe Custer's position. Accordingly, he and an orderly set out. Seeing them go, Lieutenant Edgerly jumped to

*First Lieutenant De Rudio was still in the woods and did not rejoin the command until after nightfall.

the conclusion that Weir had been told to move, and he promptly ordered Company D to follow the captain.

Company D had been gone for a quarter of an hour before Benteen discovered its absence. Profoundly aggravated, he set out in pursuit with troops H, K, and N. He had proceeded only a short distance when he saw Weir and Edgerly's men retreating under a concentrated Indian attack.

Before this sortie by the Sioux hostiles, Weir and his orderly had advanced to the top of a knob subsequently called Weir's Peak. They heard no firing to the north. With glasses they could discern dust rising from a distant hillside and scores of Indians riding about, appearing to be in confusion and shooting at objects on the ground. They decided that if Custer had been on that hillside, he had withdrawn from it.

After the pack train arrived, Reno and the rest of the command moved out. Since many of the horses had been killed by Indian gunfire, some of the troopers were forced to travel on foot. Those wounded unable to walk or ride under their own power were transported in horse blankets. The entire advance was necessarily slow and arduous, the pace being governed by the speed with which the wounded could be carried.

Benteen, meanwhile, was able to get Captain French's company into action, but it broke under the impact of a fierce Indian charge. The line was finally established when Lieutenant Godfrey came up, dismounted his men, and covered the withdrawals of Weir and French. Under accurate and heavy fire from Godfrey's troopers the hostiles were halted.

When H troop finally returned to its first position on the bluff, Benteen ordered the men to stop and summoned Lieutenant Wallace to his side.

"Put your troops over here," Benteen directed.

"I have no troops," Wallace replied. "I have only three men."

"Well put them here and stay with them," Benteen ordered. "Don't let them get away."

This was the beginning of the solidification of the command's defense perimeter. As the rest of the troops marched back to the bluff, Reno and Benteen set about directing their disposal to planned positions.

One of the first things Reno did was to make specific provisions for the wounded. A hospital area was established along the upper rim, about a hundred feet above the river, believed to be the safest place on the height. Slowly and carefully the wounded were taken to it, each litter being carried by six troopers. The horses and mules, some of them staggering with weakness and maddened by thirst, were led into a small depression toward the rear.

Lieutenant Godfrey's Company K, covering the withdrawal, were subjected to heavy fire from pursuing Sioux. As other companies took positions, the Indians launched a ferocious attack. The firing continued unabated until darkness drew a merciful shroud over the men on the bluff.*

It was nine P.M. when the Sioux withdrew toward the village, leaving only a few snipers to harass the troops.

Major Reno at once ordered the entrenchments strengthened. Feverishly, thankful for the respite, the troopers began to dig in. They had few tools with which to work, and every piece of equipment was employed—plates and cups and cooking utensils— with which the dry earth could be scraped from pits.

Major Reno went alone to the edge of the bluff and sat on a rock. As far as he could see, Indian campfires made bright yel-

---

*Severe criticism has been applied to Reno for not attempting to reach Custer. This is both undeserved and patently foolish. The attempt by Weir was not only ill-advised but endangered all men of Reno's command, as Benteen well understood.

It would have been suicidal for Reno to have attempted to reach Custer, who had promised to support him. Perhaps no one stated the situation as clearly and concisely as General Philip H. Sheridan, who said: "The reasons given why Major Reno should have remained where he was driven, on the top of the bluff, that he afterwards fortified and held, are very good; but there are other reasons no less strong. For instance, he could not abandon his wounded, who would have been slain by the enemy, and furthermore, he had no knowledge of the whereabouts of Custer nor of the straits he was in, and it is natural to presume that he supposed Colonel Custer would return to his support when he discovered the superiority in numbers of the Indians, in order that the regiment might be reunited."

low holes in the purple night, and the throaty sounds of drums beat out the rhythm of the Scalp Dance.

An orderly had reported to him that eighteen men had been killed in the late afternoon and evening fighting. As many more had been wounded. Under the protection of the darkness men were crawling down the bank to the stream to obtain water in canteens and cooking pots and buckets for both the animals and the wounded, but enough to quench the terrible thirsts of either could not be obtained.

Burning in Major Reno's mind was the question: What happened to Custer?

He saw himself as a prisoner on the height. With so many wounded, even a retreat was impossible. Against the formidable forces facing him, any charge would have been suicide. He wondered if Terry had received any message from Crook. What the devil was Crook doing?*

Major Reno asked himself how long he could hold out, but he gave himself no answer. If enough water could be obtained, he might hold out several days. Yet a full-scale assault from all sides could overrun the position.

Terry and Gibbon were scheduled to enter the valley of the Little Big Horn at its northern end on the next day, June 26. Unless he could be reunited with Custer, they were his only salvation.

Wearily he got up and moved along the line. He stopped to gaze at the prone figure of Lieutenant Edgerly. "My God, how can he sleep?" he muttered, and went on.

The orders he had given Benteen had been thoroughly and efficiently executed. On the northerly side were McDougall's Company B, Wallace and the survivors of Company G, French's Company M, Godfrey's Company K, and Weir's Company D. In an attack the pressure would be heaviest from that direction. On the eastern line was Moylan's Company A, and Gibson's Company H had dug in on the south. There was little chance that the Indians would attempt to ascend the bluff from the

*Crook was still in his base camp, to which he had retreated after his defeat on the Rosebud. He would remain there until late in July.

174

river. In addition to their shallow entrenchments, the troopers had dragged dead horses to the parapets, and piled saddles and breadboxes and stones about individual holes. Ammunition and rations had been distributed.*

Major Reno sprawled on the ground and after a time fell into a light doze. Later, he rose to stalk restlessly about the camp. There could be no rest, no sleep, for him. The hundreds of fires still burned down the valley. The drums still sounded.

The first gray streaks of light were showing in the sky when Major Reno was brought to full attention by the crack of two Winchester rifles. The battle that ensued is, perhaps, best revealed in Reno's own words, taken from his subsequent report to the War Department:

This was the beginning of a fire I have never seen equalled. Every rifle was handled by an expert and skilled marksman and with a range that exceeded our carbine, and it was simply impossible to show any part of the body before it was struck. We could see as the day brightened countless hordes of them pouring up the valley from out the village, and scampering over the high points to the places designed for them by their chiefs, and which entirely surrounded our position. They had sufficient numbers to completely encircle us, and men were struck from opposite sides of the line. . . . I think we were fighting all the Sioux Nation, and also all the desperados, renegades, halfbreeds and squawmen between the Missouri and the Arkansas and east of the Rocky Mountains, and they must have numbered at least twenty-five hundred warriors.

The Indians actually numbered closer to four thousand, although many of them were armed only with bows and arrows. Benteen signaled for more men on the south, and Reno threw Company M into that sector. Benteen at once launched an attack, and the Indians fell back. He then suggested that a similar

*Incidentally, during the night Reno had asked that Indian scouts make an attempt to reach Custer or General Terry to inform them of their situation. Purportedly several scouts were assigned to the mission. There is doubt that any of them made a diligent attempt to break through the hostile lines in view of the fact that the country was swarming with Sioux and Cheyenne warriors. In any event, none of the scouts did get through.

charge be undertaken on the north. Reno led it, and drove the Indians on that side into a retreat without loss of a trooper.

Returning to his trench, Reno requested Lieutenant Godfrey to go with him to survey conditions. As they started out, bullets suddenly showered down about them. The major fell behind some saddles and laughed. "Damned if I want to be killed by an Indian," he said. "I've been through too many fights to end that way."

At nine-thirty A.M. the Indian firing suddenly slackened. The thought that they might be running out of ammunition was soon shown to be fallacious. They were reorganizing for a massive assault, a desperate effort to break into the lines of the troopers on the hill.

It came at ten o'clock. The heaviest pressure was against the sectors held by Companies H and M.

. . . In this charge they came close enough to use their bows and arrows, and one man lying dead within our lines was touched with the coup stick of one of the foremost Indians . . . some idea of the desperate and reckless fighting of these people may be understood. This charge of theirs was gallantly repulsed by the men on that line led by Colonel Benteen. They also came close enough to send their arrows in the line held by Co's. D and K, but were driven away by a like charge of the line which I accompanied. We now had many wounded. . . .*

At eleven o'clock the Indian fire once more diminished. The main assault had been stopped. Groups of hostiles began to withdraw from the field.

Meanwhile, the need for water on the heights was desperate. A skirmish line was formed under Captain Benteen to protect men who volunteered to descend the hill in front of his position to the stream with canteens. Enough of the precious water was obtained to relieve the torture of the wounded, but six troopers were shot in carrying out the mission.

Gradually the numbers of the attackers decreased, until at two P.M. only scattered groups remained to keep up a desultory

*Reno's report.

and ineffective fire. Major Reno quickly took advantage of the lull to obtain more water. Every available vessel was filled.

Strangely, the Indians continued to withdraw, and at last the battlefield became ominously silent. Major Reno harbored the thought that troops—from either Custer, Crook, or Terry and Gibbon—must be coming up the valley, but he refused to let himself believe it. Perhaps the Indians, convinced they could starve him out, were merely withdrawing to rest.

Sometime during that long afternoon Reno made another attempt to communicate with General Terry. He called on some of the Ree and Crow scouts to take a message through the Indian lines to convey to Terry the present position of his troops and (according to some authorities) possibly to request medical assistance. The scouts were reluctant to take on the assignment, but finally agreed. Four copies of a written message to Terry were prepared and given to the Rees and Crows. They rode away, only to return in a short time, indicating that they could not get through. It is not known if they really tried to make the trip or not. In any event, there is no record of what happened to the actual messages.

Meanwhile, thick smoke had begun to rise over the valley, and it soon became obvious to the command that the grass was being fired. The smoke increased in density until it concealed the Indian village. For three hours the troopers watched and waited, fearing to accept the opinion of a scout that the hostiles had lighted the grass fires to conceal the fact that they were packing and preparing to leave.

The shadows were long on the hills when a fresh breeze cleared the Little Big Horn Valley of the smoke haze. The thousands of tepees were gone. And out of the level plain along the left bank of the stream wound what appeared to be an endless procession of Indians, a great snake curving for miles into the western hills and out of the valley.

We had a close and good view of them as they filed away in the direction of the Big Horn Mountains, moving in almost perfect military order. The length of the column was fully equal to that of a large division of the Cavalry Corps of the Army of the Potomac as I have seen it in its march.*

The scouts told Major Reno that no less than fifteen thousand ponies were in the line weaving its way out of the valley of the Little Big Horn. On them and trudging with them were from four to five thousand warriors and their wives and children.

It was the greatest Indian spectacle ever seen in all the West, and as the last riders and travois vanished into the sunset, an age came to an end.

21

*T*he men on the hill could not discover the reason for their deliverance, but they fervently offered their thanks to God. But Major Reno gave neither himself nor anyone else time to speculate on the mystery. Details were sent out to recover the bodies from the timber and the river crossing. Graves were prepared in a designated area below the height. A new position was established and strengthened along the stream. Pickets were placed in strategic locations, both on the valley floor and on the surrounding bluffs.

The starving animals were moved to a grazing ground a short distance above the camp, and a strong guard placed over them. Before he sank into a troubled sleep, Major Reno wrote messages to General Terry and called for volunteers to attempt to break through to him. Several troopers offered themselves, and three were selected. They would depart the next morning if, after a study of the situation, conditions seemed favorable.

At sunrise on the twenty-seventh of June, 1876, Major Reno ascended the highest point of the hill on which his stand had been made. He swept the valley of the Little Big Horn with

*Reno's report.

his glasses. He could see nothing moving, but presently he picked up a distant dust cloud. It grew as he watched. His first and immediate fear was that the dust marked the return of the Sioux. But the slow approach of the distant figures finally convinced Reno that it was a column of troops. A subsequent survey through the field glasses soon verified this.

There was a considerable division of opinion about the identity of the troops. Some officers believed it was General Crook's command, though Crook was scheduled to arrive from the opposite direction. Others estimated it to be the Terry-Gibbon forces.

Though he inclined toward the belief that it was Crook, Reno scrawled a quick message, addressing it to Terry, and handed it to Lieutenant Hare. With Lieutenant Walker and two Ree scouts accompanying him, Hare rode away at a gallop.

On the evening of the twenty-sixth of June, Terry, leading Gibbon's column, was nine miles from the great village in the valley of the Little Big Horn. Two Crow scouts, riding horses that were on the verge of collapse, arrived and were immediately taken before him. They told him that Custer had been badly defeated. The scouts had been attached to Custer's column, but had dropped behind as Custer advanced down the Little Big Horn. The intelligence that Custer had been surrounded and wiped out had been obtained from other scouts who claimed to have witnessed the massacre from a distant hilltop.

Terry and Gibbon refused to believe the report, and a message was quickly written to Custer advising him that they would proceed to his assistance at dawn. The message was given to a white scout, Muggins Taylor, who at once rode away with it into the night.

Terry's approach had been carefully observed by the Sioux, and it was for that reason that they gave up the fight against Major Reno and vanished westward toward the Big Horn Mountains.

At dawn Terry was pushing up the Little Big Horn Valley. The sun was no higher than a man above the eastern horizon when his outriders, commanded by Lieutenant J. H. Bradley, saw the white clumps that were the naked bodies of Custer and his men on a hillside above the Little Big Horn.

Wild cheering rose from the troopers of Major Reno's command as Terry rode toward them. The Major stepped forward to grip his hand, and others crowded about, but as they saw the expression of grief on the general's face, the cheering quickly died.

Terry told them that Custer and his entire command had been wiped out.

Lieutenant Bradley stepped forward. "We counted a hundred and ninety-seven bodies," he said. "I don't suppose anyone escaped."

While preparations to evacuate the wounded were being made, General Terry wrote a report to give the world the news of the disaster. In it he said nothing regarding Custer's disobedience. When staff officers asked his reasons for omitting the significant fact, he replied that he, not Custer, had been in command, and that he would bear responsibility for what had occurred.

Muggins Taylor left with the report for Bozeman, the nearest telegraph office.

The slow work of carrying the wounded to the Steamer *Far West*, anchored at the junction of the Big and Little Horn rivers, was begun. It was two A.M. on the morning of June 30 before the last litter was carefully placed on the grass-covered deck of the boat.

General Terry handed Captain E. W. Smith, who would travel with the *Far West*, a second report of the Custer massacre to be transmitted to the East from Bismarck. It was addressed to General Sheridan, and labeled "CONFIDENTIAL." In it General Terry gave a detailed account of the Battle of the Little Big Horn, including Custer's actions as far as they could be determined.

"For whatever errors he may have committed," Terry said of Custer, "he has paid the penalty."

As he said good-bye to the captain of the *Far West*, Terry

told him: "You have on board the most precious cargo a boat ever carried. Every soldier here who is suffering from wounds is the victim of a terrible blunder."

Captain Marsh made the run downstream to Bismarck in record time. The *Far West* started from the Big Horn shortly after four P.M. on July 3. A short stop was made the next morning at Powder River to bury Trooper William George, one of the wounded who had died during the night. A second stop was made at Fort Buford to land a wounded Indian scout. Fort Lincoln was reached when July 6 was only a few minutes old.

The 710 river miles had been traveled in less than fifty-seven hours, a record that was never broken by a steamboat on the Upper Missouri–Yellowstone journey.

Meanwhile, for two days the survivors of the 7th Cavalry not engaged in removing the wounded had been digging graves on a hillside above the valley of the Little Big Horn.

22

*B*enteen was gone into the hills, Reno had crossed the Little Big Horn and was charging down the valley. Custer led his five companies along the right bank of the stream. It ran slightly west of north.

Custer had advanced only a short distance when from a rise he had his first good view of the Indian encampment. Its size astounded him. For miles tepees stretched down the valley. Cheers rang out as the troops came into position to obtain a clear view of the enormous village, but no cheer came from Custer. He at once understood that the reports of his scouts as to the numbers of the enemy had been accurate, and he ordered Tom Custer to send for reinforcements and the pack train.

Sergeant Kanipe was dispatched by the captain on the mission. Kanipe was told to locate Captain McDougall and deliver instructions to him to "bring the pack train straight across to high ground."

"Tell him," Tom Custer said to the sergeant, "if packs get loose don't stop to fix them, cut them off. Tell him to come quick. We've found a big Indian village."

After giving the orders to McDougall, Kanipe was to find Benteen and give him the same information.

Custer continued on the eastern side of the river for more than a mile, then halted his command. With Cooke, Tom Custer, his nephew, Armstrong Reed, and Trumpeter Martin, Custer ascended to the top of a hill. Trumpeter Martin said later:

Several hundred tepees were in plain sight. There were no bucks to be seen; all we could see was some squaws and children playing and a few dogs and ponies. The General seemed both surprised and glad, and said the Indians must be in their tents, asleep.

We did not see anything of Reno's column when we were up on the hill. I am sure the General did not see them at all, because he looked all around with his glasses, and all he said was that we had "got them this time."

He turned in his saddle and took off his hat and waved it so the men of the command, who were halted at the base of the hill could see him; and he shouted to them, "Hurrah, boys, we've got them! We'll finish them up and then go home. . . ."

Then the General and I rode back down to where the troops were, and he talked a minute with the Adjutant. . . . We rode on, pretty fast, until we came to a big ravine that led in the direction of the river, and the General pointed down there, and then called me. This was about a mile down the river from where we went up on the hill. . . . It must have been about three miles from where we left Reno's trail.

The General said to me, "Orderly, I want you to take a message to Colonel Benteen. Ride as fast as you can and tell him to hurry. Tell him it's a big village and I want him to be quick, and to bring ammunition packs." He didn't stop at all when he was telling me this, and I just said, "Yes, sir," and checked my horse, when the Adjutant said, "Wait, orderly, I'll give you a message," and he stopped and wrote it in a big hurry in a little book, and then tore out the leaf and gave it to me.

And then he told me, "Now, orderly, ride as fast as you can to Colonel Benteen. Take the same trail we came down. . . ."

My horse was pretty tired but I started back as fast as I could go. The last I saw of the command they were going down into the ravine. The gray horse troop was in the center and they were galloping.*

Custer, in the lead, was riding Vic, a sorrel with four white feet and legs and a blaze in the face.

He carried a big Remington sporting rifle with an octagonal barrel; two Bulldog, self-cocking, English pistols with white handles and butt rings for lanyards; a hunting knife in a beaded fringed scabbard; and a canvas cartridge belt.

He wore a whitish-gray hat with broad brim and low crown, and a buckskin suit with fringed welts on the outer seams of the trousers and the arms of the blouse. The blouse was adorned with two rows of military buttons. It had a fringe on the bottom of the skirt.

The long yellow hair which Indians had seen on his previous campaigns, and which had won him his nickname, had been cut short.

The words spoken by Custer to Martin comprised the last order given by him for which there is factual substantiation.

The message scribbled by Cooke on the leaf of the notebook was the last to be dispatched from Custer's command. It said:

BENTEEN. COME ON. BIG VILLAGE. BE QUICK. BRING PACKS.   W. W. COOKE.   P.S. BRING PACKS

Moving at a fast trot (his horse was too exhausted to gallop), Martin passed over the hill crest from which Custer had first seen the village.

"I heard firing back of me," Martin reported, "and I looked around and saw Indians, some waving buffalo robes and some shooting. They had been in ambush."

Only Indians who survived the battle, or observed it in part, could tell what truly happened on that afternoon of June 25, 1876. No one else lived.

*This was in substance the story Martin gave to Captain Benteen and Major Reno, and it was later printed in several books and periodicals by the noted student of the Custer massacre, Lieutenant Colonel W. A. Graham.

A number of Indian scouts testified later, giving their versions of what occurred during the battle. Excerpts from their comments follow:*

Curley, the Crow scout, who was seventeen, spoke:

After Custer sent his message away [with Trumpeter Martin] he rode to an officer who seemed to be in command of one of the troops [gray horses] and gave him an order. Immediately the troop turned its direction toward the Little Big Horn. Custer with the remainder of his command continued going northward—his trail was about one and one-half miles from the river. In the meantime, Mitch Bouyer told Curley to leave the command and go to Terry.

"Curley, you are very young," Bouyer told Curley. "You do not know much about fighting. I am going to advise you to leave us and if you can get away by detouring and keeping out of the way of the Sioux, do so, and go to the other soldiers [meaning Terry] and tell them that all are killed. That man [pointing to Custer] will stop at nothing. He is going to take us right into the village where there are many more warriors than we have. We have no chance at all."

The two men hastily shook hands and Curley departed. He immediately turned his bay horse around and retraced Custer's trail as he was instructed by Mitch Bouyer. Curley rode back to the creek where Custer and his men halted a few minutes before and then followed its meanderings up until he came to a tributary that took him in a northerly direction. He followed this tributary until he reached the high ridge east of the battlefield. From this place [about a mile and a half from the battlefield] Curley with field glasses could see the battle. He saw how the Indians circled Custer's men. After being satisfied that what Mitch Bouyer said came true, he rode away toward the Pine Hills.**

The Crow scout, Goes Ahead, said:

Custer had told the Crow Scouts to stay out of the fight and they went to the left along the ridge overlooking the river while he took his com-

*All of the Indian testimony on this page and following pages is taken from *The Custer Myth* by W. A. Graham, published by The Stackpole Company, and reprinted with their permission.

**Interpreted and recorded by Russel White Bear, noted Crow leader.

mand to the right. . . . At this point both Curley and Black Fox, Arikara Scout, disappeared. The three Crow Scouts rode [on] along the ridge, keeping back from the view of the Dakotas [Sioux] till they came to the end of the ridge and to the bluff just above the lower ford. There they dismounted and fired across into the Dakota camp, the circle of tents they could see over the treetops below them. They heard two volleys fired and saw the soldiers' horses standing back of the line in groups. Then in accordance with orders Custer had given them about staying out of the fight, they rode back along the ridge and met the Arikara Scouts and pack mules. Then they rode away around the highest point of the hill. . . . After riding all night they reached the mouth of the Little Big Horn by daylight. Here Terry met them. He asked about Custer and they told him Custer had been wiped out. He asked them four times.

The Crow scout, White Man Runs Him, stated:

The scouts took up a position on the high bluffs where we could look down into the Sioux camp. As we followed along the high ground, Custer had come down Medicine Tail Creek and was moving toward the river. The Indians [Sioux] saw him there, and all began running that way. There were thousands of them. Custer tried to cross the river at the mouth of Medicine Tail Creek, but was unable to do so. This was the last we saw Custer. Mitch Bouyer said to us: "You scouts need to go no further. You have guided Custer here, and your work is finished, so you had better go back to the pack-train and let the soldiers do the fighting." Mitch Bouyer said he was going down to join Custer, and turning his horse galloped away. This is the last time we saw Mitch Bouyer. . . . We went back along the ridge and found Reno's men entrenched there.

The Crow scout, Hairy Moccasin, said:

Mitch Bouyer was ahead with the four scouts right behind. Custer was ahead of his command a short distance behind us. Custer yelled to us to stop, then told us to go to the high hill ahead. From there we could see Reno fighting. . . .

We four scouts turned and charged north to where Custer was headed for. Three of us stopped to fire into the village [across the river]. We saw no more of Curley after that. I don't know where he went. When we met Custer, he asked, "How is it?" I said, "Reno's men are fighting hard." We went with the command down into a dry gulch where we could not see the village. Custer told Mitch Bouyer to tell us to go back to the pack-train, which we did.

In the spring of 1876, many of the Indians at Standing Rock Agency were starving. Without permission, Kill Eagle, a chief of the Blackfoot, led twenty-six lodges westward to hunt and trade with hostile Indians. He and his people had no intention of fighting the soldiers. All they wanted was food.

Their hunt was successful, and they soon had fat bellies. Reaching the great village on the Little Big Horn, they were welcomed by Sitting Bull, who pleaded with them to join in the war against the white men. When they refused, their horses were shot or stolen. They became prisoners, and were brutally treated by Sitting Bull. After the fight on the Rosebud against Crook, Kill Eagle was beaten with the arms cut from the body of a dead trooper. Food and possessions were taken from his band.

Kill Eagle was an unwilling spectator to the fighting. During the entire battle with Reno and Custer, he remained in the village.

His statements were interpreted in this way:

The fight with Reno commenced about noon, the Indians all rushing to oppose his advance, until the approach of Custer from the lower end of the village was announced, when the wildest confusion prevailed throughout the camp. Lodges were struck and preparations made for instant flight. Vast numbers of Indians left Reno's front and hastened to the assistance of their red brethren engaged with Custer, who was steadily forced back and surrounded until all were swept from the field by the repeated charges of the Indians as if they had been carried into eternity by the irresistible.

He described the firing at this point as simply terrific, and illustrated its force by clapping his hands together with great rapidity and regularity. Then came a lull in the fearful storm of iron hail and his hands were still again. The storm beat fast and furious as the thought of some loved one nerved the arm of each contending trooper. Then the movement of his hands gradually slackened and gradually grew more feeble. A few scattering shakes, like rain on a window pane, and then the movement ceased as the last of Custer's band of heroes went down with the setting sun. It was dusk as the successful combatants returned to camp littered with their dead and wounded.

He is very positive, however, that no prisoners were taken.

Kill Eagle says he got the following information from Sitting Bull himself: "After crossing the creek with his warriors he met the troops [Custer] about six hundred yards east of the river. He drove the soldiers back up the hill. He then made a circuit to the right around the hill and drove off and captured most of the horses. The troops made a stand at the lower end of the hill, and there they were all killed."*

Kill Eagle says it seems as if every one [Indians] was wounded, and places the number as high as six hundred. They kept continually coming in with wounded thrown over horses, with their heads hanging down and blood running out.

An interpreter repeated statements made to him by seven unidentified Sioux warriors who were in the battle:

The hostiles were celebrating their greatest of religious festivals—the Sun Dance**—when runners brought news of the approach of cavalry. The dance was suspended and a general rush—mistaken by Custer, perhaps, for a retreat—for horses, equipment and arms followed.

Major Reno first attacked the village at the south end and across the Little Big Horn.

*This was obviously an account by Sitting Bull of his strategy and conduct of the battle. He directed the fighting, but did not actually participate in it.
**A cousin of Sitting Bull, Mrs. Spotted Horn Bull, told interviewers of how Sitting Bull had a vision of victory more than a week before the Little Big Horn battle. Her husband, Spotted Horn Bull, was a participant in the fight, and she witnessed much of it from the Sioux camp. Eleven days before the hostiles met Custer and Reno, she related, the Sioux were camped some distance from the Little Big Horn and held a Sun Dance. Sitting Bull was one of the men tied to the "suffering pole" by thongs through the muscles of his breasts. For two days and two nights he suffered without food or water, and on the morning of the third day became unconscious. When released and revived, he stated that in a dream during his suffering he had been told that his people would soon meet Custer's soldiers and would annihilate them. Mrs. Spotted Horn Bull's story was confirmed by other Sioux who attended the Sun Dance.

... runners arrived from the north end of the village with news that the cavalry had attacked the north end of same—three or four miles distant. . . . A force large enough to prevent Reno from assuming the offensive was left and the surplus available force flew to the other end of the camp, where, finding the Indians there successfully driving Custer before them, instead of uniting with them, they separated into two parties and moved around the flanks of his cavalry. They report that he crossed the river, but only succeeded in reaching the edge of the Indian camp. After he was driven to the bluffs the fight lasted perhaps an hour.

After the battle the squaws entered the field to plunder and mutilate the dead. A general rejoicing was indulged in, and a distribution of arms and ammunition hurriedly made. Then the attack on Major Reno was vigorously renewed.

Sitting Bull was neither killed nor personally engaged in the fight. He remained in the council tent directing operations. Crazy Horse and Black Moon were the principal leaders.

The Indians were not all engaged at any one time: heavy reserves were held to repair losses and renew attacks successively.

They report . . . that in the three fights [with Crook, Reno, and Custer] they had with the whites they have captured over four hundred stand of arms—carbines and rifles, revolvers not counted—and ammunition without end.

The Sioux chief, Red Horse, one of the head councilmen of the great village, spoke:

The attack [by Custer] was made on the camp about noon. The troops, it appears, were divided, one party charging right into the camp. We drove them across the creek. When we attacked the other party, we swarmed down on them and drove them in confusion. The soldiers became panic-stricken, many of them throwing down their arms and throwing up their hands. No prisoners were taken. All were killed; none left alive even for a few minutes. These troops used very few of their cartridges. I took a gun and a couple of belts off two dead men. Out of one belt two cartridges were gone; out of the other, five. It was with the captured ammunition and arms that we fought the other body of troops [Reno on the second day].

If they had all stayed together they would have hurt us bad.

The party [Custer's troops] we killed made five different stands. Once we charged right in until we scattered the whole of them, fighting among them hand to hand. One band of soldiers was right in rear of us; when they charged we fell back and stood for one moment facing each other. Then the Indians got courage and started for them in a solid body. We went out but a little distance when we spread out and encircled them. All the time I could see their officers riding in front, and hear them shouting to their men. It was in this charge that most of the Indians were killed.

We lost 136 killed and 160 wounded.

Crazy Horse appointed Horned Horse to make a statement for him. Horned Horse spoke through an interpreter, and his narrative was reported in this way:

The village was divided into seven different bands of Indians, each commanded by a separate chief and extended in nearly a straight line. The bands were . . . commencing from the lower end . . . first, the Hunkpapas, under Sitting Bull; second, the Ogallalas, under Crazy Horse; third, the Minneconjous, under Fast Bull; fourth, the Sans Arcs, under Red Bear; fifth, the Cheyennes, under Ice Bear; sixth, the Santees and Yanktonais, under Red Point of the Santees; seventh, the Blackfeet, under Scabby Head.

The village consisted of eighteen hundred lodges, and at least four hundred wickayups. Each of the wickayups contained four young bucks, and the estimate made by Crazy Horse is that each lodge had from three to four warriors. Estimating at three made a fighting force of seven thousand Indians. This is the lowest estimate that can be made, for there were a good many Indians without shelter. . . .

The warriors . . . divided their forces into two parts, one intercepting [Custer] . . . and the other getting in his rear. Outnumbering him as they did, they had him at their mercy, and the dreadful massacre ensued.

Horned Horse says the smoke and dust was so great that foe could not be distinguished from friend. The horses were wild with fright and uncontrollable. The Indians were knocking each other from their steeds, and it is an absolute fact that the young bucks in their excitement and fury killed each other, several dead Indians being found killed by arrows.

Horned Horse represented this hell of fire and smoke and death by intertwining his fingers and saying: "Just like this, Indians and white men."

While the butchery was going on, Reno was fighting in the upper part of the village, but did not get in so as to get surrounded, and managed to escape. They [Crazy Horse and Horned Horse] say had he got in as far, he would have suffered the same fate as Custer, but he retreated to the bluffs, and was held there until the Indians fighting Custer . . . could join the northern portion in besieging him. These Indians claim that but for the timely arrival of General Terry they would have certainly got Reno.

In both the Rosebud fight and the Custer massacre . . . he [Crazy Horse] rode unarmed in the thickest of the fight invoking the blessing of the Great Spirit on him . . . that if he was right he might be victorious and if wrong he might be killed.

Sitting Bull spoke:

I was lying in my lodge. Some young men ran into me and said: "The Long Hair is in the camp." I jumped up and stepped out of my lodge.

I tell no lies about dead men. These men who came with the Long Hair were as good men as ever fought. When they rode up their horses were tired and they were tired. When they got off from their horses they could not stand firmly on their feet. They swayed to and fro—so my young men have told me—like the limbs of cypresses in a great wind. Some of them staggered under the weight of their guns. But they began to fight at once; but by this time . . . our camps were aroused, and there were plenty of warriors to meet them. They fired with needle guns. We replied with magazine guns—repeating rifles. . . . Our young men rained lead across the river and drove the white braves back . . . and then they rushed across themselves. . . .

The trouble was with the soldiers, they were so exhausted and their horses bothered them so much that they could not take good aim. Some of their horses broke away from them and left them to stand and drop and die. When the Long Hair, the General, found that he was so outnumbered and threatened on his flanks, he took the best course he could have taken. The bugle blew. It was an order to fall back. All the men fell back fighting and dropping. They could not fire fast enough, though.

None of them died on horseback.

. . . there were a great many brave men in that fight . . . they were shot down like pigs. They could not help themselves. One by one officers fell. . . .

The Long Hair stood like a sheaf of corn with all the ears fallen around him. . . . He killed a man when he fell. . . . He laughed as he fired his last shot. . . . He rose up on his hands and tried another shot, but his pistol would not go off. . . . All this was far up on the bluffs. . . .

At one time . . . I started down to tell the squaws to strike the lodges. . . . I was overtaken by one of the young warriors who had come down from the fight. He called out to me: "No use to leave the camp. Every white man is killed."*

*Most historians discredit and disregard Indian accounts of the Little Big Horn campaign for the reason that the Indian in battle is an individualist and too often tends to glorify his own personal exploits. In addition, many Indians had the habit of telling white listeners what they felt the latter wanted to hear. Others were inclined to color their accounts because they feared they might suffer reprisals from having participated in the massacre. However, they serve as valuable contributions to the over-all picture. Many of them throw light on events and details which otherwise would remain in shadow.

23

Captain Weir's hand holding his field glasses trembled. "My God, how white they look!" he said in a strained voice.

It was sunrise on the morning of June 28, 1876. Major Reno had led his men to the bluffs above the Custer battlefield. As he gazed down on the carnage his face had the immobility of brown marble. He said nothing as he started down the slope toward the Little Big Horn.

The 7th had buried its dead below Reno Hill, more than half a hundred of them, and now it had come to dig more than two hundred shallow graves in which to place the remains of the men who had died with Custer. There would, in the end, be 266 names recorded on the death roster of the Battle of the Little Big Horn.

The warriors had their bloody scalps to prove their bravery. The squaws had done well their plunder and mutilating. From the bluffs the naked bodies had looked like white boulders scattered over the hills and slopes. As the troopers came close to them they were horrified and sickened. Bowels were slashed open, penes and testicles had been torn out. After their lives had been extinguished, the troopers had been stabbed, shot, and beaten. Skulls were smashed, limbs broken, faces were unrecognizable pulpy masses.

The harrowing sight of the dead bodies crowning the height on which Custer fell, [Major Reno wrote] and which will remain vividly in my memory until death, is too recent for me not to ask the good people of this country whether a policy that sets opposing parties in the field, armed, clothed and equipped by one and the same government should not be abolished.

Gentle words, without condemnation of the corrupt bureaucracy that had permitted the Indians to be supplied with the weapons that had destroyed the men sent to subdue them. Soft words, without reprobation for the religious hypocrites who prayed each Sunday and on every other day desecrated their God, and violated every principle of good He ordained.

The male members of the Custer clan had been exterminated. Custer's two brothers, Tom and Boston, his nephew, Arthur Reed, and his brother-in-law, Jim Calhoun, were gone.

Custer was found between the bodies of two troopers who were lying one across the other. Godfrey was one of the officers called upon to identify it, and he reported that Custer's naked body was "in a sitting posture between and leaning against them, his upper right arm along and on the topmost body, his right forearm and hand supporting his head in an inclining posture like one resting or asleep. . . . He had been shot in the left temple and the left breast. There were no powder marks or signs of mutilation."*

Mitch Bouyer had ridden down into the valley to his death after sending scouts to Terry for help. Colonel Sturgis' young

*Chief Gall, who had been a leader of the hostile Indians in the battle, later declared that the "Big Chief" had not been mutilated because the Sioux respected his rank and his bravery.

son, Lieutenant James G. Sturgis, only a few months out of West Point, had died in the first battle of his career. Mark Kellogg, the correspondent whom Custer had been forbidden to take with him, had covered his last assignment.

The troopers had little equipment with which to perform their gruesome, heart-rending tasks.

> The burials did not amount to much, [said Sergeant John Ryan of M Company], as we had only a few tools, so we simply dug up a little earth beside the bodies and threw it over them. In a great many instances their arms and legs protruded. . . . Some of the companies burying those men had no shovels. They had a few axes and chopped down some sagebrush and put it over the bodies.

It was the best they could do. The 7th Cavalry rode away, out of the valley of the Little Big Horn, toward the Yellowstone.

24

*I*n the chapel at Fort Abraham Lincoln, the Rev. Richard Wainwright conducted a memorial service for George Armstrong Custer and the men of the 7th Cavalry who had died with him. Elizabeth Bacon Custer fainted and was carried out. For several days she remained in a kind of trance, seeming to hear nothing that was said to her, lost in a world of insupportable grief, but at last her strength and her consciousness returned. Quietly she directed that her household goods be packed, and as quietly she departed.

When Libby Custer started back to her family home in Monroe, Michigan, she was embarking on a new career. She was to devote the remaining years of her life to the glorification of the name of George Armstrong Custer. As long as God permitted her to live, she would seize upon every opportunity to exalt her beloved Autie.

Even in the confusion and depths of her sorrow, she understood that someone had blundered, as General Terry had said—and the realization became increasingly clearer as the days passed—but it could not have been Autie. She would never believe that.

When the reports of General Terry were published, she decided that he was the culprit, that he had sent her husband to his death. As she learned more details of the Battle of the Little Big Horn, her views changed, and at last she absolved Terry and pointed the finger of guilt at Captain Benteen and Major Reno. This was a situation more to her personal satisfaction, for she despised both officers.

Shaping the strategy of her campaign in the quiet environment of her Michigan home, Elizabeth Custer one day opened a copy of the *Army and Navy Journal* in which she read an article on the Battle of the Little Big Horn. The author was Frederick Whittaker. Elizabeth Custer knew at once she had found the man for whom she had been looking.

Frederick Whittaker was born in England on December 12, 1838. His father was a solicitor who had been forced to flee to the United States to escape imprisonment for debt. He had endorsed some notes for a client wno had defaulted.

The family settled in Brooklyn. Frederick's only formal education had consisted of six months in a private school. In compliance with his father's desire that he study law, he became a clerk in the New York City office of an attorney, N. Dane Ellingwood. He soon lost interest in his work, and announced his intention to become an architect, but this ambition quickly failed. Shortly before the Civil War, he had tried his hand at writing. When the *Great Republic Monthly* purchased one of his stories, he felt that he had found his true calling.

On November 11, 1861, Whittaker enlisted as a private in the Union Army. In the Battle of the Wilderness he was shot through the lung. On August 9, 1865, he was discharged with the rank of second lieutenant. He maintained that he had been breveted to a captaincy, but military records did not support his claims.

He also boasted that he had become a close friend of General Custer and his wife during the war, but neither Custer nor Libby was known to have mentioned his name or to have been in touch with him up to the time of the Battle of the Little Big Horn. When she wrote to Whittaker at the *Army and Navy Journal,* Libby Custer gave no indication that she knew him.

As the result of a small inheritance, Whittaker had been able to marry, purchase a home in Mount Vernon, New York, and devote himself to writing. He was prolific, and nickel and dime thrillers flowed freely from his pen. It was in 1874 that he accepted a post as National Guard editor of the *Army and Navy Journal.*

Meanwhile, an avalanche of stories and articles about Reno, Custer, and the Battle of the Little Big Horn—almost all of them without documentation—were appearing in the nation's newspapers and periodicals. It was during this period, when the name of Custer was on the public's lips and very much in the public's thoughts, that Whittaker resigned his editorial post in order to write a book about the controversy that raged about Custer and Reno.

It is not known that Libby Custer actually commissioned Whittaker to take on the project, though a number of historians believe that this was the case. In any event, Whittaker wrote and delivered to Sheldon and Company a bulky manuscript that was, in large part, the general's autobiography, *My Life on the Plains,* rewritten and rearranged. To it had been added a few chapters about the Little Big Horn fight. These latter were largely figments of his imagination.

The book was titled *A Complete Life of General George A. Custer* by Frederick Whittaker, Brevet Captain, Sixth New York Veteran Cavalry. From the day of its publication in the fall of 1876 it was a best-seller.

The section called "The Last Battle" strongly defended Custer from the criticism that he had disobeyed his orders, and excoriated Major Reno and Captain Benteen. Whittaker seized upon Major Reno's retreat from the timber as an example of his cowardice, declaring:

If Reno could get no farther, he could at least defend himself, die in his tracks if need be like a soldier. Instead of this, he tried to escape by running away from an enemy who had the advantage in speed. . . . By his inexperience in Indian warfare, Major Reno thus gave himself up helpless to the favorite style of fighting of his enemies. . . . Looking for personal security, he took the course least adopted to serve it.

Whittaker charged that Benteen had deliberately sacrificed Custer.

Looking at all the testimony impartially from this distance of time, the conduct of Benteen is far worse than that of Reno.* The major did his best in his fight, and it was nothing but want of experience in command and in Indian Warfare that caused his defeat. Benteen's case is different. He was an old Indian fighter, a man of remarkable personal courage, as he proved in the subsequent battle, had often fought under Custer and knew his business perfectly. That he should have, as his own testimony confirms, deliberately disobeyed the peremptory orders of Custer to "come on," argues either a desire to sacrifice Custer, or an ignorance of which his past career renders him incapable.

In his violent prejudice, Whittaker gave no consideration to the facts that during the Civil War Major Reno had successfully commanded a company, a regiment, and a brigade, that he had been in combat with Indians in the Northwest as early as 1858, before "old Indian Fighter" Benteen had seen a western savage, even before Benteen had become a soldier.

While Whittaker was furiously writing his dishonest and unfounded accusations, and reveling in the anticipation of his royalties, Libby Custer was enjoying the first fruits of her campaign to enshrine her Autie. July, 1876, was a particularly rewarding month for her. Custer's last letter to the *Herald*, in which he condemned Major Reno and put himself in the role of saving the campaign, was published. The newspaper declared the letter provided "something for Sherman and Sheridan to investigate."

This was very pleasing in itself, but she found even greater

*The "distance of time" was a few weeks.

satisfaction from a dispatch written by the *Herald*'s correspondent, Mark Kellogg, the day before he rode away with Custer on the fateful march to the Little Big Horn. Kellogg accused Major Reno of disobeying the orders given him by General Terry:

> Major Reno made an error in that he crossed . . . from the forks of the Powder to the Rosebud River, where he found a fresh hostile trail. General Terry had planned to have Major Reno return to the column, marching down the valley of the Tongue River; and after he had formed the junction General Custer was to organize his regiment for a scout up the Tongue, thence across to the Rosebud, striking it near its head; thence down the valley toward General Terry, who in the meantime would move by steamer to the mouth of the Rosebud, join General Gibbon's command, march up that valley until he met and joined General Custer. The plan was an excellent one, and but for the unfortunate movement of Major Reno the main force of Indians, numbering 1,500, would have been bagged.

Kellogg was greatly impressed with the beauties of the western country, and he described it at length "for the thousands of readers of the *Herald*," but he was equally ecstatic in his praise of Custer.

> And now, a word for the most peculiar genius in the army, a man of strong impulses, of greathearted friendships and bitter enmities, of quick, nervous temperament, undaunted courage, will and determination; a man possessing electrical mental capacity and of iron frame and constitution; a brave, faithful, gallant soldier, who has warm friends and bitter enemies; the hardest rider, the greatest pusher, with the most untiring vigilance, overcoming seeming impossibilities, and with an ambition to succeed in all things he undertakes; a man to do right, as he construes the right, in every case; one respected and beloved by his followers, who would freely follow him into the jaws of hell. Of Lieutenant-Colonel G. A. Custer I am now writing. Do not think I am overdrawing the picture. The pen picture is true to life, and is drawn not only from actual observation, but from an experience that cannot mislead me.

Kellogg's letter was a guide for Whittaker, and he followed it faithfully in his own descriptions of Custer.

25

*S*itting Bull had not been able to hold the hostile bands together. From the Platte to the Canadian border they were being pursued by a score of Army columns operating under similar orders: force the runaways to return to their reservations or kill them.

The 7th Cavalry was not permitted to convalesce. Reinforcements and supplies were sent out to its camp on the Yellowstone, and to Crook, whose defeat had at last been disclosed. The assignment to restore the regiment to the high level it had previously reached as an efficient and well-disciplined fighting force was given to Major Reno, the senior officer. It was a difficult and unrewarding task. The ranks were filled with raw recruits, many of whom had never seen a wild Indian, and the spirit of both officers and men who had been through the fight on the Little Big Horn was at a low ebb.

A few officers—notably Godfrey and Weir—were critical of Reno and Benteen for their actions in the battle. Both the major and the captain attributed the carping to hindsight and personal animosity, and ignored it. No serious criticisms came from their superiors, or from headquarters, and the attitude of the great majority who had suffered the ordeal was highly laudatory of them.

The respect and gratitude of the enlisted men were made apparent in tangible form. On their own initiative they took steps to have Major Reno promoted to lieutenant colonel to fill the vacancy created by Custer's death, and to have Captain Benteen promoted to the rank of major.

In a petition addressed to President Grant and the Congress they declared the action would confer

a bravely fought for and justly merited promotion on officers who by their bravery, coolness and decision of the 25th and 26th of June, 1876, saved the lives of every man now living of the 7th Cavalry who participated in the battle, one of the most bloody on record and one that would have ended with the loss of life of every officer and enlisted man on the field only for the position taken by Major Reno, which he held with bitter tenacity against fearful odds to the last.

To support this assertion—had our position been taken 100 yards back from the brink of the heights overlooking the river we would have been entirely cut off from water; and from behind those heights the Indian demons would have swarmed in hundreds picking off our men by detail, and before midday June 26th not an officer or enlisted man of our Regiment would have been left to tell of our dreadful fate as we then would have been completely surrounded.

On the petition were the signatures of 29 sergeants, 6 corporals, 10 trumpeters, 5 saddlers, 3 blacksmiths, 3 farriers, and 180 privates, a total of 236 troopers, comprising approximately 80 percent of the survivors of both Reno's and Benteen's commands.

The plea of the men was not granted, but it evoked a sympathetic response from the Commander of the Army, General Sherman. He wrote them:

The judicious and skillful conduct of Major Reno and Captain Benteen is appreciated, but the promotions caused by General Custer's death have been made by the President and confirmed by the Senate; therefore this petition cannot be granted. When the Sioux campaign is over I shall be most happy to recognize the valuable services of both officers and men, granting favors or recommending actual promotion.

Promotion on the field of battle was Napleon's favorite method of stimulating his officers and soldiers to deeds of heroism, but it is impossible in our service because commissions can only be granted by the President on the advice and consent of the Senate.

Far out on the Yellowstone, Major Reno was unaware of the plotting of Libby Custer and her literary hatchetman, Fred

Whittaker. His first intimation of the gathering storm he would be obliged to face came in the July 8 issue of the St. Paul *Pioneer Press and Tribune.*

The newspaper had expressed the opinion that the Little Big Horn disaster was the result of reckless indiscretions on the part of Custer. This editorial judgment brought down upon it severe condemnation from one of its most prominent readers, Thomas Lafayette Rosser, railroad executive and former Major General of the Confederate Army.

Declaring that he failed to find anything rash in Custer's actions, Rosser, in a letter to the editor which was printed, voiced his conviction that "Custer would have succeeded had Reno, with all the reserve of seven companies, passed through and joined Custer after the first repulse."

Without official reports or other documentation to support the contention, Rosser accused Reno of agreeing with Custer on a place of junction, and then "instead of an effort being made by Reno for such a junction, as soon as he encountered heavy resistance he took refuge in the hills, and abandoned Custer and his gallant comrades to their fate."

Although admitting that he had known Custer since his boyhood, and had great admiration for him as a soldier, Rosser did not trouble to add that he had been Custer's roommate and close companion at West Point, that following the war their friendship had been renewed, and that he had often been entertained by General and Mrs. Custer.

"As a soldier," he told the editor of the *Pioneer Press and Tribune* emotionally, "I would sooner today lie in the grave of Gen. Custer and his gallant comrades alone in that distant wilderness, that when the 'last trumpet' sounds I could rise to Judgment from my post of duty, than to live in the place of the survivors of the siege on the hills."

Greatly to Libby Custer's satisfaction, the letter was reprinted in the New York *Herald.*

Both angered and deeply perturbed, Reno and Benteen, with the help of other officers, drafted a reply in which they gave a detailed account of the action on the Little Big Horn. Not only had Custer not named a point of junction, but he had not proposed a plan of attack, they declared.

Reno recited the orders Custer had given him, which were to attack the village, and which he had carried out. He had sent word to Custer that he had the enemy in front of him in force. At that time Benteen had not yet joined him. Thus he was not commanding seven companies.

"You see by this," Reno wrote, "I was the advance and the first to be engaged and draw fire, and was consequently the command to be supported, and not the one from which support could be expected."

Stating that Custer had promised that he would "be supported by the whole outfit," Reno continued: "All I know of Custer from the time he ordered me to attack till I saw him buried is that he had not followed my trail, but kept on his side of the river and along the crest of the bluff on the opposite side from the village and from my command."

Had Benteen been twenty minutes later in coming to his support, said Reno, "not a man of that regiment would be living today to tell the tale."

Major Reno expressed the assumption that as a soldier Rosser had in him a spirit that would give him no rest until he had righted "the wrong that was perpetrated upon gallant men by your defense of Custer." He requested that Rosser publish his letter "with such comments as that spirit will dictate."

Major Reno handed a copy of his letter to James J. O'Kelly, a correspondent for the New York *Herald*. O'Kelly reported to his paper his own opinion that Major Reno would be "the last person in the world to leave a comrade in trouble without trying to save him." He spoke of Benteen as "the savior of the 7th," describing him as a kindly man with a gentle expression that belied "the decision of character he had shown in the battle." The officers of the regiment, declared O'Kelly, were "annoyed by the incorrect and garbled accounts published in some papers."

Not all the 7th's officers held such feelings. Weir and Godfrey were annoyed because Reno's report to headquarters failed to recognize their contributions and efforts during the battle on the bluff, and they set out to make a friend of O'Kelly, and furnished him with material purported to be the "inside truth" of the Little Big Horn massacre. It placed themselves in the roles of outstanding heroes and not only gave little credit to Reno and Benteen but cast reflections on them that were seriously damaging to both their characters and their competence as officers.

The undercover efforts of Godfrey and Weir paid dividends. When he returned to Bismarck, O'Kelly wrote a long report in which he completely reversed his opinion of Reno and Benteen. On the basis of information furnished him by Godfrey and Weir, O'Kelly charged that the defeat was caused by a "blundering want of soldierly sympathy . . . a failure on the part of men to do their duty or lukewarmness in supporting General Custer that might be called an ugly name."

O'Kelly declared that in his charge toward the Indian village Reno had faced only fifty Indians, and that in breaking out of the timber Reno had not conducted a charge but a retreat, "because there were no Indians in the way to be charged." He neglected to state that in that mad ride more than a score of officers and men had been killed.

There were, O'Kelly said, men in the 7th who wanted to tell the truth but could not speak against their superiors. He called for a searching official investigation of the battle to bring out the facts.

Major Reno's letter to Rosser appeared in the *Herald* on August 8, 1876. Rosser's reply contradicted Reno's statements and comprised a maudlin eulogy of Custer and a scurrilous attack on Reno's honesty, competence, and record as an officer.

He termed Custer "immortal" and declared, "I am proud to know that he sleeps today in an honored grave, and all patriots and lovers of heroic deeds, performed in devotion to duty, will join in his requiem."

Rosser's second letter appeared in the *Herald* edition of August 22. "The errors which I believe you committed in that engagement," he told Reno, "were attributed to what I believed to have been a lack of judgment and a want of experience in

Indian warfare, as I understand that you have seen but little service with your regiment on the plains."

He accused Reno of

gently pushing a line of skirmishers down toward a mounted force of Indians when it was expected that you would attack vigorously with your entire command.

The fact of your dismounting and taking to the point of timber . . . was an acknowledgment of weakness, if not defeat, and this, too, when your loss was little or nothing.* This was an act which I condemn. You had an open field for cavalry operations, and I believe that if you had remained in the saddle and charged boldly into the village the shock upon the Indians would have been so great that they would have been compelled to withdraw their attacking force from Custer, who, when relieved, could have pushed his command through to open ground, where he could have maneuvered his command, and thus greatly have increased his chances of success.

Rosser's comments were widely disseminated by Libby Custer, and they were paraphrased and plagiarized by a growing number of persons rallying to the defense of Custer. Because of a lack of time, Major Reno gave up any attempt to prove Rosser in error. He had taken it upon himself to send a personal letter of condolence to the family of every man who had died on the Little Big Horn. To accomplish the immense task he was forced to spend every evening at the little desk in his tent for several weeks.

The commands of Terry and Crook were at last united, and a column of more than four thousand men began a largely fruitless search for Indians. The 7th came under Gibbon's command, much to the dissatisfaction of most of its officers. Even Godfrey, who had no wish to see Reno promoted, wrote in his diary:

Something must be wrong about General Terry that he cannot hold control of the Cavalry and Infantry without having merely nominal command.

*At this point Reno's casualties were quite heavy, and by the time the troops reached the bluff his losses had risen to fifty percent of his command.

Orders precluded the possiblity of granting leaves, and when Godfrey was refused permission to travel by steamer to Fort Abraham Lincoln to see his wife, he unleashed his wrath on Reno. "Major Reno has been playing ass right along," he confided to his diary, "and is so taken up with his own importance that he thinks he can snip everybody. . . . Reno's self-important rudeness makes him unbearable."

Following the massacre a number of newspaper correspondents had rushed to the West. When their hopes of covering stirring engagements were not fulfilled, they turned to writing critical essays on the Sioux campaign, setting themselves up as authorities on Indian warfare. The representative of the Chicago *Times* wrote:

One good battle and a decent windup of this wretched business would just about suit me now, but I fear very much that the last shot of this section of the campaign has been fired. This comes of the official imbecility which, at the outset, sent an insufficient force to fight a powerful enemy, and in the end sent green infantry to impede our movements, and left us cavalry horses fit only for the purposes of a glue factory.

O'Kelly had changed his direction once more, switching from attacking Reno and making General Crook his target. He termed the maneuvers "theatrical" and wrote of Crook: "The conduct of this officer through the campaign has been, to say the least, peculiar."

It was on the twenty-sixth of September that the 7th Cavalry came in sight of Fort Abraham Lincoln. A reporter wrote that it appeared to be a regiment of ghosts, "like scarecrows more than human beings." No band welcomed them with "Garry Owen." No one cheered.

The thought immediately uppermost in Major Reno's mind was to soak in a hot tub and don fresh linens. That accomplished, his next goal was to consume a good steak—beef, not the buffalo on which he and his troopers had subsisted for weeks.

At the post club he was joined by other unattached officers, among them Varnum, Weir, and Hare. Each bite of steak was followed by liberal gulps of good red wine. Newcomers to the garrison were introduced and joined the gathering: Lieutenant W. W. Robinson, Jr.; Lieutenant Herbert J. Slocum, who had failed at West Point, but for whom his influential family had secured a commission; and Lieutenant John A. Manly of the 20th Infantry, who had risen from the ranks.

Heavy drinking was continued throughout the evening. Major Reno had reached unsteadiness when Manly began to comment on the adverse publicity the regiment had received. His comments suggested an agreement with the opinion of Rosser, O'Kelly, and others who had written derogatorily of the retreat from the timber to the height above the Little Big Horn.

Leaping up in fury, Major Reno struck the young lieutenant. They clinched, fell, and thrashed about the floor. Struggling to separate the two antagonists, others became embroiled. Tables were upset, bottles and dishes were broken. The fighting was nearing a dangerous stage when Weir mounted a chair and shouted that he would have everyone placed under arrest unless it was halted. The threat had the desired effect, and the officers left the club.

The next morning the drunken brawl appeared to have been forgotten. Major Reno, once more the commanding officer of Fort Abraham Lincoln, assumed his duties with a dark blotch beneath one eye, a cut on one cheek, and a headache.

He applied by telegraph to St. Paul for a leave of thirty days, anticipating a reunion with his son and a rest in the comfortable homes of the Rosses and the Haldemans in Harrisburg. Refusal of his request came within a few hours with the explanation that in view of present plans for a continuance of the Sioux campaign his services were required.

In the ensuing month he gave frequent dinners and accepted numerous invitations. A Fall Hop was held. During an intermission in the dancing, while refreshments were being served, Major Reno found himself cornered by Emiline Bell and Mary Godfrey. If the attacks on him had influenced the attitudes of their husbands, they appeared to be unaffected by them. Both expressed the opinion, with appropriate giggles, that he had grown much more handsome, and each asked for a copy of a photograph of him which stood on a table in his parlor. When he protested that he had no copies, Emiline Bell said in a tone of warning, "Well then, we'll just have to take such action as we see fit."

The next day, while he was in Headquarters and his house-keeper was shopping at the post trader's store, Emiline Bell and Mary Godfrey entered his quarters and took the photograph. Emiline concealed it in a trunk beneath clothes. Neither she nor Mary mentioned their adventure to their husbands.

On October 20 Major Reno was ordered to disarm and dismount all Indians on reservations west of the Missouri River in Dakota Territory. Five troops were assigned to him for the mission. He found the duty easier than he had expected it to be, for the Indians appeared to have no desire to oppose him. On November 4 he was back at the fort with several wagons heavily loaded with guns, and his troopers driving a herd of a thousand confiscated Indian ponies.

He found that Colonel Sturgis had returned from his long tour of detached duty, and had resumed command of both the 7th Cavalry and Fort Abraham Lincoln.

26

On a cold day shortly before Christmas, in 1876, a big man wrapped in a buffalo coat and wearing a fur cap and fur gloves drove a one-horse cutter southward from Fargo, Dakota Territory, on a rutted icy road that ran along the bank of the Red River of the North. There was without doubt no more lonely officer in the United States Army than Major Reno as he traveled over the empty whiteness of the plains.

Reno had been ordered by Colonel Sturgis to assume command of Fort Abercrombie. To an officer of Major Reno's rank, experience, and outstanding record it was a not too welcome assignment. The frontier having been pushed westward, beyond the Missouri River, Fort Abercrombie stood in the backwash of the Indian Wars. It was small, remote in its location thirty miles south of Fargo, the nearest town with railroad facilities, and of no strategic or military importance. Plans for its abandonment in the spring of the coming year already had been announced. Its garrison was comprised of Company F of the 7th Cavalry and one company of the 17th Infantry, both below normal strength. As its commander, Major Reno's chief duty would be that of a caretaker.

The prospect of an insufferably dull winter, locked in by deep snow and subzero temperatures, was not, however, the entire foundation for the feelings of frustration and futility that filled him. His request for a leave so that he might go to Harrisburg for the holidays had been rejected.

Contributing greatly to his melancholia was the mounting flood of criticism of his actions on the Little Big Horn which had appeared in newspapers immediately following the publication of Whittaker's biography of Custer. He had obtained a copy in Grant's Book Store in Fargo, and an hour's perusal of it had been sufficient time for him to realize the full extent of its dishonesty and malevolence.

The sight of the somber log post in the cold blue light of the late afternoon did nothing to lighten his morosity. Westward the white prairie reached into the rosy sunset. Beside the road the Red River of the North, a wide ribbon of ice, curved away through bare trees.

Alerted that a new commanding officer might be expected, the sentry at the main gate reported the approach of the cutter when it was several miles distant. As Major Reno passed through the stockade he stopped only long enough to ask the location of the headquarters building. He found awaiting him on the steps Captain William Van Horne, the post commander whom he was to relieve, and the adjutant, Lieutenant W. W. Robinson, Jr., whom he had first met on the evening of the brawl at Fort Abraham Lincoln. They gave him an enthusiastic and most cordial welcome, and escorted him to the commanding officer's quuarters, a two-story frame house conveniently adjacent to the headquarters offices.

Major Reno was unaware that his arrival was being thoughtfully observed, from behind a protective shield of lace curtains, by Emiline Bell, whose husband had shortly before been assigned to Fort Abercrombie to command the small company of cavalry stationed there.

When he had warmed and refreshed himself, Major Reno walked alone to the home of Captain Van Horne, who had invited the garrison's officers and their wives to a dinner in his honor. Emiline was vivacious and appeared delighted to see him. He was presented to Mrs. Van Horne, Mrs. Robinson, Lieutenant and Mrs. Thomas G. Troxel, Lieutenant Herbert J. Slocum, Surgeon and Mrs. W. J. Hatch, and Mr. and Mrs. John Hazelhurst. Hazelhurst was the post trader and maintained clubrooms in which the officers might drink and play billiards.

Throughout the dinner Captain Bell appeared moody and depressed. He disclosed at last that he had received a telegram from his mother in Altoona, Pennsylvania, that his father was near death. He was planning to leave the following morning. Early in the evening he excused himself with the explanation that he wished to pack and visit the stables to arrange for a cutter in which he would drive to Fargo. Emiline remained, appearing not to share her husband's concern.

On Tuesday morning, December 19, Emiline Bell opened her door to say good morning to Major Reno as he passed on his way to headquarters. He inquired if she would care to accompany him on a sleigh ride to inspect the post. She declined the offer, but suggested that she would be glad to receive him if he would call that evening. The major thanked her for the invitation, touched his hat, and proceeded on his way.

Major Reno was admitted shortly after seven o'clock that evening by Emiline Bell's Negro maid, Eliza Galloway, and ushered into a sparsely furnished parlor, typical of that provided company-grade officers on western posts.

In the center of the room stood a round table with a marble

top over which a fringed lace cover had been thrown. On the table sat a tall brass oil lamp with a red glass shade. The other furniture consisted of three uncomfortable straight chairs and a rocker. On one wall were framed oval photographs of Captain Bell's parents. Through an archway hung with portieres Major Reno could see into another room which contained a heavy mahogany bureau, a large brass bed, a small dressing table, and two chairs. A narrow stairway led to the second floor.

Major Reno was somewhat startled when Lieutenant Slocum emerged from the bedroom. Under one arm he carried a book.

"Good evening, sir," the lieutenant said pleasantly. "Sorry, I must be on my way. Work to do."

Emiline, appearing a few moments after the lieutenant had departed, greeted the major in her usual buoyant manner. "This back room is really warmer," she said. "Let's sit in there. We really use it more during this cold weather than the parlor. The upstairs rooms are very difficult to keep warm. How nice it was of you to come."

The Bells' quarters adjoined those of the Van Hornes. A single storm vestibule served both houses. The Major and Emiline had no more than seated themselves when Captain and Mrs. Van Horne, without overcoats, came in. Mrs. Van Horne wanted to talk with Major Reno about plans for celebrating Christmas.

When the Van Hornes departed, at the end of half an hour, Emiline took up some sewing and sat in a chair between the dressing table and the bed. The major, seated across the room beside the bureau, inquired if he might smoke. Emiline suggested they move into the parlor as she preferred not to have tobacco smoke in her bedroom. In the parlor they sat on straight chairs on opposite sides of the marble table.

Finishing his cigar, Major Reno arose and announced his intention to leave. Quickly Emiline dropped her sewing on the table and got up. She straightened the major's cravat, saying, "Colonel, you really should wear a coral stickpin. It would suit your complexion."

The major laughed, took her hands, and thanked her for a pleasant conversation. Then he donned his overcoat. Emiline again offered her hand, and in taking it the major's fingers missed their intended mark slightly and gripped her wrist. He quickly released it. Emiline giggled.

"Is that the Masonic grip, Colonel?"

Again the major laughed. "Yes, and I have a book on the subject. Would you like to read it?"

Emiline only giggled in reply.

"Good night," the major said and went out.

Major Reno had been an officer of the Regular Army almost twenty years, and the larger part of that period had been spent in remote posts and on the frontier. He understood that maddening boredom, confinement in winter, and an environment that was the epitome of dreariness frequently opened the minds of intelligent men and women to the fogs of pettiness, perversity, and juvenile caprice. Trivialities often assumed false proportions.

In his own case, to such pressure and conditions were added the heavy burdens of frustration, resentment, disappointment, and anger. Yet he appeared to make no use of his knowledge, to give no heed to the lessons he had learned from experience, nor to analyze his own situation. He seemed to be blind to what was occurring, what was happening to him—until it was too late to take remedial steps.

27

$W_{ednesday}$, *December 20:* Major Reno officially took command of Fort Abercrombie, Dakota Territory. After a busy day in his office with Captain Van Horne, he felt quite tired. Had he not agreed to call at the Hazelhurst home in the evening, he would have retired at an early hour. He remained at Hazelhursts only a quarter of an hour and, pleading weariness, returned to his quarters. During his brief visit at the trader's,

Emiline Bell had been playing an organ in an adjoining room, and he had not spoken to her.

Thursday, December 21: In the late afternoon Major Reno went to the Bells' quarters. Lieutenant Robinson's sister, who had been visiting him, was leaving the post, and the major had been invited to accompany Emiline Bell and Captain and Mrs. Van Horne to pay a farewell call on her.

To reach the quarters of Lieutenant and Mrs. Robinson, it was necessary to proceed along the plank walk which skirted two sides of the parade ground.

"If you don't take my arm," Emiline Bell told the major, "I shall take yours. The persons who built this walk were certainly short of lumber."

The mission to bid good-bye to Lieutenant Robinson's sister was completed in a few minutes. When he returned with Mrs. Bell to her home, the major did not remove his overcoat.

"I must get along. My housekeeper will have dinner ready for me," he said.

Emiline appeared to be disappointed. "Isn't it rather early for dinner?"

"Perhaps, but I said I would be there."

"I am planning to play whist at the Van Hornes this evening," Emiline murmured in a rather vague manner.

The major opened the door leading to the vestibule.

"I think I'll go there now," Emiline said.

Turning, the major placed his arm about her waist in the act of helping her pass through the door before him.

"Oh, naughty, naughty!" Emiline said with a girlish laugh.

The major quickly withdrew his arm. "Good night," he said with a smile and left.

When Mrs. Van Horne opened her door, Emiline at once whispered that Major Reno had tried to embrace her.

Friday, December 22: Major Reno sent a note to Emiline asking if he might escort her to the post Christmas party in the evening. He received no reply. On his way to the party he knocked at Emiline's door. Although he could see a light, there was no response. He was turning away when Lieutenant Slocum appeared.

"Good evening, sir," the lieutenant said, and knocked loudly on the door.

Major Reno concluded that Emiline had an escort to the party. "Good evening. I could get no answer," he said and left.

Shortly after he had arrived at the party, Emiline and the lieutenant entered. Dancing later with Emiline, the major said in a humorous tone, "All the knocking at your door this evening wasn't done by me, I see."

A shadow crossed Emiline's face. When the dance ended, she turned abruptly away from the major and rejoined Lieutenant Slocum.

"The major was insulting to both of us," she said as if she were deeply pained. In repeating the major's remark about the knocking she gave to it an inflection that was suggestive.

Lieutenant Slocum told her angrily, "I shall speak to him and demand an apology." He turned away and immediately sought out the major on the opposite side of the room. "I should like to see you later, sir," he said.

Major Reno nodded. "Very well."

A short time afterward, the major paused before a sofa on which Emiline was sitting alone while the lieutenant had gone for refreshments. "What the devil does Slocum want?" he asked her.

She only shrugged and averted her eyes.

A few minutes later the major left the party and went to his quarters. He was having a lonely nightcap when Lieutenant Slocum arrived. His face was flushed.

"Mrs. Bell informs me you have insulted her and me, and we should like an apology," he said in an angry tone.

The major laughed. "Oh, for Christ's sake, go home and go to bed," he said.

The lieutenant's flush gave way to a pallor. He stared at the major momentarily, then turned quickly and went out.

Major Reno poured himself another drink and sat before his

fire. Perhaps, he thought, he had made a mistake in showing any attention to Emiline Bell. Stories he had heard of her repeated themselves in his thoughts. Before he retired he sat at his desk and penned a short note to her. He had reached the decision that his future relations with her would be conducted on an unquestionably formal basis. The note requested her to return the photograph of him which she had taken without his permission. "It is the only copy I have," he wrote.

Saturday, December 23: Major Reno's note was delivered to Emiline in the morning. Immediately she dispatched her maid to him with the photograph and a terse note.

"Enclosed, Major Reno will find the photograph he requested me to send him," she said.

During the day, often with tears in her eyes, and pretending to be hurt and chagrined, she showed Major Reno's note, asking that the photograph be returned, to several women, on each occasion declaring with indignation: "Just look what this man has done to me!"

Several officers, passing through the country, had arrived at the post for a brief stay. The Van Hornes quickly arranged a whist party for them and the staff of the garrison. Emiline took the opportunity to invite, in quiet private conversations, each of the guests, with the exception of Major Reno, to her home on Christmas night.

Monday, December 25: The Christmas party for the officers of Fort Abercrombie and their ladies was held in the home of Captain and Mrs. Van Horne. Each of the wives contributed a dish especially cooked for the occasion, and after breakfast the guests gathered about a Christmas tree for an exchange of gifts. Major Reno had no gifts to give, but he received a number, and seemed to be deeply appreciative. Emiline, who distributed the packages, did not speak to him.

The major was aware that he had been ostracized by Emiline, and in the evening he went alone to the clubrooms maintained by Hazelhurst. For a time he played a lone game of billiards.

After that he conversed with the bartender, the only person present. During the evening he consumed a number of drinks. With each highball his resentment at being snubbed increased, and by midnight, when Hazelhurst came in from Emiline's party, his attitude had become touched with belligerence.

"Well, what went on at her fine party?" he demanded.

Hazelhurst shook his head in concern. "I'm afraid she's thrown down the gauntlet, Major." His tone became one of sympathy. "I can't blame you for being mad. Someone ought to make it hot for her."

The major only nodded, and left.

Friday, December 29: McCauleyville was a tiny crossroads settlement across the Red River of the North from Fort Abercrombie. During the afternoon, the Rev. Richard Wainwright, Episcopal missionary in Fargo, got off a stage there. He expected to be met by a cutter from the post, for he had written that he would arrive on the twenty-ninth to hold religious services on the last day of 1876. Finding no one waiting for him, he had set out across the river ice on foot.

Wainwright was forty-five, a man of forthright manner and great physical stamina. He had been born in Manchester, England, of a poor Methodist family. Because of a lack of funds, he had been able to study only a semester at the University of Edinburgh. Obliged to seek a means of livelihood, he had emigrated to Canada. There he had forsaken the religion to which he had been born, joined the Church of England, and received religious instruction from the Bishop of Quebec.

After becoming a deacon, he had been sent as a missionary to the Eskimos in Labrador. On his return from Labrador his first assignment after his ordination had been the region of the Great Lakes. In 1875 he had been assigned by the American Episcopal Church to an immense parish reaching for more than four hundred miles through the Sioux country of Dakota Territory. He established a home for his wife and three daughters in Fargo, and thereafter spent almost all of his time preaching in trading posts, frontier forts, and the small communities of settlers on the vast plains.

Upon his arrival at Fort Abercrombie, Rev. Wainwright was cordially welcomed by Major Reno, who apologized for the failure to meet him, and at once sent a sleigh to bring his luggage from McCauleyville. When they were seated before the open fire in his quarters, the major invited the clergyman to be his guest.

"I've been invited to stay with Captain and Mrs. Bell," Wainwright said. "They're very old friends of mine."

"Captain Bell is on leave," said the major. "Illness in his family."

Wainwright appeared to be surprised. "Well, I'll go see Mrs. Bell, and if she isn't expecting me to stay there, I'll be glad to accept your hospitality."

Wainwright left Major Reno's quarters.

That evening, the major went to the officers' club, where he joined Captain Van Horne and Lieutenants Robinson and Troxel in a game of pool. Lieutenant Slocum, Hazelhurst, and a bartender also were present.

During the game Robinson remarked, "I wonder why Wainwright isn't with us?"

"I presume he's writing his sermon," said Van Horne.

Major Reno grunted. "Perhaps he's more pleasantly employed."

"Well, I hear there was a preacher in McCauleyville last year who seduced the schoolteacher," Robinson said.

"A preacher must have his goose," said Troxel, "the same as any other man."

Shortly afterward Major Reno retired.

Saturday, December 30: The Rev. Wainwright appeared at Major Reno's office to speak about holding church services Sunday morning. Major Reno approved the plan and promised whatever facilities the minister might require. Wainwright thanked him and left.

Hazelhurst soon came in.

"I don't like this social war business," he said, "and I want to make sure I stay out of it. If Wainwright is going to hold church in the morning, and Mrs. Bell is going to play the organ, I guess I'll take my family over to Morehead for the day and see some friends. You said I might use one of the post sleds for the trip."

Major Reno smiled. "You can use the sled, but don't take this too seriously."

Hazelhurst looked grave as he left.

Major Reno and Lieutenant Robinson drove in a cutter on a tour of inspection about the post.

"Major," Robinson said, "I'm sorry about this business with Mrs. Bell."

"Mrs. Bell should know better than to commence a fight with me," the major said. "Her character is too vulnerable for that."

"Well, I am very sorry to have it happen," Robinson told him.

At noontime an enlisted man delivered a note from Major Reno to the Rev. Wainwright at the home of Emiline Bell. It said:

Sir: My attention having been called again to the subject of your holding services, I am convinced it is in the interest of peace and harmony that you should not do so. I need scarcely assure you of the deep regret with which I make you acquainted with this decision.

Wainwright went at once to the major's quarters and requested an explanation of the note.

"Since I saw you this morning," Major Reno told him, "I had a conversation with a member of the garrison who said that if you hold services in the fort, he will take his family to Morehead."

"Who was the officer?" Wainwright demanded.

"I didn't say he was an officer. I said he was a member of the garrison."

"Who was this man?"

"I don't care to tell you," the major said. "Now, if you don't mind, Doctor, I should like to give you a bit of advice. Last night several unfortunate remarks were made about you in the club. The statement was made that a preacher must have his goose as well as any man."

"I'd like to talk with the man who said that," Wainwright told the major with some heat. "Will you arrange a meeting for me?"

"Perhaps," Major Reno said.

Later, when the three men got together, Wainwright accosted Hazelhurst, asking, "If it was you who said he would take his family to Morehead if I preached here, I wish you would explain."

"Oh, I didn't mean anything by it," Hazelhurst replied. "I'll tell you what, if you preach here, I and my whole family will be present." He turned to the major. "I certainly have no objection to services being held."

The major appeared to be provoked. "Well," he told Wainwright, "I shall withdraw my objection. Go ahead with your services as you planned. I'll announce them at retreat."

Wainwright, his face taut with anger, left.

At five o'clock Major Reno summoned Wainwright to his quarters. He spoke in a blunt tone. "I understand from others that you have made up your mind to remain at Mrs. Bell's."

"I have," said Wainwright.

"Well, I think you should consider the propriety of such a thing," the Major said. "It's caused considerable unfavorable talk about you around the garrison."

Wainwright snorted. "I don't see why it should. It's something that occurs frequently. It's not unusual for me to stay at the house of a friend when the husband is away. For example, when I was at Fort Abraham Lincoln, General Custer was in Washington. I stayed with Mrs. Custer. If my remaining with Mrs. Bell casts an imputation, I should like to know why."

"Doctor, I'm thinking about the looks of it, the welfare of your own church, and the good of the services," the major explained. If you don't want to stay in my house, go to Captain Van Horne's. He'd be glad to have you. If you don't want to do that, then go to the hotel in McCauleyville. I'll see that your expenses are paid."

"I shall consider the matter," Wainwright said and left. He

spent an hour going about the post and asking several officers to meet with him in the quarters of Lieutenant Slocum. To each one he said:

"Major Reno says Mrs. Bell's reputation is like a spoiled egg, there's nothing you can say that will hurt it. The major told me she was a notorious woman in the regiment, and that he had heard immoral stories about her from Captain Benteen, Lieutenant Wallace, and Lieutenant Hodgson, and they had asked to have her expelled."

Mrs. Van Horne repeated to Emiline Bell the story as recounted by Wainwright. Captain Van Horne spoke about it to Major Reno.

"I never said any of those things," the major told Van Horne.

Subsequently, Slocum, Robinson, Van Horne, Troxel, and Hatch responded to Wainwright's call for a conference.

Van Horne appeared to be somewhat annoyed. "You're not doing anybody any good, least of all Mrs. Bell, circulating this story," he told the minister. "I'd suggest that, if you want to carry it on, you write Captain Bell and tell him of the situation. It's his problem."

"Well, I certainly think it's my problem, too," Wainwright answered.

The others agreed with Van Horne's suggestion, and Wainwright accepted the assignment. He wrote the letter to Captain Bell at Captain Van Horne's home. Then he sent a note to Major Reno:

... I communicate my decision on the subject of staying at Captain Bell's quarters. Whilst I am at Abercrombie, I have decided not to change, as I find I cannot remove without offering a slight to Captain Bell in the person of his wife.

Sunday, December 31: Major Reno issued an order that the organ in the officers' club was not to be taken to the post library, where Wainwright was to hold church services. To an appeal from Lieutenant Robinson for cancellation of the order, Major Reno said: "Well, you can have the organ moved, but Mrs. Bell is not to play it."

Emiline Bell announced her intention to defy Major Reno, but was dissuaded by the Rev. Wainwright.

The religious service was conducted without organ music.

Tuesday, January 2, 1877: Mrs. Bell complained that she was not well, and Dr. Wainwright moved to the home of Captain and Mrs. Van Horne. He announced that he intended to remain at Fort Abercrombie until Captain Bell had returned.

Friday, January 5: Captain Bell returned. He went at once to Captain Van Horne's quarters, where he talked with Wainwright and the captain. They went to Major Reno's quarters. There they were joined by Lieutenant Robinson. Bell informed the major of what Wainwright had related to him.

Major Reno's face hardened as he replied to Bell. "Captain, I deny everything that this supposedly holy Christian man, this meddler, has said."

Wainwright leaped up in indignation. "Major Reno," he demanded, "if you never said anything derogatory to me about Mrs. Bell, how did I get the names of Benteen, Wallace, and Hodgson as the men who wanted her expelled from the regiment?"

"I wouldn't know," Reno replied and spoke again to Bell. "Captain, you know as well as I do of the gossip that has gone around. You know of the difficulties in Shreveport. You know the trouble with Major Hall. But I deny ever saying anything of that nature about your wife."

Captain Bell appeared to be embarrassed, but no anger was revealed in either his words or his manner. "I guess we've talked enough about it," he said and went out. Captain Van Horne, Lieutenant Robinson, and Wainwright, who was looking crestfallen, followed him.

"Look here," Wainwright said to Bell when they were outside, "you can't let this matter drop. You've got to file charges against Major Reno. I'll see that they are prepared for you. I'm leaving tomorrow."

"I'll think about it," Bell said, and when Wainwright had

walked away he told Captain Van Horne, "I'm glad he's leaving."

Saturday, January 6: Captain Bell announced that he would go to St. Paul to ask the advice of General Terry in regard to placing charges against Major Reno.

Monday, January 8: After a meeting with Captain Bell, General Terry sent a telegram summoning Major Reno to headquarters of the Department of Dakota, and granted Captain Bell permission to remain at the Hotel Metropolitan in St. Paul pending a resolution of the difficulties.

In the mail Captain Bell received a long communication from Wainwright in which the missionary repeated his account of Major Reno's actions.

Thursday, January 11: General Terry met in his private office with Major Reno, Captain Bell, and Wainwright. Major Reno denied categorically making any advances toward Mrs. Bell. He admitted an attempt to induce Wainwright to seek other quarters at the post to halt unpleasant gossip.

"All I told Dr. Wainwright about Mrs. Bell," he said, "was that stories had been bandied about the regiment. I did not repeat the stories, nor do I know if they are accurate. Captain Bell is fully aware of them. It was in the interest of both his and his wife's name that I asked Dr. Wainwright to move."

Captain Bell again mentioned his inclination to let the matter drop, and General Terry agreed that such a decision might be advisable.

Wainwright leaped up in fury. He not only demanded that Bell bring the charges against Major Reno and call him as a witness, but he threatened that if they were not filed at once he would find other means of invoking them.

Friday, January 12: Captain Bell formally charged Major Reno with conduct unbecoming an officer, to wit: making immoral overtures to Mrs. Bell during her husband's absence.

Wednesday, February 28: Major Reno received telegraphic orders to relinquish command of Fort Abercrombie to Captain Van Horne and proceed to St. Paul to stand trial on the charges filed there against him by Captain Bell.

28

*T*he court-martial of Major Reno began at St. Paul on March 8, 1877, after an unsuccessful conference between General Terry and Wainwright and Bell, at which time the general requested that Bell withdraw his charges against Reno. When Bell remained adamant, there was nothing for Terry to do but to let the trial proceed.

The military court consisted of nine members, led by the president, Colonel William Babcock Hazen. The others were: Colonel George Sykes, 20th Infantry; Lieutenant Colonel George F. Buell, 11th Infantry; Lieutenant Colonel Pinkney Lugenbeel, 1st Infantry; Lieutenant Colonel Lewis C. Hunt, 20th Infantry; Lieutenant Colonel Daniel Houston, Jr., 6th Infantry; Major William P. Carlin, 17th Infantry; Major Robert E. A. Crofton, 17th Infantry; and Major Charles G. Bartlett, 11th Infantry. Defending Major Reno was the former governor of Minnesota, Cushman Kellogg Davis.

The Rev. Wainwright had done well his work of preparing the specifications against Reno. They were eight in number:

Major Marcus A. Reno did, during the temporary absence from Fort Abercrombie of Captain James M. Bell, visit the quarters of said Bell, and then and there take improper and insulting liberties with the wife of the said Captain Bell . . . attempt to draw her person close up to his own . . . placing his arm around her waist . . . failed to receive an invitation to the home of Mrs. James M. Bell . . . said "This means war! Mrs. Bell has thrown down the gauntlet, and I will take it up. Perhaps these people do not know the power of a commanding officer. . . . I will make it hot for her! I will drive her out of the regiment!" . . . told the Reverend Wainwright of the mention of his name and that of Mrs. Bell in the presence of other officers, connected together in a licentious and obscene expression. . . . "Mr. Wainwright would have his goose as well as another man, and he could have it with Mrs. Bell," statements wilfully and maliciously false, given for the dishonorable purpose of injuring the good name and repute of Mrs. Bell. . . . Major Reno said to the Reverend Wainwright: "Mrs. Bell's reputation is like a spoiled egg —you cannot hurt it. She is notorious in the regiment as a loose character." Major Reno said to Lieutenant Robinson: "Mrs. Bell ought to know better than to make a fight with me; her character is too vulnerable." Major Reno . . . sought to bribe a colored servant, Eliza Galloway . . . to obtain testimony for his defense . . . all to the scandal and disgrace of the military service.

"Major Reno, how do you plead?" Colonel Hazen asked.

"Not guilty, sir," he replied.

"Very well," said Colonel Hazen. "The prosecution may call its first witness."

Major Thomas F. Barr, a judge advocate of the Regular Army since 1865, arose. "I call Mrs. James M. Bell," he said in a quiet voice, and moved quickly to assist Emiline to the witness chair.

If she appeared to be distraught, Emiline Bell's memory was remarkably clear. She described in the minutest detail the furnishings of her bedroom and parlor.

"The major took my hands and tried to pull me toward him. I took my hands away. Before he left he took my hands again and slipped his fingers up toward my arm. . . . When I started out to go to the Van Hornes, he put his arm around my waist. . . ."

"How did you conduct yourself during these attempts of Major Reno to make advances toward you?" Barr asked.

Emiline twisted her lips in a look of indignation. "I conducted myself as any lady would."

"Cross-examine," said Major Barr.

"Mrs. Bell," Governor Davis inquired in a gentle tone, "did

you adjust Major Reno's stickpin and tell him he should wear a coral pin to match his complexion?"

Emiline covered her eyes with a hand and appeared to be suffering from a headache. "Oh, dear, perhaps something like that happened."

"Did you enter Major Reno's quarters at Fort Abraham Lincoln without his knowledge and take a photograph of him?"

Emiline seemed to have difficulty with her memory.

"Did you, Mrs. Bell?"

Emiline nodded, and gestured in a manner intended to show that she considered the incident a harmless prank. "Yes," she said in an almost inaudible voice.

Governor Davis smiled at Emiline. "Mrs. Bell, two days after the date on which you charge that Major Reno took your hands did you voluntarily permit him to escort you to the quarters of Lieutenant Robinson?"

"Well—it was . . ."

"Did you, Mrs. Bell?"

"Yes, but . . ."

"Mrs. Bell, while walking along a board sidewalk to Lieutenant Robinson's quarters did you say to Major Reno, 'If you don't take my arm, I shall take yours'? "

"Yes, the walk is very narrow."

"Did you feel at that time that Major Reno had made improper advances to you, Mrs. Bell?"

"Well . . ."

"Were you angry at him?"

"Yes."

"And yet you were willing to accompany him and to take his arm? I believe that is all, Mrs. Bell," Davis said, bowed, and sat down.

The Rev. Wainwright took the witness stand and delivered an eloquent recital of the words Major Reno had uttered to the defamation of a good woman whose husband was not present to protect her.

Major Barr apppeared both pleased and satisfied as he turned the minister over to Governor Davis.

223

"You took it upon yourself to protect the good name of Mrs. Bell?" Davis asked.

"I did."

"Why did you run around the post telling every officer what you allege Major Reno said of her?"

"Sir, I did it as a gentleman and a Christian."

Governor Davis permitted a slight smile to cross his lips, and Wainwright's face clouded with anger.

"Why did Major Reno suggest that you stay in his quarters?"

"That was an affront to Mrs. Bell."

"Wasn't it because Major Reno did not think it proper for you to stay with Mrs. Bell when her husband was away?"

"I resent that!"

"No need to lose your temper, Reverend," Davis said calmly. "Wasn't it because there was gossip about you and Mrs. Bell?"

"The gossip came from Major Reno. Again I say I resent your implications. I have been a guest in numerous homes when the husband was away. That is an outrageous implication."

"When Captain Bell told you he was inclined to make no charges against Major Reno, did you insist that he do so, and did you prepare charges for him to submit?"

"I did. One cannot stand idly by and let these immoral actions go unpunished."

"Didn't Mrs. Bell plead with you not to press the charges?"

"She was confused and frightened. This is an ordeal for a gentlewoman."

"Didn't she express the fear that certain unpleasant incidents in her own life might be revealed at a court-martial?"

"Sir, that is an affront to her I must protest!"

"I think you protest too much, Reverend," Davis said with a smile. "That's all."

Lieutenant Robinson testified that Mrs. Bell's name had never been mentioned in the officers' club in a derogatory manner. "The remark that a preacher must have his goose was directed at another preacher who used to be in McCauleyville," he said, "but it did follow remarks about Wainwright. It was the next day that Major Reno said to me that Mrs. Bell ought to know better than to start a fight with him, as her character was too vulnerable for that."

Lieutenant Slocum gave support to the testimony of Robinson. "I was only in the clubroom fifteen minutes the night after Dr. Wainwright arrived," he said, "and I didn't hear either Mrs. Bell's or Dr. Wainwright's name mentioned. I do recall that something was said about the preacher in McCauleyville."

Captain Van Horne's memory of the incident in the officers' club was equally vague. He denied saying that Wainwright was "probably writing his sermon."

"There was a stage driver there, and I think he did say something about the minister of McCauleyville," the captain said.

Lieutenant Troxel demonstrated that he had the poorest memory of anyone who had been present in the club at the time the derogatory remarks were made against Mrs. Bell.

"Someone said something about some other preacher, but I don't remember what it was," he told the court.

The post trader, John Hazelhurst, appeared to be extremely unhappy to be summoned to testify. He declared that he had made every effort to avoid being involved in the unpleasantness, and that he had not repeated any gossip which he might have heard. He had heard nothing said in the club about Mrs. Bell.

Major Barr did not appear to be confident of success as he announced that the prosecution rested.

Governor Davis was prepared and rapidly moved his case ahead with smooth efficiency.

"I never asked Major Reno to have Mrs. Bell expelled from the regiment," Lieutenant Wallace said.

"What is Major Reno's reputation?" Davis asked.

"I have known him since 1874, and his character as an officer and a gentleman has always been good."

"Have you any knowledge as to Mrs. Bell's reputation?"

"I have frequently heard her discussed unfavorably by officers of the 7th Cavalry."

"In what way did the remarks you have heard about her reflect on her character?"

"That she was not a true wife. She was involved in a scandal in Shreveport, Louisiana," Wallace replied.

Captain Benteen's great mane of white hair gave him the appearance of an old lion.

"I did not suggest to Major Reno that Mrs. Bell be expelled, nor to anyone else. Never," he said.

"What is your opinion of Major Reno's character?" Davis inquired.

"It is first-rate. I have known him intimately since 1869."

"Have you ever heard the character and reputation of Mrs. Bell discussed?"

"Frequently."

"In terms of approval or disparagement?"

"In terms of disparagement, by officers of the regiment."

Major Lewis Merrill had been in Shreveport during the time Captain Bell had been assigned there.

"I heard many critical remarks about Mrs. Bell's conduct," Major Merrill said.

Davis addressed the court. "I shall read a detailed statement prepared by Major Reno," he said. "In it each and every charge as set forth here will be categorically denied. The true facts will be presented."

At ten o'clock on the morning of March 20, 1877, Colonel Hazen asked Major Reno to stand before him.

The court-martial had found him guilty of conduct unbecoming an officer and a gentleman, and had recommended that he be dismissed from the service.

Pending approval of the court's findings by Secretary of War George W. McCrary and President Rutherford B. Hayes, Major Reno was ordered to remain in St. Paul. Robinson, Slocum, Rev. Wainwright, and James and Emiline Bell returned to Fort Abercrombie. The following month Fort Abercrombie was deactivated and the three officers were transferred to Fort Abraham Lincoln.

In May dispatches from the Department of Dakota headquarters brought news that struck them with dismay. If they did not know what had prompted President Hayes' reduction of the Reno court-martial sentence, they knew that the action might result in serious consequences for them.

What they did not know was that Hayes, harassed by political troubles and struggling under countless executive problems of far more import and urgency, had not concerned himself at all with the Reno verdict. He had simply taken the advice of the War Department, dictated a hasty note, and forgotten the matter.

Hayes ordered that the major's sentence be reduced to suspension without pay for two years.

Major Reno's offenses, grave as they are, [he said] do not warrant dismissal and all its consequences, upon one who has for twenty years borne the reputation of a brave and honorable officer, and has maintained that reputation upon the battlefield of the rebellion and in combat with Indians.

As a result of Hayes' action, Robinson, Bell, and Slocum prepared a new set of charges against their former commander. These charges, which were placed before Colonel Sturgis, specified that Reno had been drunk on duty on September 26, 1876, at Fort Abraham Lincoln when the post was in danger of being attacked by hostile Sioux Indians, that he made malicious and insulting remarks to a brother officer, thereby provoking a personal encounter, that he did

engage in a fisticuff and rough and tumble fight . . . did roll on the floor of the officers' club room . . . in the slops and filth caused by spittle and the spilling of liquor . . . did use arbitrary and abusive language . . . did allow pistols to be sent for, for the purpose of engaging in a duel . . . all this in the presence of civilians and junior officers . . . to the disgrace of the Military Service . . . for which Major Reno should be brought to trial.

It was soon demonstrated that Robinson and Slocum were not alone in the desire to damage the career of Major Reno.

Supporting the charges were the names of Captain McDougall, who had commanded the pack train at the Battle of the Little Big Horn; Captain Myles Moylan, Custer's protégé; and Lieutenant De Rudio, the Italian soldier-of-fortune and assassin. They were successful in inducing several young officers who had seen the fight in the officers' club, but who had never before known Major Reno, to offer themselves as witnesses. Captain Bell was at last persuaded to affix his own name to the formal document.

Robinson and Slocum had felt they could count on the cooperation of Colonel Sturgis, and they were astounded and chagrined when he rejected the petition with a volley of blasphemy.

In sending on the charges to General Terry, as he was required by regulation to do, Sturgis wrote:

I strongly disapprove. If Major Reno is guilty of the conduct herein alleged, charges should have been preferred against him at the time. They appear now with bad grace and do not carry with them the idea that they proceed from conscientious motives. I was not at Fort Lincoln at the time of the occurrences. I am credibly informed that the occasion was the return of the Regiment from the field . . . that the debauchery was pretty general and in my opinion it would be difficult to get at the real state of the facts, notwithstanding the large array of witnesses.

General Terry agreed with Colonel Sturgis, and so informed the Secretary of War. The Secretary of War agreed with General Terry, and ordered the charges dropped.

Lieutenant Robinson and Slocum were depressed and fearful men as they went into the northern plains for the campaign of the summer of 1877.

When he was informed of the President's reduction of his sentence, Major Reno applied for permission to leave for Europe with his son. The request was denied. The War Department granted him permission to leave the Department of Dakota, but he was not to travel beyond the boundaries of the United States during his suspension.

The gratification he had felt with receipt of the word that he was not to be dismissed in disgrace was overshadowed by thoughts of the unpleasant situation he would face in Harrisburg. Even though he looked forward to seeing Ross with great eagerness, he knew a profound feeling of loneliness as he took the train for the East.

29

A year and a half after its publication, sales of Whittaker's *Life of Custer* were rapidly falling off. Newspapers appeared to be losing interest, and for some months the attacks on Major Reno which had appeared in print had gone unanswered. Inquiries revealed that Major Reno purportedly was living quietly in Harrisburg, seemingly unperturbed by the spasmodic efforts to blacken further his name and character.

Accordingly, on May 18, 1878, from his home in Mount Vernon, New York, Whittaker wrote a long letter to his friend, W. W. Corlett, delegate to Congress from the Territory of Wyoming:

Having been called upon to prepare the biography of the late Brevet Major General George A. Custer, U.S.A., a great amount of evidence, oral and written, came into my hands tending to prove that the sacrifice of his life and the lives of his immediate command at the Battle of the Little Big Horn was useless, and owing to the cowardice of his subordinates.

I desire, therefore, to call your attention, and that of Congress, through you, to the necessity of ordering an official investigation by a committee of your honorable body into the conduct of the United States troops engaged in the Battle of the Little Big Horn, fought June 25, 1876, otherwise known as the Custer Massacre, in which Lieut. Col. Custer, Seventh United States Cavalry, perished, with five companies of the Seventh Cavalry, at the hands of the Indians.

The reasons on which I found my request are as follows:

First: Information coming to me from participants in the battle, written and oral, is to the effect that gross cowardice was displayed therein by Major Marcus A. Reno, Seventh United States Cavalry, second in command that day: and that owing to such cowardice, the orders of Lieut. Col. Custer, commanding officer, to said Reno, to execute a certain attack, were not made.

That the failure of this movement, owing to his cowardice and disobedience, caused the defeat of the United States forces on the day in question; and that had Custer's orders been obeyed, the troops would probably have defeated the Indians.

That after Major Reno's cowardly flight, he was joined by Captain F. W. Benteen, Seventh United States Cavalry, with reinforcements, which were placed under his orders, and that he remained idle with this force while his superior officer was fighting against the whole force of Indians, the battle being within his knowledge, the sound of firing audible from his position, and his forces out of immediate danger from the enemy.

That the consequences of this second exhibition of cowardice and incompetency was the massacre of Lieut. Col. Custer and five companies of the Seventh United States Cavalry.

Second: The proof of these facts lies in the evidence of persons in the service of the United States Government, chiefly in the Army, and no power short of Congress can compel their attendance and protect them from annoyance and persecution if they openly testify to the cowardice exhibited on the above occasion.

Third: The only official record of the battle now extant is the report written by Major Reno, above named, and is, in the main, false and libelous to the memory of the late Lieut. Col. Custer, in that it represents the defeat of the United States forces on that occasion as owing to the division by Custer of his forces into three detachments, to overmanning his forces, and to ignorance of the enemy's force,—all serious charges against the capacity of said Custer as an officer; whereas the defeat was really owing to the cowardice and disobedience of said Reno and to the wilful neglect of said Reno and Capt. Benteen to join battle with the Indians in support of their commanding officer when they might have done it, and it was their plain duty to do so.

Fourth: The welfare of the United States Army demands that in case of a massacre of a large party of troops, under circumstances covered with suspicion, it should be officially established where the blame belongs, to the end that the service may not deteriorate by the retention of cowards.

Fifth: Justice to an officer of the previously unstained record of Lieut. Col. Custer, demands that the accusation under which his memory now rests, in the only official account of the Battle of the Little Big Horn now extant, should be proved or disproved.

I have thus given you, as briefly as I can, my reasons for asking this investigation, and the facts I am confident of being able to prove. My witnesses will be all the living officers of the Seventh United States Cavalry who were present at the battle of June 25, including Major Reno and Capt. Benteen;—myself to prove statements of an officer since deceased, made me a few days before his death; F. F. Girard, Indian Interpreter to the United States forces; Dr. Porter of Bismarck, D. T., contract surgeon at the battle in question; Lieut. Carland, Sixth Infantry; Sergeant Godman, now of the Signal Service, and others whose names I can find in time for the committee's session, should the same be ordered.

Trusting, dear Sir, that this letter may result in an investigation which shall decide the whole truth about the battle of the 25th June, 1876, and the purgation of the Service.

I am your obedient servant.

Taking no chances that his letter might be pigeonholed or delayed by red tape, Whittaker made it public in the form of a press release. The precaution was hardly necessary. Delegate Corlett promptly sent the letter to the Committee on Military Affairs.

On June 13 newspapers throughout the nation informed their readers that Major Reno had been accused of cowardice, and that an investigation was probable.

The House Committee on Military Affairs [said a wire story] decided today to report favorably to the House a resolution directing an investigation of the Custer Massacre. Mr. Bragg will present a resolution for a subcommittee to sit in recess and send for persons and papers.

Looking back through the past few years, Major Reno might well have wondered if he was destined to continue to the end of his days under the shadows of ill-fortune and the burdens of new tragedies. He had lost Mary Hannah, and had not been permitted to see her in death before she was laid to rest. He had been through terrible combat against the Sioux, and he had been condemned for the foolhardy actions of another.

He had returned to Fort Abraham Lincoln to be denied a leave so that he might spend Christmas with his only child. He had been affronted and insulted by an assignment to an insignificant post that was to be abolished because it was no longer of military value. He had—and he freely admitted that he had not shown good judgment—been the victim of a silly, conscienceless female. He had returned to Harrisburg to take rooms in the Locheil Hotel, where he lived quietly by himself.

As he read the story from Washington that new charges of cowardice and disobedience of orders had been brought against him, this time in the Congress of the United States, he understood that his silence was no longer possible. It was obvious that Whittaker did not intend to abandon the campaign against him until he had ruined him and driven him forever from the Army, a broken man.

Reno resolved to fight, to fight in the open, and to fight with no quarter asked.

In a dignified letter that did not reflect the fury seething within him, he wrote the House Committee on Military Affairs, joining unqualifiedly and enthusiastically in the request made by Whittaker.

He was disappointed to learn a few days later that Congress had adjourned without taking action on the issue, but he was not diverted from his determination to take up the challenge thrown at him.

At once he sent another request to Washington. It was dated June 22, 1878.

His Excellency, The President:

A letter addressed to the Hon. W. W. Corlett, Delegate to Congress from Wyoming Terr'y., and by him referred to the House Committee on Mil. Affairs, and thus made semi-official, appeared in the press of the

13th inst. As the object of this letter was to request an investigation of my conduct at the battle of the Little Big Horn river, and was also the first time various reports and rumors had been put into definite shape, I addressed a communication to the same Committee, through its chairman, urging that the investigation be resolved upon. The Congress adjourned without taking any action, and I now appeal to the Executive for a "Court of Inquiry" to investigate the affair, that the many rumors started by camp gossip may be set at rest and the truth made fully known.

The letter to Mr. Corlett which is referred to, is hereto attached.

I am, Sir, Very respectfully, Your Obed't. Ser't.

As the weeks of the summer dragged away without a response from the White House, Major Reno began to fear that the investigation would not be ordered until Congress had reopened and a new resolution had been introduced. He had nearly given up hope when, in August, he was informed in a communication from the Adjutant General of the United States that his request for a Court of Inquiry had been granted. It would be convened after the return of his regiment from its summer campaign on the western plains, and the necessary witnesses could be obtained without incommoding the service.

Although delighted that he would have an opportunity to defend himself under the aegis of an official inquiry, Major Reno was concerned that the expense would be more than he could meet. It would be necessary for him to retain counsel, and if in addition he was obliged to travel and to pay the expenses of his attorney and himself, his available funds would be depleted to a dangerous extent. He had already asked Lyman D. Gilbert, a young Harrisburg lawyer he had known for several years and a close friend, to defend him. He wrote Secretary of War McCrary:

I will be compelled to go to some strange place and be at quarters other than I can afford. I have, therefore, to ask that my pay at least in part be restored to me. Have I not been punished far beyond my guilt, even if guilty as charged? The amount of my fine has already reached the sum of $4,600—more than any jury would award as damage under the same circumstances. I appeal to you as a lawyer and one acquainted with the character of the woman in this case if this statement is not true.

Does it not strike you that all just demands have been fully satisfied in this case?

Secretary McCrary submitted the appeal to General Sherman, who replied:

The case was fairly tried and the sentence should be enforced. In the event of a Court of Inquiry being ordered, Major Reno will receive transportation and issue of quarters while the court is in session.*

The administrative mill of the War Department ground slowly. It was not until the twenty-fifth of November that Major Reno received Special Order No. 255 from Headquarters of the Army directing that the Court of Inquiry he had requested be convened in Chicago on January 13, 1879.

30

*T*he Palmer House, an old gray masonry pile rising at Monroe and State streets, in the heart of downtown Chicago, had been selected as the place in which the Reno Court of Inquiry would sit. In its furnishings and decorations it represented, with each plaster angel cornice, each fringed chair and draped divan, each velvet portiere and pile carpet, the tortured

*A Military Court of Inquiry is an investigatory body that inquires into the truth or falsity of charges that have been directed against a member of the military service. Unlike a court-martial, it does not try a person formally charged with a crime. Its sole purpose is to establish facts. If its findings warrant, it may recommend that additional actions be undertaken.

grandeur of the Victorian Age. Its mahogany bars and paneled dining rooms served excellent liquors and passable French cooking, modified by such midwestern specialties as corn-on-the-cob, corn pone, corn oysters, and apple pie à la mode. Silver dollars adorned the corners of the tiles of the barbershop floor. Tall brass spittoons stood at strategic locations throughout its public salons.

In a red plush anteroom, Colonel John H. King of the 9th Infantry, the senior officer and president of the court, shook hands with his colleagues, Colonel Merritt and Lieutenant Colonel W. B. Royall of the 3rd Cavalry, both of whom he had known for many years. Upon being informed that Major Reno's counsel, Lyman D. Gilbert, could not arrive from Harrisburg until the next day, the court members agreed to appear only long enough to complete the necessary formalities of opening the inquiry.

They entered the hearing room, and Colonel King inquired of Major Reno if he objected to any member of the court.

"No, sir," Major Reno said.

The court was sworn by the recorder, First Lieutenant Jesse M. Lee of the 9th Infantry. After presenting Whittaker, Lee asked for the court's ruling as to whether the accuser of Major Reno would be permitted to suggest the names of witnesses or offer evidence which might illuminate the investigation. Major Reno announced that in the absence of his attorney he was not ready to proceed, but the court ruled in the affirmative as to the question of the position Whittaker might assume.

Colonel King stated that the court would not be confined, however, to the allegations in Whittaker's letter. "We expect to go over the whole ground. The recorder will proceed in his own way to prove whatever matters he chooses to allege against Major Reno," King said.

The taking of testimony was postponed until the following day, when Attorney Gilbert was expected to be present.

At the age of thirty-three, Gilbert's reputation as a competent and shrewd attorney had been established. Among his clients in

Harrisburg were the Pennsylvania Railroad and the Standard Oil Company. He came of a wealthy and prominent Front Street family, long had been a neighbor and close friend of both the Rosses and the Haldemans, but it had not been because of Reno's affiliation with them, nor because of neighborliness or friendship, that he had agreed to accept the case before the Court of Inquiry. He had taken it at the small fee Major Reno could afford to pay for the personal publicity it would bring him. His affiliation with such a celebrated and controversial issue would place him in the spotlight of public attention. It was an opportunity to add to the national stature he was striving to achieve. Moreover, he had convinced himself through study and analysis of all evidence available to him that he could not lose. He would have been less willing to accept the role of defense counsel had he believed there was even a reasonable danger of being defeated.

Another advantage he saw for himself was the inexperience and lack of training of his opponent, the recorder, Lieutenant Lee. For some unaccountable reason, the Army had seen fit to appoint a prosecutor without courtroom training and who admittedly did not aspire to a career in law, but intended to continue as a professional soldier.

As to the three members of the court, he could find no objection. He had looked into their careers, and he had found nothing to suggest that prejudice might influence their decisions. Each was a veteran combat soldier, skilled in military tactics. Each had served brilliantly in the Civil War and in campaigns against Indians. Two were cavalry officers fully capable of judging Major Reno's conduct at the Little Big Horn. Perhaps more important than anything else, in Gilbert's judgment, was the fact that all three had long known both Major Reno and Colonel Custer, and were in a position to compare the characters and competency of both men.

There were, also, political angles to the case that Lyman Gilbert probably found intriguing and which he thought might prove to be beneficial to him and his client.

Gilbert had in his papers a note to remind himself that in 1876, a few months before the Little Big Horn massacre, President Grant, a Republican, had removed Custer, a prominent Democrat, from command. Grant at last had permitted Custer to go on the ill-fated campaign, but not until after he had been bitterly assailed by the Democratic press for his treatment of the glamorous and popular officer. After Custer had been killed, poor Grant was criticized by the same newspaper for permitting him to ride off to his death, and bitterly attacked when he placed the blame for the disaster on Custer's incompetence and foolhardy actions.

There had been no disagreement with Grant's views voiced by any member of the Army's high command, nor had any of them indicated the opinion that Reno had been culpable or had not demonstrated his ability as a military leader.

Grant was gone, but Gilbert found significance in the fact that the Army's leadership was virtually the same as it had been under him. Gilbert shrewdly deduced that if the Army had felt that Major Reno had been cowardly or derelict in his duty, he would have been court-martialed before the Court of Inquiry had been ordered. The Army obviously felt that it had nothing to hide.

"I call Lieutenant Edward Maguire," Recorder Lee said when the court convened on the morning of Tuesday, the fourteenth of January, 1879.

The lieutenant, an engineer, presented and explained a map he had prepared from personal observation of the Little Big Horn battlefield.

The parade to the witness stand had begun, and for twenty-five days it continued, broken only by the interruption of four Sundays. Under oath twenty-three men, officers, and civilians who had taken part in the battle gave their direct testimony and were subjected to cross-examination. Eleven documentary exhibits were received into evidence. Under the flashing, seemingly tireless pen of the reporter, H. C. Hollister, a voluminous record built up until it had consumed thirteen hundred foolscap pages.

Lieutenant George D. Wallace:

Gen. Custer's order was about this: "The Indians are about 2½ miles ahead on the jump. Follow them as fast as you can and charge them wherever you find them, and we will support you." . . . When Reno received the order to charge he had 22 Indian Scouts and 3 companies of cavalry; average 35 to 40 men. They had been marching for 3 or 4 days, making long marches; up all the night before and moved that morning with little or no breakfast. The men were tired and the horses worn out. . . . We came to a ford on the Little Big Horn that had been used by the Indians. It was about belly deep to the horses. We crossed and halted to reform. Companies A and M were formed in line with the Indian Scouts under Varnum and Hare ahead; and my company in rear in line as a reserve. There were 22 scouts. We moved forward first at a trot and then at a gallop. The Indians when the order was given were apparently running. There was a big dust; but as that cleared we saw them coming back. After moving some distance my company was brought to the left of the line and the command moved in that way until near the timber. There the command was halted, dismounted and prepared to fight on foot. The horses were put in the timber and the men deployed, with the right on the timber and the left extending toward the bluff. The line was only a few hundred yards long. The Indians, instead of pressing our front, passed to our left and opened a flank fire. When we went on the skirmish line I for the first time saw the village and the Indians were thick on our front and were passing to our left and rear. After a short time it was reported that they were coming to the opposite bank and were trying to get our horses. Company G was taken off the line and put in the timber. The skirmish line soon had to fall back into the timber on account of exhaustion of ammunition and Indians on left and rear. After being there some time the Indians commenced firing from across the stream 50 yards from us and in our rear in the timber. There was no protection where we were and on the other side was a bank. Word was passed that we would have to charge them, as we were being surrounded and no assistance had come, and we must get to a better defensive position. The companies were mounted and commenced getting out. I could not find Lt. McIntosh commanding Company G, and so I mounted what men I could find and started. When I got out I saw the troops in column of fours at a gallop. I followed along with my men. The command did not follow its own track, but crossed lower down and were making towards the bluff. The Indians were in the bottom and we rode through them. They would ride along beside the column and fire into it. At the creek they halted and fired at the men as they crossed. They came over with the rear of the column and one or two men were killed there. After getting to the top of the hill we halted and prepared to stand them off. Soon afterwards it was reported that Benteen was coming up, and he joined us. We were out of ammunition, had several wounded, and I could find but seven of my company. We waited then for the packtrain to come up. Then we got ammunition and attempted to move on, but Capt. Moylan could not move his wounded. It took 6 to carry one and the Indians were coming up thicker, and we had to fall back and take position. The men worked all night the 25th. There were only 3 spades and with these and tin cups they scraped and dug rifle pits. In the morning of the 26th the Indians opened at daylight. After 12 the fire was not so heavy, except from prominent points, where they located sharp-shooters. Some time near sunset we saw the village moving off. . . . My opinion is that the Indians knew what we were doing and exactly what our movements were from the time we left the mouth of the Rosebud the 22nd. Our scouts saw their scouts that morning [i.e., 25th] watching us and saw them riding back into the village. They knew of our approach and were ready. After we crossed the stream their running was only a sham. They ran and then turned back to meet us. They probably did not notice Reno's command until it crossed, but they knew we were coming and could see the dust for miles. . . . I think Reno did the only thing possible under the circumstances. If we had remained in the timber all would have been killed. It was his duty to take care of his command and to use his best judgment and discretion. I think his conduct as to courage was good, I saw no evidence of fear then or at any time. Before we re-tired from the timber, Indians were crossing the river on our right and firing on us from the right bank. . . . I can recall no act of Maj. Reno dur-ing those two days that exhibited any lack of courage as an officer and soldier, or that I can find fault with; nor any lack of military skill.

F. F. Girard, civilian interpreter:

I heard Gen. Custer give the order to Reno. The General hallooed to Reno and beckoned him over. Maj. Reno rode over and Custer said "You will take your battalion and try to bring them to battle and I will support you"; and as the Major was going off he said "And take the scouts with you." . . . I think Reno could have held out against all the

Indians as long as his ammunition and provisions held out if he were determined and resolute. . . . When we got to the ford, and I saw the Indians I said "Major Reno, the Indians are coming up the valley to meet us." He looked at me, looked at the valley and gave the order "Forward." The Indians were two and a half miles away and in large numbers coming. . . . Major Reno dismissed me from my position of interpreter and Gen. Custer reinstated me, but I have no unkind feeling toward Maj. Reno.

Lieutenant Charles A. Varnum:

The position in the timber was as good as any place on the left bank, but I don't think we had enough men to hold it and keep the Indians out of it. The front was good; but I don't know about the rear. Of course, the position threatened the village to some extent and kept a containing force of Indians there. These were withdrawn when we left and I think that the attack made elsewhere was made about the time we left the timber,—but I don't think the entire force was at any time attacking us, because we could see parties a long way off, after we got on the hill. But I think the main force was against us when we were dismounted. . . . I suppose everybody felt as I did—wondering what had become of Custer and where he was. I don't know that there was any special worry—he had 5 companies with him. I don't think there was any idea or thought in the command that he was in the fix he was. The command felt in doubt—wondering if he was corralled as we were, or had been driven away to Terry; but that he had been wiped out— there was no such thought. I had no such idea, because when Gen. Terry came up, the first thing I and others asked was "Where is Custer; do you know what has become of Custer?" and I supposed the cavalry of Terry's command was Custer. . . . I think there was plenty of courage with the officers and troops and everybody. There were no signs of fear or anything of that sort. I don't know whether Benteen could have joined Reno in the timber or not, if the Indians had seen him. It would depend on how much they opposed him. They might have driven him into the timber and prevented him from joining us. As it turned out, he could have done so when the Indians turned back and left us and went the other way. Such a junction would have kept a large containing force of Indians there, but we could not have united with Custer, except by going through the village to him or his coming through to us. I do not think either force could have done that. As to Col. Reno's conduct, I have nothing to say against him and nothing in particular for him, either one way or another. Certainly there was no sign of cowardice or anything of that sort and nothing especial the other way. I didn't see anything special to say on either side. . . . If Reno thought he could not hold the timber, and saw no troops coming, it was for him to use his own judgment and leave it for a place he could defend better. Capt. Benteen united with Reno 20 to 25 minutes after he left the timber, and the command moved down river in about an hour or an hour and a half. . . . On the 26th Reno tried to get a letter thru to Gen. Terry. The scouts returned the letter to him. It described our position and the fight, stated that he did not know where Custer was, and asked for medical aid and assistance, and that he was holding the Indians in check. . . . The Indians did not get away with Gen. Forsyth at the Republican River in 1869. And they did not get away with Maj. Reno at the Little Big Horn.

Dr. H. R. Porter:

At the time I heard Reno say we would have to get out and charge them, he moved out and the men followed from all directions. They had a great deal of trouble finding their horses, but as soon as they mounted they went out. I stayed a few minutes with the wounded men and when I got out the men were all running and the Indians too, within a few yards of me. There were a few Indians between me and the command. I went out expecting to see the command charging the Indians, but instead the Indians were charging the command. They were all on the run. I let my horse out and got to the edge of the river and he jumped in and crossed with the rest. There was a great deal of dust, hallooing and confusion. The wounded man was left in the timber.

The first officer I saw on the bluffs was Lt. Varnum. He had his hat off and said "For God's sake, men; don't run. There are a good many officers and men killed and wounded and we have got to go back and get them."

When I saw Major Reno I said to him "Major, the men were pretty well demoralized, weren't they?" He replied "No, that was a charge, Sir."

The command was demoralized. They seemed to think they had been whipped.

In a few minutes I saw some troops coming and some of the men shouted "Here comes Custer"; but it was Benteen and his battalion.

Then the command felt pretty good; they thought they were going to have some help. . . .

I saw nothing in the conduct of Maj. Reno particularly heroic or the reverse. I think he was a little embarrassed and flurried. The bullets were coming thick and fast and he did not know whether it was best to stay there or leave. That was my impression at the time.

Captain Myles Moylan:

An immense dust was seen down the valley, with a little opening in it occasionally when we could see figures moving. After the line was formed the command moved again in line and the dust seemed to recede until the command passed a mile further when it stopped. Then we could see Indians coming out of the dust, mounted. They were so numerous that I suppose Maj. Reno thought it was more force than he could attack mounted. Consequently he dismounted his command. At that time we had reached the point of timber and the command was given to halt and to fight on foot.

The horses were led into the timber for protection and the men deployed as skirmishers, G on the right, mine in the center, and M on the left. . . .

We remained there twenty-five or thirty minutes under heavy fire till the Indians seemed to be withdrawing from our front and working around to the left. . . .

The order was then given to mount. . . . Maj. Reno was on his horse overlooking the formation. He asked my opinion as to the point we better retreat to, as it had been evident we would be entirely on the defensive, on account of the force of Indians in sight and coming. He designated a high point on the opposite side where we would go and establish ourselves and await developments. The command moved forward at the trot and then at the gallop. At gallop, the heads of the companies were almost in line, and the Indians closed in on both flanks and fired into the columns. There were many Indians in the woods. The firing into the rear was very severe. A good many men were wounded and some killed. When I reached the river I found it full of horses and men. . . .

I have no doubt Reno's column was discovered before it crossed the Little Big Horn. . . . There were, I think, enough Indians within 500 yards to warrant Reno's halting and dismounting. . . .

The object of leaving the timber was, if possible, to save the command. In going to the river I lost 4 killed and 4 or 5 wounded. I took 38 men into the fight and lost 11 killed and wounded. The loss was about the same in the other companies, I think.

If we had stayed 30 minutes longer in the timber, unsupported, I doubt whether we would have gotten out with as many as we did. If we reached the other bank there was a possibility of aid coming up. We could not have successfully resisted the force of Indians if they had followed to the river; we had not sufficient ammunition. The command was not, however, actually driven from the timber. It was virtually so, however, and would have been actually, in a very short time. . . .

Maj. Reno gave his orders during the advance in the bottom as coolly as any man under the circumstances. He was in front of the command all the time. During the afternoon of the 25th he seemed perfectly cool. I saw nothing indicating cowardice. After dark, the 25th, I laid down beside him, talking with him. I saw very little of him on the 26th and received no orders from him that day. . . .

I saw nothing in Maj. Reno which betrayed evidence of cowardice; there was a certain amount of excitement visible in his face, as well as that of anybody else, but no trace of cowardice.

In my judgment if Reno had continued to charge down the valley he would have been there yet. The purpose of leaving the timber was to save the command, which without assistance, would, in my judgment, have been annihilated in the timber. If the Indians had followed and closed in on the retreat to the bluffs the same result would have followed.

George Herendeen, civilian scout:

About a mile or a mile and a half from the village I heard Gen. Custer tell Maj. Reno to lead out and he would be with him. Those are about the words I understood him to use. It was about three quarters of a mile from the crossing right beside an Indian lodge. Directly after, Custer said "Take the scouts with you, too." We started at a lope and went to the Little Big Horn. . . . I am not saying Maj. Reno is a coward.

Whittaker was obviously displeased with the manner in which the recorder was proceeding. Very little, if any, testimony damaging to Major Reno had been heard. He was especially disappointed with the questions asked of Herendeen. In several conversations he had had with the scout, Herendeen had expressed a willingness to discredit Major Reno and brand him a coward. That had not been done.

Whittaker submitted a list of questions to be asked of Herendeen by the prosecution, all of which were designed to show that the major was stricken with fear in the battle and had thought only of his own safety. Whittaker wrote below the questions:

I further desire leave respectfully to submit to the court that in case these questions should lead to fresh ones by Major Reno's counsel I should be permitted to ask questions if necessary in my own person of this or any other witness, subject to the discretion of the court in the same manner as Major Reno and his counsel.

Recorder Lee was clearly aggravated by Whittaker's request as he submitted it to the judges for a ruling. He told the court:

As far as I am concerned as Recorder, I have not considered that I was here as the prosecutor of Major Reno. I have desired to elicit all the facts in the case, whether they are for or against Major Reno; and while I have not a very exalted opinion of my own abilities in the matter, still I feel that I am, if I may be allowed to say so, competent to go on with the matter as I have done heretofore, because if I had not felt so, I should have asked the Court before this time for assistance in this matter.

Defense Counsel Gilbert was given permission to address the court:

There are many of these questions that I shall not object to, but in regard to the request of Mr. Whittaker to appear as assistant prosecutor, I think that it is evident to the Court that the Recorder does not require it. If the Court then thinks or feels that this man, Mr. Whittaker, can be any addition—any desirable addition, to these proceedings, then of course I withdraw my objection, but as far as I can understand the course of procedure to be, it is that the War Department designates the officer who shall take charge of the eliciting of testimony, and I

244

submit that it is entirely against the spirit of the law, and against the substance of this order to permit the authority given to the Recorder, which is not only that of a prosecutor, but is of a semi-judicial character, to be delegated to anybody else. It is entirely apart from this case.

After a brief conference with his colleagues, Colonel King informed the attorneys:

The request of Mr. Whittaker to appear before the Court as an accuser or assistant to the Recorder will not be allowed. The Court determines that the matter of all questions proposed by Mr. Whittaker shall be decided by the Recorder, in whose abilities to conduct the case to a thorough investigation, the Court has the utmost confidence.

Whittaker, his face dark with anger, wrote furiously on a large pad as Recorder Lee called the next witness.

Captain John Scott Payne:

In August, 1878, I measured the distance between Reno's hill position and the spot where Gen. Custer was killed. It was 4 miles, 160 yards.

Lieutenant L. R. Hare:

There were probably a thousand Indians opposing Reno on the bottom. The constant firing came from only a part of them, probably 200. The command left the timber about thirty to forty minutes after the skirmish line was formed. . . .

I heard no bugle calls in the timber; and when I got on the hill, most of the men had come up and Capt. Moylan was forming the skirmish line. Maj. Reno was standing there where he could supervise, but I did not hear him give any orders. . . .

The command was scattered, but not demoralized. They rallied and formed promptly. Before I got to the top I heard Lt. Varnum calling to the men to halt and when I got there Capt. Moylan was forming the skirmish line. If the Indians had followed us in force to the hill-top, they would have got us all, though not before Benteen came up. The hill position was much better than the timber. I think the difference in the positions more than balanced the loss sustained in getting there. If the

Indians had charged us in the timber we could not have stood it but a few minutes; but Indians don't do that. We could have stood them off for perhaps thirty minutes by using our ammunition judiciously. . . .

The supposition was that Custer would support Reno by following. He had not done that; he had plenty of time to follow. . . .

Whether such an attack on the flank as Custer made would have supported Reno would depend entirely on what disposition the Indians made. As it was, it was no support at all and did not amount to anything. The results of the battle show that. . . .

On the retreat Capt. Weir and Capt. French were the only ones engaged until within three of four hundred yards of the final stand; then Capt. Godfrey engaged them and held them in check till we took position. The general engagement began at once, about an hour and a half after Capt. Weir started on his advance. I heard Capt. Benteen say to Maj. Reno that the position we took was the best place to make a stand and he agreed. Maj. Reno gave no orders that I heard: the captains put the men in position. . . .

Maj. Reno stayed in the timber till all hope of rear support from Custer had vanished. I think the reason we left was because if we stayed much longer, say twenty minutes, we could not have gotten out at all. . . .

My impression of the retreat from the timber was that Maj. Reno thought we would be shut up there, and the best way to get out was to charge out. I did not think it absolutely necessary at the time.

If the command had been pursued by the one thousand Indians who were about us, we would all have been killed; it would not have lasted ten minutes. . . .

I saw the village move away on the evening of the 26th. It was two or three miles long—a dark moving mass. I estimated about 20,000 to 25,000 ponies in the herd.

I know of but one instance of gallantry on Reno's part, and none of cowardice. When Capt. Benteen joined, Maj. Reno turned and said in a very inspiriting way to his men, "We have assistance now, and we will go and avenge the loss of our comrades."

I can only estimate his conduct by the way it turned out. I think his action saved what was left of the regiment. His conduct was always good. I didn't see anything particularly inspiriting about it, except what I told you. He seemed to be very cool at all times. . . .

If Reno had continued to advance mounted, I don't think he would have got a man through; the column would not have lasted five minutes. His dismounting and deploying was the only thing that saved us.

As to the retreat from the timber, there is certainly always more or less disorder about a cavaly column moving at a fast gait; but I don't think that command was much demoralized, because when I got on the hill the men were halted in column and moving into line without any difficulty.

I can't think Maj. Reno lost much time in moving in Custer's direction; I went to the pack train and then to Capt. Weir, who had moved out during my absence; and when returning from Capt. Weir, met Reno advancing. He could not have moved to where I met him if he had lost much time. His column moved altogether and about a mile or maybe a little more.

I reported to Maj. Reno that Capt. Weir had ceased his forward movement because the whole country was covered with Indians; at least fifteen hundred in sight, and the country was favorable for concealment of a larger force. I do not think that Reno's consultation with Benteen as to the best place to make a stand indicated cowardice or indecision. . . .

I saw no evidence of cowardice upon Reno's part. The command was under good control and the disposition as good as possible under the circumstances. . . .

I was mistaken when I said I did not hear Maj. Reno give any orders on the hill. I did hear him directing the deployment into skirmish line just as I reached the top of the hill. This was immediately after the retreat from the timber.

I did not report to him that I heard firing from Custer's direction.

Lieutenant Charles De Rudio:

As soon as we cleared the woods, Reno called the battalion into line and moved at a gallop. He was ahead of me about fifteen yards. He was continually checking the men and keeping the line in good order. The horses on the right were unruly and excited after the long gallop. We galloped about two and a half miles across the plain which was sandy and full of sage brush. When we got near the woods, which were on the right of the line, I heard some bullets whistling, but not the sound of firing. In our front was an immense dense dust and we could see the shadows of Indians in that dust. Pretty soon Reno gave the command "Dismount and prepare to fight on foot." The battalion halted promptly and dismounted; and deployed very nicely. It surprised me because we had many recruits and green horses. . . .

As soon as the line was deployed, Indians came out of the dust and went to our left, on the high bluffs. Came all around and soon were on our flanks. The line advanced seventy-five to a hundred yards and when the fire got on the left flank, it turned. Our fire was striking short, though theirs reached us. They continued to come out and soon their fire was all around us to the front, left and rear; the only place we were not shot at was from the right, next the woods. The line remained there about ten minutes, during which time I saw Maj. Reno encouraging the men. He stood there and directed the fire. . . .

During the ten minutes I observed Maj. Reno on the skirmish line I admired his conduct. All officers and men did well. . . .

I think Maj. Reno had more Indians around him the evening of the 25th than were in the attack on Custer. I saw those around Reno, and make my estimate by comparison of the number in the village. . . .

I saw no indications of cowardice on Reno's part; nor any want of skill in the handling and disposition of the men. When he halted and dismounted I said "Good for you," because I saw that if we had gone five hundred yards further we would have been butchered.

Sergeant Edward Davern:

I saw no evidence of cowardice at any time on the part of Maj. Reno.

Sergeant F. A. Culbertson:

The firing I heard downstream while on the hill was no heavier than we had on our skirmish line, and I don't think anybody had any impression that Gen. Custer was having any more trouble than we were. Maj. Reno exercised caution over his command on the 25th and I saw him in very dangerous and exposed positions during the afternoon and evening and also on the 26th. . . .

I saw no evidence of cowardice on the part of Maj. Reno at any time.

John Martin, Trumpeter:

I was orderly trumpeter to Gen. Custer on June 25th. At the tepee on the right side of the river Maj. Reno's column took off to the left and we took off to the right. It was at a ravine; we could see hills on both sides. We remained on the right side of the river and went on the jump all the way: Gen. Custer did not go near the river at all: he halted only once, at a little creek to water the horses for about five minutes. We were there about ten minutes altogether, and the General directed the commanders not to let the horses drink too much.

He left the watering place and went about three hundred yards in a straight line; then turned to the right a little and traveled four or five hundred yards and then there was a big bend on the hill; he turned these hills and went on top of the ridge. All at once we looked on the bottom and saw the Indian village; at the same time we could only see children and dogs and ponies—no Indians at all. Gen. Custer appeared to be glad to see the village in that shape and supposed the Indians were asleep in their tepees.

We could see the bottom from the ridge but could not see the timber because it was under the hill—nor anything of Maj. Reno's column.

I rode to the left and rear of Gen. Custer, and about two yards from him. That was my position as orderly.

The gray horse company was in the center of the column. We could see the river while on top of the ridge, but after we went down a ravine we could not see the river or timber or anything else. We heard no firing as we went down. Gen. Custer's column moved always at a gallop. It was about a mile and a half from the watering place to the point on the ridge where we could see the village.

After he saw the village, he pulled off his hat and gave a cheer and said, "Courage, boys, we will get them, and as soon as we get through, we will go back to our station."

We went more to the right from the ridge and down to a ravine that led to the river. At the time Gen. Custer passed the high place on the ridge or a little below it he told his Adjutant to send an order back to Capt. Benteen. I don't know what it was. Then the Adjutant called me. I was right at the rear of the General. He said "Orderly, I want you to take this despatch to Capt. Benteen and go as fast as you can." He told me if I had time and there was no danger to come back, but otherwise to remain with my company which was with Capt. Benteen.

My horse was tired and I went through as fast as he could go. The Adjutant told me to follow the same trail we came down.

After I started back I traveled five or six hundred yards, perhaps three quarters of a mile, and got on the same ridge where Gen. Custer saw the village. I looked down and saw that Maj. Reno's battalion was engaged. I went on to about three or four hundred yards above the watering place and met Capt. Benteen. I delivered my despatch to him and told him what Lt. Cooke had told me. Capt. Benteen read the despatch and put it in his pocket and gave me an order to Capt. Mc-Dougall to bring up the pack train and keep it well up.

Capt. Benteen asked me where Gen. Custer was. I said I supposed that by that time he had made a charge through the village. I said nothing about Maj. Reno's battalion. He did not ask about it.

When I left Gen. Custer he was going ahead: the Adjutant stopped to write the despatch. It took me three quarters of an hour to get back to Capt. Benteen: it was fifteen or twenty minutes after I looked down from the ridge and saw Reno in action before I met Benteen.

I went at once to Capt. McDougall about 150 yards. He was in front of his troop, and the packs were pretty well together. I delivered my message and joined my company.

After delivery of Custer's despatch to Benteen, he moved a little faster. The packs were coming on—some walking, some running, some trotting.

We followed Gen. Custer's trail till we got on the same ridge where I saw Reno engaged. About the time we got there we saw Reno's battalion retreating to the same side of the river we were on. We joined Reno and the packs came up in about fifteen minutes. After the packs were all up, we moved down the river in about one and a half hours. I was right in front of the column and could see Indians after we got to the head of the first ravine. We halted then and Capt. Weir wanted to take his company down the stream to see Gen. Custer. He went a little to the right and came back again. The Indians were leaving Gen. Custer and coming back to us, firing; the bulk of them came to where we were. The column then turned back as it was in a bad position; the Indians were on both flanks and the ravine was very deep and we could not go through. We took position a little further down the steam from where we first saw Maj. Reno.

I saw Maj. Reno when we took position and again that night at twelve P.M., when he sent an order to sound reveille at two A.M. No calls were sounded that night. The Indians commenced firing after reveille and kept it up. Maj. Reno was in the center of the corral at reveille and afterwards was around the skirmish line examining the position.

I was the only one who sounded calls. The second day, after the Indians left, I sounded retreat, recall and march, so that if there were any of our friends in the ravine they would hear and come up.

I judge it was about noon when Gen. Custer and I were on the ridge and saw the village. I did not see Gen. Custer after that. His command was galloping when I left. When I saw the Indian village there was no dust at all; just dogs and children playing around the tepees. Gen. Custer said "Courage, boys, we have got them; the Indians are asleep in their tepees." I was sent back from about the head of the ravine that Custer went down toward the river.

After I saw Maj. Reno engaged, I traveled about two miles to Capt. Benteen. It took about three quarters of an hour to come back with Benteen's command.

Captain F. W. Benteen:

When the command came up I ordered a trot and went on ahead to the crossing of the Little Big Horn at the ford. That was my first sight of it. There I saw an engagement going on and supposed it was the whole regiment. There were twelve or thirteen men in skirmish line that appeared to have been beaten back. The line was then parallel with the river and the Indians were charging through those men. I thought the whole command was thrashed and that was not a good place to cross. To my right I noticed three of four Indians four or five hundred yards away from me. I thought they were hostile, but on riding toward them found they were Crows. They said there was a big "pooh poohing" going on. Then I saw the men who were up on the bluff and I immediately went there and was met by Maj. Reno. I did not consider it necessary for me to go back for the pack train as it was coming, and the Indians could not get to it except by me. . . .

Reno's men appeared to be in good order, but pretty well shaken up. Men climbing a big bluff on foot would be pretty well blown, and so would the horses. They were not in line of battle but scattered around, I suppose to the best advantage. They all thought there was a happier place than that, I guess. . . .

Reno was just as cool as he is now; he had lost his hat in the run down below. . . .

I think that his conduct was all right; I saw him every fifteen or thirty minutes those two days and during the night of the 25th was with him nearly the whole time. I could have tried to join him in the timber, but would not have attempted it without first getting the pack train; but my losses would have been much greater. . . .

The position in the timber first taken by Reno was an A-1 defensive position, and could have been held five or six hours, depending on the size of the attacking force. Against nine hundred it was defensible; but the nine hundred would have been reinforced by another nine hundred, and the next morning they would all have been killed. . . .

If I had joined Reno in the timber with the pack train, it could not have made a particle of difference so far as Custer was concerned. The seven companies would have been as completely corralled there as on the hill. Gen. Custer would have had to look out for himself the same as he did; and how he did, you know. Doubtless the abandonment of the timber by Reno released numbers of Indians for attacking Custer, but I don't think they had any use for them down there. There was not a foot of unoccupied ground in that country; there were Indians everywhere, from 12 feet to 1200 yards away. . . .

I saw no evidence of cowardice on Reno's part. I found it necessary at one time to caution him about exposing himself. I told him to be careful how he stood around in front of the point, where we were making rifle pits, as volleys were coming constantly. At that particular time the fire was irregular and not very heavy.

When I received my orders from Custer to separate myself from the command, I had no instructions to unite at any time with Reno or anyone else. There was no plan at all. My orders were "valley hunting ad infinitum." The reason I returned was because I thought I would be needed at the ridge: I acted entirely upon my own judgment. I was separated from Reno possibly fifteen miles when at the greatest distance.

Trumpeter Martin came at a jog trot, and told me the Indians were "skedaddling." I moved at a trot from then till I joined Reno. I moved at a trot all the time from when I left Custer till I met Reno except when watering the horses. . . .

If there had been any plan of battle, enough of that plan would have been communicated to me so that I would have known what to do under certain circumstances. Not having done that, I do not believe there was any plan. In Gen. Custer's mind there was a belief that there were no Indians nor any village. . . .

I am convinced that when the order brought by Martin reached me

252

Gen. Custer and his whole command were dead. It was then about three o'clock. It was not evident to me that he expected me to be on the trail; he could have expected no such thing; from the orders I started out with, he could not possibly have known where to find me within ten or fifteen miles. My going back was providential or accidental or whatever you may please to term it.

Lieutenant W. S. Edgerly:

When I first arrived Maj. Reno was excited, but not enough to impair his efficiency, or have a bad effect on the troops. He did everything that was necessary, which was little, because all the officers could see what ought to be done. There was no occasion for any particular control by the Commanding Officer. So far as I could see the company commanders fought their own companies to a great degree. I saw Reno walk across the line as I saw other officers, and he seemed very cool; and I think the position we had was the best possible within a radius of many miles.

The men, too, were very cool. I don't think any particular man inspired them with courage or coolness. I have no doubt that when Capt. Benteen was on the ridge every man admired him; but I don't think it necessary to inspire the men. . . .

I do not pretend to give the history of all Maj. Reno did—only my own personal knowledge. I never expected him to be ubiquitous. The nature of the fight was such that no special directions from him were necessary. I saw no evidence of cowardice on his part. I distinguish excitement from fear, most emphatically. In the charge suggested by Capt. Benteen, Maj. Reno accompanied the troops. Capt. Benteen did not.

Lyman Gilbert's experience had taught him to expect the injection of surprise evidence. When it had not come during the testimony of fifteen witnesses, he had begun to believe that Lee and Whittaker had none to offer. The fallacy of his assumption was quickly demonstrated with shocking force.

B. F. Churchill, civilian packer:

From the hill position I could see a few tepees in the village. There were not many Indians attacking us at the time, but when they came back they came in force. The firing I heard appeared to come from the lower end of the village. Others heard it, and spoke of it. . . .

I did not see Maj. Reno that afternoon; but did after dark, about nine or ten o'clock. A Mr. Frett was with me. We had started out on the line to get our blankets and something to eat, and saw Maj. Reno standing there, though we did not notice him till he spoke to Frett. He asked Frett what he wanted. Frett said he was after something to eat. Maj. Reno then asked him if the mules were "tight." It sounded like "tight" but Frett thought he meant "tied," and said "yes." Maj. Reno again asked if the mules were "tight" and words passed between them and Maj. Reno made a pass to strike Frett; and some whiskey flew over me and Frett. At that Maj. Reno stepped back and picked up a carbine —whether he intended to strike Frett with it I don't know. I took Frett by the shoulders and pulled him away. That was the last I saw of Reno that night. He was, I thought, under the influence of liquor.

Lieutenant Edgerly, recalled by Gilbert:

I saw Maj. Reno the night of the 25th about nine o'clock. He came along toward where I was from the direction of Capt. Benteen's line, and was perfectly sober. There was no evidence that he had been drinking at all. It was at that time that I reported the gaps in the line and he told me to have them filled up.

I saw him again at two o'clock, and he was perfectly sober then. I never heard the faintest suspicion of intoxication until I came to Chicago this time. If he had been stammering and staggering and acting like a drunken man the officers would not have permitted him to exercise command.

Captain Benteen, recalled:

I may say I was with Maj. Reno all the time the night of the 25th. I saw him every fifteen or twenty minutes till 3 A.M.; I laid down in his bed. He was sober as he is now. He is entirely sober now and he was then. There was no time during the 25th or 26th when there was any indication of drunkenness on the part of Maj. Reno. He could not have been staggering and stammering without my knowing it.

I know nothing about any altercation with a packer except by hearsay. I know they robbed the packs and robbed me, and I also know there was not whiskey enough in the whole command to make Reno drunk. I saw him every fifteen or twenty minutes throughout the night, except after the last time I left him, about 2:30. The Indians opened up about 3, and there may have been a half to three quarters of an hour that I did not see him.

If he had been drunk between nine and ten o'clock I would have known about it; and had I known he had any whiskey I would have been after some myself.

Captain E. S. Godfrey:

Upon joining the command I was asked by Maj. Reno to get into line quick. I was not assigned a position; my men were mixed with those of B, M, G, and D. The attack began immediately. In fact it began before I got there; it followed me right in. It was then after six P.M. and the engagement lasted until dusk.

I don't recall seeing Maj. Reno on the hill during the fight that afternoon. I had no orders from him. When the fire of the Indians ceased that night, we dug rifle pits and put the men in them, and the companies were changed around so as to have them in order, and each was assigned to a position. . . .

Capt. Benteen came over during the afternoon of the 26th and said we would have to drive the Indians from our front because they were firing over on the rear of his line. He had to repeat the request several times to Maj. Reno before the charge was ordered. But it was made, Capt. Benteen giving the order.

Some time afterwards he came to the rear of my position and said he was going over to look for a new position. We started across together. While going over the rise, the Indians set up a pretty heavy fire on us. Reno dodged and said in a laughing manner: "Damned if I want to be killed by an Indian. I've gone through too many fights for that." Then he went on over to Benteen's line.

I had no talk with him on either day as to what had become of Custer. I saw very little of him the first day or night. I was not particularly impressed by Reno's qualifications as to courage, coolness or efficiency. There was little to do the 26th except to lie and shoot—no supervision was required; but what was done outside the line was done by Benteen. I don't think Reno's conduct was such as tended to inspire the command with confidence in resisting the enemy. It was my opinion that Capt.

255

Benteen was principally exercising the functions of commanding officer. . . .

I have described only such acts and doings of Maj. Reno as came under my personal observation, and necessarily, among a large number of officers there are differences of opinion as to how best to conduct an engagement. . . .

The firing I heard was not sufficiently severe or continued to make me believe that Gen. Custer and his command were destroyed. Such a thought did not cross my mind at all. . . .

Maj. Reno's hesitation in accepting Capt. Benteen's suggestion did not, in my opinion, indicate cowardice; nor did his dodging bullets when he said he didn't want to be killed by Indians indicate fear.

Whittaker understood that the testimony of the packer, Churchill, had been well countered by Edgerly and Benteen, but he had anticipated the development and had prepared for it with another witness to corroborate the evidence that during the fight on the hill Major Reno had been drunk.

John Frett, civilian packer:

The first time I saw Maj. Reno was after the firing ceased. I went over where we put the packs into breastworks and passed an officer. When almost in front of him I saw it was Maj. Reno. I saluted and said "Good evening." The first he said was "Are the mules tight." I said "tight," what do you mean by "tight". He said "Tight, God damn you"; and with that slapped me in the face and leveled a carbine at me and said "I will shoot you." Then a friend of mine named Churchill pulled me back and that was the last I saw him till the next day.

He had a bottle of whiskey in his hand and as he slapped me the whiskey flew over me and he staggered. If any other man was in the condition he was I should call him drunk. . . .

Capt. Benteen at no time to my knowledge came to the packs to drive out skulkers. At least I did not see him

I know of no complaints made about stealing in the pack train.

I have no bitter feeling against Reno because he slapped me in the face—not in a place like this.

I would say he was drunk—very drunk. He staggered and stammered; his language was not very plain and he braced himself against a pack.

I did not see him the next morning; not till the afternoon. That was the only time I saw him drunk there.

Captain Benteen, recalled:

I had occasion to go to the pack train many times during the 25th and 26th to drive out skulking soldiers. I did not go there for that purpose the afternoon of the 25th; but I did many times on the evening of the 25th and during the day of the 26th.

There was much complaint about stealing in the pack train: they stole everything I had.

Captain E. G. Mathey:

When Maj. Reno first came up, he was somewhat excited, as any man would be under such circumstances. It was not long since he came out of the fight and that would be the natural condition for a man to be in. I did not think to question his courage and saw no act to indicate lack of courage, or cowardice. I received orders from both Reno and Benteen. The latter was second in command and I obeyed his orders without question.

On the 26th Maj. Reno had a bottle with a little whiskey in it. Some one spoke of being thirsty and he said he had some to wet his mouth with to keep from getting dry. I don't know whether it was a quart flask or a pint. There was very little in it the morning of the 26th.

I saw no indication of drunkenness on his part, and never heard any intimation of it till last spring. I do not think excitement means fear; a man can be excited and not afraid. . . . I don't know whether there was any belief in the command that Custer needed support more than we did. We had so many wounded that we could not have moved with safety. Nobody seemed to think Custer had been destroyed.

The night of the 25th we had all we could attend to. I was so exhausted that I went to sleep standing up.

Captain Thomas M. McDougall:

As to Maj. Reno's conduct, when I found him he seemed perfectly cool; had nothing to say; and during the day I did not see him till he asked me to go round with him. He was perfectly cool then. He had no enthusiasm as far as I could observe, but was as brave as any man there; they were all brave; I saw no officer or man show the white feather.

I think Maj. Reno would make as stubborn a fight as any man, but don't think he could encourage men like others. Men are different; some are dashing and others have a quiet way of going through. I think he did as well as anyone could do. I thought when he asked me to walk around with him that he had plenty of nerve. The balls were flying around and the men in the intrenchments firing. We took it easily and slowly. . . . The position we took was the best position we could get in that country. We retired because we could go no farther and were attacked within five minutes by an immense number of Indians. I saw no evidence of drunkenness on Reno's part and never heard any intimation of it.

Recorder Lee read into the record the message sent by Major Reno to General Terry on June 27, 1876. It said:

I have had a most terrific engagement with the hostile Indians. They left their camp last evening at sundown moving due south in the direction of Big Horn Mountains. I am very much crippled and cannot possibly pursue. Lieutenants McIntosh and Hodgson and Dr. De Wolf are among the killed. I have many wounded and many horses and mules shot. I have lost both my own horses. I have not seen or heard from Custer since he ordered me to charge with my battalion (three companies) promising to support me.

I charged about two P.M., but meeting no support was forced back to the hills. At this point I was joined by Benteen with three companies and the pack train rear guard (one Co.). I have fought thousands and can still hold my own, but cannot leave here on account of the wounded. Send me medical aid at once and rations.

As near as I can say now I have over 100 men killed and wounded.

Lieutenant Wallace, recalled by Attorney Gilbert:

I saw no evidence of inebriety on Reno's part at any time during the 25th and 26th June, and the first mention of it I ever heard was during this inquiry here in Chicago. . . .

At no time did I observe any failure upon Maj. Reno's part to do the duty expected and required of a commanding officer.

Lieutenant-Colonel M. V. Sheridan, called by the defense:

I visited the Custer field in July 1877 to bring away the bodies of officers killed there. . . . I don't think the struggle could have lasted over an hour. . . .

I approached the field from the north, up the valley. I went up to the point known as Reno's crossing and rode over it and then went over what is called Reno's position. . . .

For several hundreds of yards above the middle ford it would not be possible for a command to cross against resistance. It would be difficult on account of bluffs, to get down there even without resistance.

It would not be practicable to cross against resistance anywhere between Reno's crossing and the middle ford.

Captain Mathey, recalled by the prosecution:

I have heard officers discuss the fight a great many times and express varied opinions. Some think it would have been better to have remained down below; others have expressed themselves in different ways. One expression particularly impressed itself on me; it was—"If we had not been commanded by a coward we would all have been killed."

I have heard officers say that they thought Reno lost his head, or words to that effect. Lt. De Rudio was the one who used the expression I remembered, and that impressed me so.

Lt. De Rudio has always told the same story to me. I know that there has been some question as to the reason he stayed in the timber; some doubted his story. I don't know whether he brought out the guidon or not.

General John Gibbon, witness for the prosecution:

Reno's position on the hill was an exceedingly weak one for defense naturally. It was commanded at tolerable long range by bordering hills on the downstream side. The country was broken by a succession of little rolling hills and valleys behind which attacking parties could conceal themselves. The manner in which the animals were exposed was very bad. I counted forty-eight dead horses in one little valley; and the place was practically cut off from water which made it weak for any prolonged defense. This is a general opinion only. I did not go over the whole line, but had a view of it from the top of the hill.

Gilbert was prepared to call a number of defense witnesses, but, feeling that Whittaker's charges already had been successfully demolished, and confident of victory, he abandoned the plan. He read into the record a portion of General Sherman's report on the Battle of the Little Big Horn:

In this engagement, the five companies of the Seventh Cavalry led by Lieut. Col. Custer in person . . . were literally obliterated, and the remaining seven companies were saved by the brave and prudent conduct of Major Reno, and the timely arrival of General Terry.

Gilbert offered in evidence the petition, signed by 80 percent of the surviving enlisted men, which asked the President to promote Major Reno and Captain Benteen as a reward for their "bravery, coolness and decision" which had "saved the lives of every man now living of the 7th Cavalry."

"I call Major Reno," Gilbert said.

31

*M*ajor Reno took the witness chair, and in a calm and firm voice told the court:

On the morning of the 25th, Col. Benteen came over to where I was, and while he was there, I discovered that the column was moving. I was not consulted about anything. I never received any direct orders, and exercised the functions of what I imagined were those of a lieutenant colonel. The division into battalions and wings had been annulled before we left the Yellowstone, and when the command moved out I followed it. At daylight, after we had marched some distance, the command halted, and I was informed only that the Commanding Officer had gone to the top of the mountain to make observation with regard to the Indians which the scouts had reported to be in sight. He called the officers together and I attended, of course. He said the Indian scouts reported a large village in view from the mountain; that he did not believe it himself, as he had looked with his glass. He then announced that the column would be formed by companies in order in which they reported ready, and this was done. I continued as before for two or three hours. About ten o'clock Lt. Cooke came to me and said, "The General directs that you take specific command of Companies M, A and G." I turned and said "Is that all?" He replied "Yes." I made no further inquiry but moved with my column to the second ridge; and between myself and Custer's column was a small ravine which developed into a tributary of the Little Big Horn. I moved parallel to Gen. Custer for some time. Previous to that Capt. Benteen had started to the left up the hill. I had no instruction as to him and asked him where he was going and what he was going to do. His reply was to the effect that he was to drive everything before him on the hill. That was all that passed between us. He had Companies H, D and K. He went over to the hills and was soon out of sight. The other two columns continued moving on opposite banks of the stream until we came in sight of the tepee that has been referred to, when the Commanding Officer beckoned to me with his hat to cross to the bank where he was. When I got there the battalion was somewhat scattered and I was about opposite the rear of his column. I there received an order from Lt. Cooke to move my command to the front. When I got up there, there was a tumult going on among the Indian Scouts. They were stripping themselves and preparing to fight. I understood that they had refused to go forward and Gen. Custer had ordered them to give up their guns and horses. I moved forward to the head of the column and shortly after Lt. Cooke came to me and said "Gen. Custer directs you to take as rapid a gait as you think prudent and charge the village afterward and you will be supported by the whole outfit."

My Adjutant, Lt. Hodgson, was on my left and Lt. Wallace on his left. He came up and said, laughing, that he was going as volunteer aide. He was not at the time on company duty.

I took a trot and proceeded to carry out my orders. I crossed the creek and formed my battalion with two companies in line and one in reserve. I had been a good deal in Indian country and was convinced that they were there in overwhelming numbers. I sent back word twice; first, by a man named McIlargey, my striker, to say that the Indians were in front of me in strong force. Receiving no instructions, I sent a second man,

Mitchell, a cook. They were the nearest men I could get hold of quick. That was some minutes after and I was convinced that my opinion was correct. I still heard nothing to guide my movement and so proceeded down the valley to carry out my orders.

My first thought was to make my charge with two companies and hold the third as a rallying point, but when I saw the number of Indians I sent my Adjutant to bring the third company on the line. I was in front near the centre and to the right. The Indian scouts had run away, except three or four, and we did not see them again until we got to Powder River, ninety miles away.

We were then at a gallop and I was about forty paces in advance. I could see a disposition on the part of the Indians to lead us on, and that idea was confirmed when upon advancing a little further I could see them coming out of a ravine in which they had hidden. The ravine was eight or nine hundred yards ahead on what are called the foothills on the left bank. There were also straggling parties of Indians making around to my rear. I saw I could not successfully make an offensive charge; their numbers had thrown me on the defensive. The village was stretched along the bank to the front and right. There were times going down when I could not see it at all.

I dismounted by giving the order to the company officers. Lt. Hodgson gave it to Company G and myself to M and A. I gave the order to dismount and prepare to fight on foot and shelter the horses in the point of timber.

I had an idea of the number of Indians from the trails, and I saw five or six hundred with my own eyes; all the evidences through the bottoms and over the trails showed Indians there. The dust on the trail I followed was four to six inches deep and there were several other trails showing that numbers of animals had gone there.

We were in skirmish line under hot fire for fifteen or twenty minutes. I was on the line near Capt. Moylan when word came to me that the Indians were turning my right. I left Lt. Hodgson to bring me word of what went on there and went with Company G to the banks of the river. I suppose there were forty men in the Company. When I got there I had a good view of the tepees and could see many scattering ones. It was plain to me that the Indians were using the woods as much as I was, sheltering themselves and creeping up on me. I then rode out on the plain. Lt. Hodgson came to me and told me they were passing to the left and rear and I told him to bring the line in, round the horses. After going down to the river and seeing the situation, I knew I could not stay there unless I stayed forever. The regiment evidently was scattered, or some-one would have brought me an order or aid; and in order to effect a union of the regiment, which I thought absolutely necessary, I moved to the hill where I could be seen, and where I thought I could dispose the men so they could hold out till assistance came. The men had one hundred rounds each, fifty in their belts and fifty in the saddle bags; their firing for twenty minutes was what I call quick fire.

At the time I was in the timber I had not the remotest idea where either the packtrain or Benteen's column were. There was no plan communicated to us; if one existed the subordinate commanders did not know of it.

I left the timber, sending Lt. Hodgson to give the order to Capt. French and giving it in person to Capt. Moylan and Lt. McIntosh, to mount their men and bring them to the edge of the timber and form in column of fours. I had no other means of accomplishing the formation.

Where Bloody Knife was shot I stood about ten minutes while the formation was going on. I had nothing to do with it. They had their orders to form the men in column of fours out of the timber. I had made up my mind to go through these people and get to the hill for the purpose of getting the regiment together, so as to have a chance to save those who got through. There was no use of staying in the timber when I could assist no one, and create no diversion. I acted on my best judgment and I think events proved me right.

The Indians were increasing, particularly on the right bank, skipping from tree to tree, keeping themselves as much under shelter as possible. They were much more cunning in woodcraft than the soldiers.

The Indians are peculiar in their manner of fighting; they don't go in line or bodies, but in parties of five to forty. You see them scattering in all directions. My opinion is that six or seven hundred Indians were there; and I had but 112 men. I thought it my duty to give those men the best chance I could to save themselves; and it was impossible to have a victory over the Indians. I thought it my duty as a military movement, and I took the responsibility.

The column was formed to go through the Indians on that side. I felt sure that some of us would go up; we were bound to; some would get hit and I would lose part of my command. I was willing to risk that in order to save the lives of the others from the desperate position we were in.

I saw Bloody Knife shot, and also a man of M Company to whom the attention of the Doctor was at once directed. Bloody Knife was within a few feet of me; I was trying to get from him by signs where the Indians were going. I did not immediately leave the glade and the timber and go on a gallop to the river. I had given orders for the formation and I went through the timber and up on the plain to satisfy myself about the Indians there. Capt. Moylan was at my side. Before Bloody Knife was killed the formation was being made to leave the timber. The column was formed, A in front, M in rear, and G in center. I was at the head of the column and the gait was a rapid one. I thought it my duty to be there, to see about the direction of the column and for observing the ford and the hill on the other side; I would be on the hill to rally and reform the men. I stopped at the river a moment. The men crossed hurriedly and it threw the rear into confusion. They were exposed to heavy fire and I lost many there. The Indians had Winchester rifles and the column made a big target and they were pumping their bullets into it. I did not regard the movement as a triumphant march, nor did I regard it as a retreat. When I reached the hill, after a glance about, I thought it as good a position as I could get in the time I had; and I immediately put in the command in skirmish line, through the company commanders.

At the time I left the timber I did not see Benteen's column, nor had I the remotest reason to expect him to unite with me. But in a short time after reaching the hill I saw him not far off and rode out to meet him. I told him what I had done. He moved his battalion to where mine was.

In crossing, Lt. Hodgson, my Adjutant, and a great favorite and friend, had been shot. In the hope that it might be only a wound, and that I might do something for him, I went to the river after Benteen's arrival with some men I called together. Sergeant Culbertson was one of them. I was gone about a half hour. Capt. Benteen was in command while I was gone, and I had complete confidence in him.

He showed me the order from Lt. Cooke about bringing up the packs. It was about this effect "Benteen—come on—big village—bring packs" and then a postscript "bring packs," and signed "W. W. Cooke." He had not had time to add his official designation as Adjutant. I took a ring and some keys from Lt. Hodgson's body and went back on the hill. The Indians had withdrawn from my front and around me, except for a scattering fire.

Ten wounded had been able to get on the hill with their horses. Most of them men of A Company, which led the column. I told Capt. Moylan to make them comfortable and do all that could be done.

The packs were not yet in sight; one of the men was sent after them to get the ammunition mules up as soon as possible. When I had time to look around I told Lt. Hare to act as my Adjutant and I sent him to the pack train to hurry it all he could. He went and returned and reported what he had done. In about an hour the packs arrived. I am not positive about the time; I had other things to do than looking at my watch. Before they came up the command was put in position; it was on this hill which I thought would enable everybody to see it, and I kept it there as a nucleus about which the scattered parties could gather, till all came together. That was the purpose for which I went there.

When Lt. Hare returned I told him to go to Capt. Weir, who on his own hook had moved out his company, and to tell him to communicate with Gen. Custer if he could, and tell him where we were. I knew in which direction to send him, as Gen. Custer's trail had been found back of the position on the hill.

The main body was kept in hand and after the packtrain came up I formed the column with three companies on the left, the packs in the middle and two companies on the right, and started down the river.

We went perhaps a mile or a mile and a half. I was at the head of the column, and skirmishers were thrown out on the flanks and some on the river bank. I regarded Weir as an advance guard and if anything came there he could check it and give up time to take position.

Lt. Hare came back and said he had taken the responsibility of using my name and ordered the return of the command on account of the number of Indians he saw. The orders were then communicated to the other officers. Capt. Weir, I was afterwards told, left one of his men down there.

I had been impressed with the position I first reached on the hill; it was nearer water and if the companies in the rear could hold the Indians in check we could get there. The column moved both down and back by my orders.

I remained at the rear as the column was put about by fours. I thought, as the Indians were coming, I would be where I could get first information. I remained there a few minutes and then galloped to the head of the column to make disposition of the troops. Capts. French and Godfrey were sent to Capt. Benteen who gave them directions while I was gone to the head. I selected the position; it appeared to me the best I could get in the time I had. I knew I would have to fight dismounted, and that I would have all I could do to take care of myself. I said to Benteen "You look out for that side and I will of the other." I took D Company with me; I spoke to the men and told them to come with me.

It was the strongest company we had and I put them in position where I thought the main attack would be made. I remained there most of the time as I knew the other flank was in good hands.

We hardly had time to dispose of the horses and get the men on the line before we were attacked in large numbers. The men threw themselves on the ground, having no protection except the "grease weed" which was no protection whatever. I cannot fix the time, except that the sun was high enough to see it over the hills below us.

The fire commenced immediately. It was very heavy and lasted till about nine o'clock P.M. Between six and nine I went over the line and felt satisfied we could hold it, and then I went to the left of D Company. About nine o'clock the fire ceased and the Indians went down and made a huge bonfire in the village, where we could see them dancing and scampering about. After nine I went around and made further dispositions; moved some of the companies and told the company commanders to protect themselves all they could and get all the shelter possible as they had to stay there; I remember saying many times that we could not leave the wounded, and we had got to stay there until relief came, that I knew could not be long as I knew Gen. Terry was in the country and I was sure to get information soon. I had been informed by one of Terry's staff that there had been a plan agreed upon between himself and Gen. Custer to meet in the vicinity of the Little Big Horn. He was to come up the Little Big Horn; so I expected to be relieved either by Terry or Custer.

The men and officers were very tired: they had been hard marched. It had been harder on the men than on the horses. The men were badly in need of sleep because they had been up in the saddle.

That evening the whereabouts of the Commanding Officer of the regiment was discussed by Capt. Benteen and myself, while he was lying on my blankets.

There was not the slightest belief or suspicion that Custer had been destroyed. It was supposed that he could take care of himself as well as we could. He had nearly as many men as I had; more than when I opened the fight.

On the morning of the 26th I went around the line and could see the Indians moving up the valley, about daybreak; the attack commenced about two-thirty, after they had formed a circle around me. The first thing I heard was two rifle shots, which attracted attention as everything was quiet. These were immediately succeeded by firing from all round the position. It was only when they fired that their position was indicated; by puffs of smoke and by the sound. There was one point behind which there were about twenty-five who fired together. They were the nearest Indians to us, and the ones who hit most of the horses. The fire was as severe as I ever experienced.

The time periods I stated in my official report were fixed by gathering information from various persons in the command. I got the best approximations available. But the nine and two-thirty times I fixed myself and think they are about right. I stated in my official report that from the best information I had, I estimated the number of attacking Indians about 2500. I think now I was below the mark. I think they were all there on the hill. The firing continued intense till about ten-thirty, and then slackened; they were removing to the bottom in the direction of the village. I thought they were gone for ammunition or reliefs. They were raising a big dust, and had set the prairie afire, so it was difficult to see what they were doing, because we could not see behind the dust and smoke. I now think they left me to meet Gen. Terry, who encamped that night eight or nine miles from where I was. In fact I know they did.

There were some high points which perfectly sheltered some of their sharpshooters who remained all day; and a few were left to annoy the command who stayed all day, annoying us particularly in the matter of getting water.

The weather was very warm. I and some other officers had gotten broad-brimmed straw hats from a trader at the mouth of the Rosebud and I wore one of these on the march. I lost it in the bottom, in the timber.

I brought my carbine with me to the hilltop. I never told anyone I had lost it. I did not fire my pistol on the hill, though I did several times while coming across the bottom; I don't think it had a charge in it when I got on the hill.

My motive in leaving the timber was that we had an immense force against us, and nobody came to our assistance. I was not certain that anybody knew where I was, unless directed by the firing. The position, in my judgment, was not tenable, and I thought by placing my command on the hill, the scattered portions of the regiment could get together. It was my opinion that was the only means of getting anybody away alive. The guidon planted by Capt. Benteen on Weir's hill was put there with the thought that it might be discovered by scattered men and detachments.

I heard no firing from down river till after we moved out in that direction and then only a few scattering shots. I thought they were from the village. It did not impress me as coming from a general engagement. Nothing that came to my attention on the 25th or 26th led me to suspect that Custer was destroyed.

My official report was made up in the manner such reports are generally made—from the best information I could obtain. There must have been matters of which I had no personal knowledge as to which I considered my information reliable; especially in regard to time.

I had some whiskey in a flask that I carried in the inside pocket of my uniform sacque; it held about a pint. I did not touch it until about midnight of the 25th. I was not drunk at any time; and the flask was not emptied till the 28th when on the Custer field; it was a most disagreeable sight and officers and men alike were much affected. The stench was sickening. I took one drink on the night of the 25th, but it did not affect me at all. I think it was the only whiskey in the command, except what the Doctor had.

On the 25th I went around the line and came to the packs, and found there a great many skulkers, and drove them out. I did this several times. The horses and mules were safe and I thought these men had no business there. The last time was after the packs had been taken off and I asked one of the men what he was doing there. I was annoyed. I cannot recall his reply, but I know it angered me and I hit him; and I may have told him if I found him there again I would shoot him. This was about 10 P.M., or between nine and ten.

I never had any intimation that Benteen was to support me in my attack on the bottom. I did not even know where he was.

During the night of the 25th I completed the line by moving some of the companies, and I told all the company commanders to shelter themselves as well as they could, as it would be impossible to leave. I went round the line several times. The Indians that were firing into the herd were able to reach the animals best through the depression, and I tried to fill that up with everything belonging to the packs. I had boxes of ammunition placed along the lines of the different companies, so the men could have all they wanted. Those were about all the orders I gave, and I went around afterward to see that they had been complied with.

On the 26th I moved about, but stayed most of the time with D Company near Lt. Wallace. I crossed the ridge several times, and recall being out in front of Benteen's line, and in Moylan's line; in fact, I was around all. After the heaviest firing was over, I was outside Benteen's position with Sgt. DeLacy, to shoot at some Indians we could see galloping around.

268

I took every means to inform myself that the officers and troops were behaving as well as possible in the circumstances. Frequent orders were not needed; and after the morning of the 26th I did not think any were necessary. I saw no occasion for encouraging either officers or men.

I remained in command after Gen. Terry's arrival, and he sent me to bury the dead, which I thought a proper duty for the 7th—to care for the wounded and bury our comrades, whom we were best able to recognize.

I received no communication from Girard at the ford "A"; he had no right to speak to me officially. I had had trouble with Girard, and discharged him because I thought he was stealing from the Government.

My effort to communicate with Custer the night of the 25th was as much for my benefit as for his. I had no more concern, nor as much, about his position as for my own.

There were two Indians, Half-Yellow-Face and a Crow, who I thought would be able to go through. I would not order a soldier to go to certain death. These Indians talked about it but would not go.

I made an effort on the 26th to communicate with Gen. Terry by a Crow scout. He took the note and left the lines but came back shortly. I do not know what became of the note. I finally got one to Gen. Terry on the 27th.

The only expectation of support I had from the order I received, was from the rear. I do not feel that I failed in my duty and think the results of those two days justify me.

The heavy dust I spoke of was on the trails we followed from the Rosebud, and which enlarged for miles before we reached the Little Big Horn. Lt. Cooke put a portion of the command off the trail because we were making so much dust.

When troops are on an expedition of this kind, it is a general order always to carry one hundred rounds of ammunition if they expect to meet anything, and I suppose all companies had that amount, as that was Gen. Custer's order.

When I say that no plan was communicated to us I mean to the regiment. I do not think there was any plan. The trail I spoke of as Custer's was one of shod horses, and could not have been made by Capt. Benteen's command.

I do not remember the exact phraseology of the message to Benteen; as near as I can recall it was "Benteen; Come on; big village; big thing; bring packs. P.S. Bring packs," and now that you call it to my attention, I remember that it also contained the words "Be quick." It did not make any great impression on me at the time, because I was absorbed in getting those packs together, and did not intend to move until I had done so. It did not occur to me that Custer with 225 men needed anyone quickly; his force could hold off quite a number of Indians if properly disposed. I mean the number I saw.

Weir moved out on his own hook; and when I sent orders to him to communicate with Custer, which I did immediately after I got hold of the pack train and the wounded were cared for, Lt. Hare told me that Weir took him out and showed him the impracticability of going any further; and it was then Lt. Hare used my name and ordered the return. I had thought he could cut through; I regarded him as the advance guard, as the whole column started toward him when the order was sent.

I do not mean to be understood that all the Indians engaged me on the hill at one time; there was not room enough; but I think there were from 1800 to 2500 engaging at a time. But I think they all came there. I imagine the circumference of the circle they formed around was about four thousand yards, and they were all the way from ten yards to twelve hundred yards from us.

I had no reason to believe that Gen. Custer would support me in any other manner than from the rear; in my opinion there was no other way. An attack on the flank would not have been a support under the circumstances, though I may have stated in my report that he intended to do so. I did not know where Benteen was; he might have gone to the mouth of the Rosebud for all I knew.

My relations with Gen. Custer were friendly enough; and if my own brothers had been in that column I could not have done any more than I did.

I had known Gen. Custer a long time; and I had no confidence in his ability as a soldier. I had known him all through the war.

The Indians I alluded to in my report as having been driven were the forty or fifty decoys sent out there. I saw no ponies being driven about. Every pony I saw had an Indian on him.

I suppose there were from six to nine hundred Indians on my left and rear when I left the timber, and there were plenty in front, between me and the village. And they were in force on the other side of the river, in sheltered places, within close range, less than one hundred yards away.

My casualties, before I decided to get out of there were, one scout killed, Sgt. Heyn of A Company hit, and two or three of M Company; that was before I mounted. The scout's name was Isaiah, a negro who had lived among the Sioux and had a Sioux wife.

The least number of men who could have held that timber was six or seven hundred; they would have to hold the outer edge all around, otherwise the Indians could creep up and get at us. I think the regiment could have done it, but not 120 men—and I did not have 120. To cover the necessary space, that number of men would be beyond speaking distance apart and their fire would be no support at all.

I suppose the Indians killed the wounded left in the timber. I could make no effort to take them out; and none was made. I do not know what became of the wounded left on the plain; the Indians would not permit me to take care of them.

I received no communication from Girard at the crossing; I would not have believed it if I had. I should have listened to him, but I repeat, I should not have believed him.

I tried to communicate with Custer the night of the 25th. I was quite as anxious to get him to aid me as I was to aid him. I did not call for volunteers; and I would not order a soldier on a mission of that kind, for I believed that would be sending a man to his death. I would have sent an Indian out, because of his peculiar ability to skulk along and get through a country without being seen when a white man would be seen.

I consider that the results of the battle justified my every act, and with the same knowledge I then had, I would again do the same thing under the same circumstances. I believe that when I came out of the timber Custer's command was all dead. This belief is based on after information: I did not think so then.

I do not remember anybody reporting to me that he heard firing on the right. If I had heard this firing as they represent it, I should have known he was engaged while I was on the hill; but I heard no such firing. Perhaps I was not in a position to hear the firing when I was down the hill by Lt. Hodgson's body, though I was nearer the battlefield then than the command was.

I consider that I obeyed orders. I did not charge into the village, but I went far enough to discover that it was impossible. Of course, ten men could be ordered to charge a million; a brilliant illustration is the battle of Balaklava. I then knew nothing of the topography, but it afterwards developed that had I gone three hundred yards further the command would have been thrown into a ditch ten yards wide and three or four feet deep. The Indians were in it; and the command would never have gotten that far; but by the time they had got within a few yards most of the saddles would have been emptied and the horses killed.

I was responsible for the union of my battalion with the rest of the regiment, and I believed I would find them on the other side of the river. I knew they were not on my side, as M, A and G were the only companies that got on the left side of the river.

I had 112 soldiers and officers when I crossed the river going to the attack, and about twenty-seven Indian scouts who didn't remain with me long.

I did everything I could to assist and cooperate with Gen. Custer as much as if he were my own brother. Never in my life did I feel more interest in the success of an engagement, because the Seventh was essentially my own regiment. I feel that I did everything possible short of sacrificing my command.

The principle that actuated me in returning to the hill was that of reuniting with Custer, not leaving him unsupported. I went out of there as much to aid him as to secure aid.

When I said in my report that Gen. Custer meant to support me by a flank attack, it was a conviction formed after the fight. I expected my support to come from the direction I had crossed. I did not see how it was possible, on account of the high banks on the other side, for support to come from the flanks. I didn't think it was practicable to get down below me.

The number of wounded had nothing to do with my action in the timber. I should have done the same thing if no man had been hit. There was no communication to me that Custer's command had been sighted from the timber.

When I retreated from the bottom I had no idea where Custer was. I knew he was not on the side where the village was, and if there was any chance for him to see me it was on this hill. I had no doubt that I could explain the retreat from my position; but I did not give it a thought. I never thought it would be questioned.

Following the closing addresses of Recorder Lee and Gilbert, the court retired behind closed doors to prepare its findings.

Whittaker, angry and depressed, did not wait for a decision to be announced. As he left Chicago, he cried "whitewash" to newspapermen.

The decision came on February 1, 1879. It said:

The Court of Inquiry assembled by Special Orders No. 255, dated Headquarters of the Army, A.G.O. Washington, November 25th, 1878, reports in obdience to that order the following facts involving the conduct of Major Marcus A. Reno, 7th Cavalry, in regard to the Battle of the Little Big Horn fought June 25 and 26th, 1876:

1st. In the morning of the 25th of June 1876 the 7th Cavalry, Lieutenant Colonel G. A. Custer commanding, operating against the hostile Indians in Montana Territory, near the Little Big Horn River, was divided into four battalions, two of which were commanded by Colonel Custer in person, with the exception of one company in charge of the pack train,—one by Major Reno and one by Captain F. W. Benteen.

This division took place from about twelve (12) to fifteen (15) miles from the scene of the battle or battles afterwards fought.

The column under Captain Benteen received orders to move to the left for an indefinite distance (to the first and second valleys) hunting Indians with orders to charge any it might meet with.

The battalion under Major Reno received orders to draw out of the column, and doing so marched parallel and only a short distance from the column commanded by Colonel Custer.

2nd. About three or four miles from what afterwards was found to be the Little Big Horn River where the fighting took place, Major Reno received orders to move forward as rapidly as he thought prudent until coming up with the Indians who were reported fleeing, he would charge them and drive everything before him, and would receive the support of the column under Colonel Custer.

3rd. In obedience to the orders (given by Colonel Custer) Captain Benteen marched to the left (south) at an angle of about forty-five degrees, but meeting an impracticable country, was forced by it to march more to his right than the angle above indicated, and nearer approaching a parallel route to the trail followed by the rest of the command.

4th. Major Reno, in obedience to the orders given him moved on at a fast trot on the main Indian trail until reaching the Little Big Horn River, which he forded, and halted for a few moments to reform his battalion.

After reforming he marched the battalion forward towards the Indian village, downstream or in a northerly diection, two companies in line of battle and one in support, until about half way to the point where he finally halted, when he brought the company in reserve, forward to the line of battle, continuing the movement at a fast trot or gallop until after passing over a distance of about two miles, when he halted and dismounted to fight on foot, at a point of timber upon which the right flank of his battalion rested.

After fighting in this formation for less than half an hour, the Indians passing to his left rear, and appearing in his front, the skirmish line was withdrawn to the timber and the fight continued for a short time, half an hour or forty-five minutes in all, when the command, or nearly all of it, was mounted, formed and at a rapid gait was withdrawn to a hill on the opposite side of the river.

In this movement one officer and about sixteen soldiers and citizens were left in the woods besides one wounded man or more, two citizens and thirteen soldiers rejoining the command afterwards.

In this retreat Major Reno's battalion lost some twenty-nine men in killed and wounded, and three officers, including Doctor DeWolf, killed.

5th. In the meantime Captain Benteen having carried out as far as was practicable the spirit of his orders, turned in the direction of the route taken by the remainder of the regiment and reaching the trail, followed it to near the crossing of the Little Big Horn, reaching there about the same time Reno's command was crossing the river in retreat lower down, and finally joined his battalion with that of Reno on the hill.

Forty minutes or an hour later the pack train which had been left behind, on the trail, by the rapid movement of the command, and the delays incident to its march, joined the united command, which then consisted of seven companies, together with about thirty (30) or thirty-five (35) men belonging to the companies under Colonel Custer.

6th. After detaching Benteen's and Reno's columns, Colonel Custer moved with his immediate command on the trail followed by Reno to a point within about one mile of the river, where he diverged to the right (or northward) following the general direction of the river to a point about four miles below that afterwards taken by Major Reno, where he and his command were destroyed by the hostiles. The last living witness of this march, Trumpeter Martin, left Colonel Custer's command when it was about two miles distant from the field where it afterwards met its fate. There is nothing more in evidence as to this command, save that firing was heard proceeding from its direction, from about the time Reno retreated from the bottom up to the time the pack train was approaching the position on the hill.

All firing which indicated fighting was concluded before the final preparations in Major Reno's command for the movement which was afterwards attempted.

274

7th. After the distribution of ammunition and a proper provision for the wounded men, Major Reno's entire command moved down the river in the direction it was thought Custer's column had taken, and in which it was known General Terry's command was to be found.

This movement was carried sufficiently far to discover that its continuance would imperil the entire command, upon which it returned to the position formerly occupied, and made a successful resistance, 'till succor reached it.

The defense of the position on the hill was a heroic one against fearful odds.

The conduct of the officers throughout was excellent and while subordinates in some instances did more for the safety of the command by brilliant displays of courage than did Major Reno, there was nothing in his conduct which requires animadversion from this Court.

It is the conclusion of this Court in view of all the facts in evidence, that no further proceedings are necessary in this case, and it expresses this opinion in compliance with the concluding clause of the order convening the Court.

General Sherman and Secretary of War McCrary approved the findings.

32

Several weeks after the Battle of the Little Big Horn, in the late summer of 1876, a detachment from General Terry's command had established a semipermanent post, comprised of a dozen huts and a stockade, at the foot of Bear Butte on the edge of the Black Hills. They named it Camp Sturgis in honor of the son of the 7th Cavalry's commander who had died with Custer.

The choice of a site had been made hurriedly, and eighteen months later the camp was moved to a better location on Bear

Butte Creek. General Sheridan characterized it as "the doorway to the Black Hills . . . the best strategic point for a military post in the entire northwest . . . centrally located with relation to all western Indian reservations."

The post having been given permanent status, funds were provided for the construction of a headquarters building, officers' quarters, barracks, stables, a quartermaster's depot, commissary, blacksmith and carpenter shops, a trader's store, an officers' clubroom, and a parade ground. Secretary of War McCrary agreed with his aides that an installation of such importance properly should commemorate a soldier of high rank and great distinction. He ordered the name changed to Fort Meade, in memory of General George Gordon Meade, the victor at Gettysburg.

In the summer of 1879, the commander at Fort Meade was Colonel Samuel D. Sturgis. He had arrived in July with his wife and daughter, Ella, still depressed by a lingering sense of despair over the death of his son.

If a quarter-century of military service, during which he fought in two major wars and numerous Indian campaigns, had changed Colonel Sturgis in any manner, it had not soothed his inherent choleric temper.

He understood that he had received the most important and responsible field assignment that might be given in the West, yet what gratification he held was colored by memories that rankled and pained him, and upon which he could not refrain from dwelling at length. He thought of the Little Big Horn, where his son had died, as being "just over the hill" from Fort Meade, and although three years had passed since that tragic event, the environment of the Sioux Country and the duties to be performed served to conjure up a parade of visions of the disaster.

He could not forget—and it was with great difficulty that he controlled the rage that came with the thought—that he had been for several years kept on detached service so that a more glamorous and popular, but far less competent, lieutenant colonel named Custer might lead the 7th Cavalry. For nearly a decade Custer had bested him and had managed through influential friends—not the least of whom were Sheridan and Sherman—to override him, to have him shoved aside. Being the thorough and loyal soldier he was, Sturgis had managed to abstain from publicly criticizing the "boy general," and, although he loathed Custer and bitterly resented the unfairness of the treatment he had received because of him, he had accepted his assignments without registered protests. The needless massacre on the Little Big Horn was more than he could bear, however, and he had unleashed his fury in letters to the *Army and Navy Journal*.

In them he condemned Custer as "insanely ambitious for glory and praise," declaring that Custer

wrote much upon the subject of Indian warfare, and the people of the country who read his articles naturally supposed he had great experience in savage warfare, but this was not so. His experience was exceedingly limited, and that he was over-reached by Indian tactics, and hundreds of valuable lives sacrificed thereby, will astonish those alone who read his articles, not those who were best acquainted with him and knew the peculiarities of his character.

The extreme possessiveness Colonel Sturgis had always shown toward his three children had been augmented after the death of his lieutenant son. With his youngest son attending an eastern school, preparatory to entering West Point, his attention was centered upon his daughter Ella. She had just turned twenty and his love for her was deep and abiding.

Major Reno had served under Colonel Sturgis only for brief periods. He had seen him for a few days at a time, and for several weeks at Fort Abraham Lincoln before he left on the ill-fated trip to Abercrombie, but there had never been a prolonged opportunity to become well acquainted. The major, for his part, was pleased to serve as executive officer for the blunt colonel, who obviously was quite competent; he became a frequent visitor at the Sturgis quarters and as the summer waned began to fall in love with their twenty-year-old daughter, Ella.

The thought of once more having a real home, of bringing his son, Ross, from the distant East, did not detract from Reno's dreams. Ella, like most women who had known him, found the major attractive. As a part of the regiment she had heard stories of his way with women. She knew of the newspaper criticism and charges of cowardice at Little Big Horn, but she knew also of his quiet thoughtfulness and courtesy, his brilliant record in the Civil War and his acknowledged military competence.

Colonel Sturgis, on the other hand, was not looking for a son-in-law. Ella, the last of his children remaining at home, had been a rock and a strong right arm during the sad and bitter days of mourning. After Jack's death she had gone West to the Little Big Horn to identify her brother's mangled body. Colonel Sturgis wanted her happy; he had no objections to young officers calling on her, but he did not want to lose her immediately. There was also resentment, on the part of the colonel, against those who had survived the battle, and he became less and less enthusiastic about Major Reno's frequent visits, and showed it in his curt words. Unfortunately for everyone concerned, Reno by early autumn had fallen desperately in love with Ella and was not to be readily dissuaded from his courtship.

At 2 A.M. August 3, 1879, the cry of "Fire!" was heard on the post. The trader's store and commissary were ablaze. The enlisted men formed a bucket brigade, but the fire had gained such headway that by dawn the building was a smoking ruin. Unfortunately Mr. Fanshawe, the trader, was in Rapid City and was not expected to return until the following evening. Mr. William Johnson, who had a small investment in the store and was accordingly a partner, was at the fort and took such steps as were necessary to protect the few articles that had been salvaged.

Reno and the Fanshawes were most congenial neighbors, since they had adjoining quarters. Immediately after breakfast, the major stopped to see the distraught Mrs. Fanshawe and offered her any assistance that he or anyone else could give. The trader's wife, who was in a highly nervous state, assured him that she would most certainly call upon him and added she would feel much better as soon as her husband returned. Later in the afternoon Reno suggested they drive toward Rapid City, intercept Fanshawe, and break the news of the fire before he reached the post. This would reassure him that his wife was safe.

She was delighted with the suggestion and they accordingly set out in mid-afternoon. They drove about seven miles without seeing any sign of the trader and, since it was growing dark, they retraced their steps. Dr. Bell, Mr. Johnson, and Lieutenant Nicholson were waiting on the porch when they drove up.

By eleven o'clock, the trader had still not yet returned. It became quite cool, as it does in the evening in that part of the country in August, and Mrs. Fanshawe asked the major if he would get her shawl, which was on the chair just inside the door.

When an ambulance was heard entering the post gates a few minutes after midnight, Major Reno suggested that he and his companions go to his quarters, since Mrs. Fanshawe would probably prefer to be alone with her husband. Before they left, she asked the men to return for supper, because she had food on the stove and their presence would help cheer Mr. Fanshawe.

While waiting a proper interval, the men had a drink with Major Reno in his dining room and after a wearisome day their spirits were renewed by the time they rejoined their hostess.

The table was abundantly laden with food. In addition there was a bottle three-quarters full of whiskey. Each of the men poured himself a drink, which they laced with water. The wood-burning stove was in the kitchen against the wall of the dining room, keeping the room comfortable during the bleak winter months, but intolerably warm in the summer.

Reno felt the contrast between the outside temperature and the over-heated room. He also remembered that he had eaten nothing since noon. Reno had barely finished his first drink when he realized the whiskey was going straight to his head. After the first couple of sips of the second drink, he pushed it aside and didn't touch it again, concentrating on his supper. Sensing that his speech was a little thick, he did not join in any of the conversation. Before the meal was finished the over-heated room plus the drinks started him hiccoughing and he was acutely embarrassed.

As they were finishing their supper, Mr. Fanshawe suggested that he would like to talk with his partner Johnson, and they withdrew into the trader's office. His wife followed and in offering cigars remarked, "For goodness sake don't offer Major Reno anything more to drink."

The gathering broke up shortly, and the guests started out the back door. The major thanked Mrs. Fanshawe for her hospitality and, as he was stepping down the high stoop, Johnson emerged from the office and offered assistance.

Reno shook his head, saying, "I can take care of myself."

He and Dr. Bell cut across the yard to his quarters, and after saying "good night" Bell went on to the infirmary.

Lieutenant William J. Nicholson, a member of the party that night, was second-in-command of Company C. Nicholson was a bachelor with an appealing personality and a pugnacious disposition not unlike that of Reno. The two, together with the post surgeon, Dr. Bell, were inseparable during off-duty hours. Nightly they could be found either playing pool at the club or having a few drinks in Reno's quarters.

Nicholson, a native of Georgetown, D. C., had an unusually diversified background. From his father, a commander in the Navy, he knew and understood things nautical. His speaking knowledge of medicine stemmed from his grandfather, Dr. William Jones, a prominent Washington physician. There was also a cultural side of the lieutenant which was the result of his aunt's efforts. She had married the banker, William Wilson Corcoran, donor of the gallery and art collection bearing his name. Raised during his formative years in a city under arms, Nicholson's ambition had always been to be an Army officer. President Grant had directly commissioned him from civilian life as a 2nd lieutenant of the 7th Cavalry.

A young man of very decided opinions supported by a belligerency toward anyone who disagreed with him, Nicholson was constantly involved in arguments with his fellow officers, one of whom was Lieutenant Godfrey. Their differences finally resulted in a fist fight and they never spoke to one another again. As late as 1901, Nicholson refused a promotion to lieutenant colonel when it involved serving under Godfrey.

During the evening of August 8, shortly after tattoo, Major Reno, Dr. Bell, Captain Benteen, and 1st Lieutenant Assistant Surgeon Louis Brechemin, a recent graduate of the University of Pennsylvania Medical School, whose commission was only a year old, were playing a four-handed game of billiards in the officers' club. All were in a jovial mood and there was much drinking and horseplay. 1st Lieutenant Douglas M. Scott was watching the game, and Joe Smyth, the bartender, was busy replenishing the glasses.

As the evening progressed and the drinks began to have more effect, the billiard game degenerated into a roughhouse affair. All kinds of silly stunts were engaged in and the major at one point mounted a chair as if it were a horse. When he dismounted, he tossed it backwards and it crashed against the window and broke a pane of glass. No one at the time thought much about it, for there was already one pane missing and they knew that Fanshawe would insist that Reno pay for both.

The party lasted until well after 1 A.M. Before the major left, he gave Lieutenant Scott, who was the most sober of those present, a ten-dollar bill to settle his account, remarking that he wanted Scott to know the bill was paid. Scott handed the money to Joe Smyth who, in spite of knowing that the note had come from Reno, gave the change to the lieutenant. When Reno objected and Scott joined in the argument, Smyth crossed the room and started to give the change to the major. The latter, intentionally or otherwise, jolted the bartender's hand and spilled the coins on the floor. Certainly it was not accidental when the silver fell on the floor a second time, and Reno was required to retrieve his own coins. The officers all left for their quarters by one-thirty.

During the short walk home, Reno was accompanied by Lieutenant Scott. Reno remarked that he was hungry and suggested they wake up his housekeeper and have her prepare a supper. Scott agreed, and they were soon eating an early morning snack.

While Colonel Sturgis was absent early in October, Major

Reno called on Ella one afternoon. Cordially received by both Mrs. Sturgis and Ella, Reno remained for several hours and was still there when Colonel Sturgis returned home. He was none too pleased to find the major visiting his daughter and was very gruff. After the caller left, Sturgis informed Ella that he was telling her for the last time, that she was not to receive the major again. Ella defended herself by saying Reno had not announced himself, but knocked and walked in the door. There had been nothing, she said, that she could have done about the matter.

In the almost nightly pool bouts, Major Reno and Lieutenant Nicholson played for high stakes, while Dr. Bell conservatively avoided being drawn into the gambling. Occasionally Lieutenant Morse would join in a wager. Often after a night at the club one of the three officers would owe several hundred dollars, but the bets after a few nights' play would generally cancel out.

After a particularly heavy night of pool on October 24, Reno wound up owing Nicholson close to three hundred dollars. This was considerably more than had been owed in the pool games in the past, and the next morning, when Reno saw Nicholson, he brought up the question of the money.

Nicholson replied, "Colonel, that's all right. Forget it."

The major insisted, however, and they agreed on a compromise amount in settlement of the obligation. Later in the day, Reno sent the lieutenant a check for what he thought was the agreed sum. That afternoon Major Reno as executive officer found it necessary to go to Colonel Sturgis' quarters to report a rumor that a large concentration of hostile Indians led by either Red Cloud or Spotted Tail were said to be in the vicinity of the fort. The colonel received him cordially, but Ella was not in evidence.

That evening they were again hard at it, playing pool and making ever-increasing wagers on the outcome of the games. In addition to the regular habitués, the heavy-drinking captain of the 2nd Cavalry, James T. Peale, and the curly haired studious lieutenant of the 1st Infantry, James S. Pettit, fresh from West Point, were in attendance.

Reno had been a steady winner, and he proposed to Nicholson

they wager a hundred dollars on the next game. The game was a tense one, but at its end the major was ahead.

As they finished, Nicholson said in a rather unpleasant and loud voice, "That leaves us two hundred and eighty dollars on pool."

Reno quickly replied that he did not owe that much. An acrimonious discussion then ensued.

Finally Nicholson said that they had better settle this in some other manner. Subsequently he declared that he "could lick Reno with both hands tied behind him, that he could lick him in two minutes in any way he wanted."

Reno paid no attention, but continued with his cue to knock the balls around the table. Nicholson, on the other hand, continued to repeat how easily he could lick him and interspersed some insulting remarks. Finally the major could stand no more, and he turned and went for the lieutenant with his billiard cue, striking him on the arm, breaking the cue in half.

As Nicholson grabbed for Reno's throat, Dr. Bell cried out, "For God's sake, don't hit him!"

The two struggling men fell to the floor. They were quickly separated by the other officers and pulled to opposite sides of the billiard table, where Reno remained quiet, but Nicholson continued to threaten in a loud voice. When it appeared that as a result of the younger man's continued remarks the fighting might be resumed, Lieutenant Pettit told Nicholson that if there were any more arguments he would put the two officers under arrest. This threat quieted Nicholson. Reno put on his coat and left with Dr. Bell for his quarters.

The news of the occurrences that evening quickly spread over the entire post. It would be unfair to Colonel Sturgis to say that he was delighted. Suffice it to say, that Ella's suitor had delivered himself into the colonel's hands. Sturgis placed Reno under arrest in quarters with permission to leave only for exercise. Nicholson, on the other hand, was not even given a reprimand. Colonel Sturgis directed that charges against Reno be immediately drawn and that he as the post commander would be the accuser.

The next morning Major Reno was served with a set of charges which read:

. . . did create and engage in a disreputable disturbance or brawl in a public billiard saloon, and did violently assault and strike 2nd Lieutenant Wm. J. Nicholson with a billiard cue, with the manifest intent of inflicting severe bodily injury . . . was drunk and disorderly . . . and did several times, wantonly and in a riotous manner, knock money out of the hands of the saloonkeeper, Mr. Joseph Smyth, scattering said money over the floor . . . did, in a riotous and wanton manner, smash in with chairs the glass of one or more of the windows . . . was in a disgusting condition of intoxication at the residence of Mr. W. S. Fanshawe, post trader . . . to the scandal and disgrace of the military service.

Fred Benteen, thinking back, could well remember the evening of November 10, 1879. Shortly after ten o'clock he had glanced out a window. A light snow had fallen during the day, but at dusk the storm had passed, and the white parade ground was swept with the brittle, wintry brilliance of the stars. He watched sadly as the shadowy lone figure of Major Reno passed along the walk and vanished. It was not until three days later that he had learned, to his dismay, what had occurred after the major had passed beyond his view.

This had happened:

Proceeding on his customary evening exercise walk, the Major had been observed by Lieutenant Ernest A. Garlington. Garlington had been calling on Ella Sturgis, and he had just emerged from her house when the major passed by.

A short distance further along the major was seen by Lieutenant Baldwin D. Spilman, who was cutting across the parade ground to his own quarters.

The next person to see the major was Lieutenant Charles Starr. They passed within a few yards of each other but did not speak.

The major had circled the parade ground when he came directly before the Sturgis home. He stopped. Ella was sitting with her back to a window of the brightly lighted parlor. He could make out no one else in the room, and he quickly stepped across the narrow dooryard.

The tapping on the window caused Ella to start and turn her head. She saw the smiling face of Major Reno. Rising quickly, she moved across the room.

"What was that?" her mother asked.

"Someone tapped on the window."

"Well, who was it?"

"I think it was Major Reno."

Mrs. Sturgis dropped her sewing and went rapidly up the stairs. Ella was peering out the window when Colonel Sturgis, his shirt off and his suspenders dangling, appeared, cane in hand, and rushed out the front door.

No one was to be seen, and shivering with cold, the colonel returned.

"Are you certain?" he demanded of Ella. When she hesitated in replying, he shouted, "Don't try to protect him. I'll find out."

"Well, I thought so, but I can't be certain," Ella said, and hurried upstairs to her bedroom.

Establishment of the fact that Major Reno had been taking his evening exercise at the time the tapping on the window occurred was not difficult. The colonel's investigation, however, resulted in the incident becoming common knowledge.

Later, Captain Benteen slipped into Major Reno's quarters. "Sturgis is raving," he said. "For God's sake, what got into you?"

"It was a stupid thing to do," the major admitted. "Just an impulse. Perhaps I should write a note of apology."

"Well, send it to Mrs. Sturgis," Benteen advised him.

Major Reno sat down at his desk, and as he wrote the captain looked over his shoulder.

"I sincerely ask your pardon," the major wrote Mrs. Sturgis, "for I do assure you, if not guiltless, the fault was in the judgment and not the heart."

Benteen nodded in approval. "Let's hope it does some good."

The additional charge was preferred as the note was delivered the next morning. It said:

. . . did, in the darkness and at a late hour in the evening, surreptitiously enter the side grounds adjoining the private residence of his commanding officer . . . and did peer into a side (and retired) window of the family sitting room . . . approaching so near and so stealthily as to very seriously affright and alarm that portion of the family . . . which had not yet retired for the night.

33

A flood of memories, many of them unpleasant, occupied Major Reno's thoughts as he looked into the faces of the seven officers who comprised the General Court-Martial before which he stood accused on the morning of November 28, 1879. He was filled with a feeling of impending doom, and he wondered if he had made a mistake in not submitting a plea of guilty, asking for mercy, and accepting without contest whatever punishment the War Department decreed.

On the previous evening he had sought to predict his fate by considering the personalities and records of the court's members and analyzing his personal knowledge of the men. The effort had brought little more than a sleepless night. He could call none of the seven a friend, and two could be placed in the category of enemies.

Perhaps his greatest antagonist would be the presiding officer, Colonel William Henry Wood. He had bested Wood in a clash of authority during an Indian campaign on the Big Sandy River in 1870. Wood had been severely reprimanded by headquarters, and he had never forgiven his defeat.

Major Reno had only a slight acquaintanceship with Colonel William R. Shafter, but by reputation he knew him as a strict disciplinarian.

The major had known Lieutenant Colonel Elmer Otis as an upperclassman at West Point. They held a mutual dislike for each other that had never diminished. Otis had let it be known that he thought Reno rather crude, to which Reno had retorted that Otis should have gone to cooking school instead of the Academy. It was Otis who had been assigned to fill the vacancy created by the death of Custer, the promotion which the 7th Cavalry's enlisted men had petitioned Washington to award to Reno.

During the Civil War, Lieutenant Colonel Andrew J. Alexander had won the sobriquet of "One Man Army." He had participated in thirty-six major battles, and his deeds of heroism were numerous. Major Reno had first known him in the Cavalry Bureau in Washington, to which both had been temporarily attached.

Major Joseph S. Conrad and Major Reno had been members of the same West Point class. Neither had bothered since to maintain their relationship, although Conrad had long been a close friend of Colonel Sturgis.

Major Bernard J. D. Irwin was a medical officer, a man of extraordinary surgical ability and with a distinguished career as a combat soldier. He had won a Congressional Medal of Honor at Apache Pass for leading a small detachment of troops to victory against a superior force of Indians after his commanding officer had been critically wounded. In another Indian campaign he had captured a chief and two warriors and hanged them over the graves of several white men they had tortured to death.

Major Reno's meetings with Major Orlando H. Moore had been few and widely separated. He was reputed to be a most conscientious officer with no small ability as a military strategist.

Colonel Wood tapped on his table with a pencil, and asked, "Major Reno, are you represented by legal counsel?"

"I am not, sir," the major replied. "I shall be my own counsel."

He had no alternative. He had been back on active duty only six months, after a suspension of two years without pay, and most of his salary had gone to meet the debts he had incurred in Harrisburg.

"I should like to make a motion, if the court please," Major Reno said.

"Proceed." Colonel Wood told him.

Major Reno moved to strike from the specifications the charge that he had been drunk and disorderly in the home of the post trader. "That does not constitute a military offense," he argued. "What events transpired occurred in a private residence of a gentleman, who with his lady was present at the supper table, and who was the proper person to rebuke any disgusting, ungentlemanly or unofficer-like conduct, which Mr. Fanshawe saw no occasion to do."

The motion was overruled. "The specifications will remain," Colonel Wood said. "Let the trial Judge Advocate proceed."

"I call Lieutenant William J. Nicholson," the prosecutor, Captain William W. Sanders, announced.

Astonishment seemed to grow in Captain Sanders as Nicholson proceeded.

"I goaded Major Reno," Nicholson said. "I told him several times that I could lick him. As to the matter of the supper at Fanshawe's, Major Reno said nothing improper."

Sanders glanced at Colonel Sturgis as he asked Lieutenant James Sumner Pettit to take the stand. From Pettit he elicited a detailed description of the fight in the club, and turned the witness over to Major Reno for cross-examination.

"Did you threaten to arrest Lieutenant Nicholson and me?" the major asked.

"Yes, but the threat was directed more toward Lieutenant Nicholson than toward you," Pettit replied. "He was attempting to renew the fight."

As if he were following his cue obediently, Bartender Joseph Smyth repeated almost verbatim the testimony of Pettit. "I think Major Reno did stagger a little when he left," he added, as if with reluctance.

Before becoming a soldier, Lieutenant Douglas Marshall Scott had served in the Navy under his father, who was an admiral. It was not a secret at Fort Meade that he had been commissioned a lieutenant of cavalry directly from civilian life by Secretary of War Stanton, coincidentally upon the recommendation of General George Meade, a close friend of Admiral Scott. It was no less well known that Colonel Sturgis was another old friend of the Scott family, and he had arranged to have the young lieutenant assigned to his staff.

"Major Reno took a good many drinks of whiskey at the club," Scott said. "He was unsteady in his gait. In my opinion, he was drunk, but he had full possession of his faculties."

Dr. Ralph Bell's testimony was peculiarly similar to that of both Pettit and Smyth. He supported it with a statement that "Major Reno was quiet. He paid no attention to Lieutenant Nicholson's taunts until they had been repeated several times. I don't think Lieutenant Pettit directed his threat of arrest to Major Reno at all."

"Oh, I guess Major Reno was a little drowsy and his talk a little thick," Fanshawe told the court. "He did not insult either me or my family."

Fanshawe's partner stated that he had attended the supper, but he had observed no sign of intoxication at the table. "Major Reno was quiet during the meal," he said. "I do remember him speaking once or twice and his words were a little thick. He left a half-glass of whiskey and water on the table during the meal."

All Lieutenant Garlington had to offer was that he had passed Major Reno on the parade ground on the evening someone tapped on the Sturgis window, and Lieutenant Spilman had nothing to say but that he, too, had seen Major Reno walking near the quarters of Colonel Sturgis, and that he, too, had seen Ella at the window. Lieutenant Starr had not seen Ella, but he had passed Major Reno while en route to his own quarters.

When he was called, Colonel Sturgis moved toward the witness stand with long strides, dramatically lifted his hand to be sworn, and gravely replied, "Yes, sir, I do," in a firm voice. He sat stiffly in his chair, his eyes resting on Captain Sanders.

"I rushed downstairs, sir," he said, as if the memory gave him pain, "to find my poor, distraught daughter cowering in the further corner of the sitting room . . . alone. I picked up a cane and rushed outside the front door, but saw nobody. I returned to find my daughter in such a nervous and shaky condition that we were fearful she might be taken by something like St. Vitus's dance."

At the adjournment for the day, Dr. Bell said to Captain Benteen, "The court was to have nine members. Colonel Townsend and Colonel Davidson were to be on it. I understand they're both ill."

"Maybe they wanted no part of a lynching bee," Benteen growled and walked away.

Colonel Wood tapped his pencil at 9 A.M. on the morning of November 29, and Captain Sanders stepped quickly across the room to assist Ella Sturgis to the witness stand. She was pale, but there was no indication that she had been afflicted with St. Vitus's dance. Her hands were relaxed, and her voice, well modulated, was clear.

"I looked into the darkness out the window, and I saw a face gradually appear," she said with preciseness. "I sat paralyzed. My eyes met Major Reno's. I saw Major Reno for at least six seconds."

Ella Sturgis drew a deep breath, as if to subdue the excitement within herself, excitement that she tried to conceal behind a forced serene manner. "My impression at first was that I would have been shot if I moved, for I knew that he must have feelings against father, and his face was very pale, and he looked as if he were about to do something desperate. I remained in the corner until father came down."

"You may cross-examine," Sanders said.

Major Reno arose slowly, and said quietly: "I have no cross-examination. However, I should like to remark that seeing me so clearly through the window in the outside darkness from a brightly lighted room was quite a feat."

During the recess which ensued, Colonel Sturgis angrily approached the prosecutor. "Look here, Sanders," he said in a strained voice, "I don't like the way this thing is going. In my opinion you're not doing everything you could."

"I have not asked for your opinion, sir," Sanders said and turned away.

Although she had sat at the same table in her home on the evening Major Reno assertedly insulted her, Mrs. Fanshawe recalled the episode in a manner entirely different from that of her husband or his partner.

"Major Reno swayed in his chair," she said in a belligerent tone. "His utterances were unintelligible, and he hiccoughed. He was very much under the influence of liquor. He was very drunk. His condition was disgustingly drunk. The disgusting part in my estimation was when Major Reno had hiccoughs. I didn't know at what moment he might be ill."

When the trial resumed the following morning, Major Reno summoned Dr. Irwin, and asked him: "Regarding the supper in the Fanshawes' where I am accused of being drunk, would going from the chilling outside air into a hot room account for the effects as testified?"

"It might," Dr. Irwin said. "Such abrupt changes produce a considerable effect on some people."

"Thank you," said Major Reno. "I'll ask Colonel Sturgis to return."

The colonel rose slowly and walked forward with deliberation.

"Do you have the note of apology I wrote to Mrs. Sturgis?" the major inquired.

"Just a minute," Sanders said quickly. "I object. The note is not referred to in the specifications and charges."

"It explains my reason for tapping on the window," the major said.

"The objection is sustained," said Colonel Wood.

Reno now became a witness in his own defense. He told of the settling of his gambling debts with Nicholson and giving him a check in full payment, of later winning a wager, with the lieutenant disputing the payment of his obligations. He said Nicholson was "grossly insulting," and continued to repeat that "he could lick me and struck the table with his fist, this last remark and action provoked me and in a fit of passion with the cue in my hand I walked toward him and struck him."

As to the events of the November evening, he read to the members of the Court his letter of apology to Mrs. Sturgis as the best evidence of his motives that evening. Reno told the court of the incidents of the night at the Fanshawes' and it was substantially as testified by all the witnesses except the trader's wife. He claimed that the breaking of the window at the officers' club in August was an accident and that he had "playfully" scattered the coins from the hands of Joe Smyth. He was asked what understanding there had been between the post trader and himself, as post commander, when the clubroom was opened.

Reno replied that, "Rules governing buildings of this kind should apply to this one . . . "that is a . . . room for [the] convenience of officers and such friends [as] they choose to invite."

After Reno left the stand the Judge Advocate addressed the Court, telling them the officer preferring the charges, Colonel Sturgis, felt that it would have been ungenerous on his part not to have accepted Major Reno's apology, had he not felt that the letter did not represent Major Reno's motives.

Accordingly he requested permission to be allowed to produce witnesses who would show that Reno was not activated by the motives as set forth in his letter of apology. Reno, of course, raised the objection that his motives could not be impeached after he had finished his testimony. The Court upheld the trial Judge Advocate.

Mrs. Fanshawe was again called and she testified that on November 9 in discussing with Reno the charges Colonel Sturgis had brought against him, the major had said that the case would not amount to much, for "Miss Ella will be on the stand. I will bring her up, you see . . ."

In rebuttal Reno called Lieutenant Garlington, who said that when he heard the story that had been spread by Mrs. Fanshawe, he told Major Reno that he should call Ella Sturgis to the stand. The major had replied that Mrs. Fanshawe "told a God damned lie."

In asking permission to call the next witness, Major Reno stated that this testimony would substantiate his motive in writing the letter of apology. Captain Benteen was then sworn in. He testified that he had been in Reno's quarters after the letter had been written and that it had been read to him. Benteen then told Reno it did not express his true motive.

At this point the choleric Colonel Sturgis could stand no more. Almost incoherent with anger, he arose and indicated that he had lost confidence in the Judge Advocate and stated that the latter had ignored one or two points in the rules of evidence. He then asked the Court for permission to appear as Assistant Prosecutor. His unusual request was too much even for that particular Court, and the request was denied. The Court thereafter adjourned, with Benteen's examination to be continued the next day.

Captain Benteen was the first witness to be called the following morning. He was asked what he meant by the statement that Reno's note of apology had not expressed "his true motive."

He replied, "I mean by this that he [Reno] did not express all that he meant and [I] felt that he was dead in love with the young lady . . ." Asked if the letter was written in good faith, Benteen was allowed to reply over objection: "I believe the [letter] was, but not fully up to what he meant and felt."

Major Reno next recalled himself, stating that he had never said he would call Miss Sturgis to the stand. When he was informed that she would be a witness, he had gone to the Judge Advocate and said that, with the permission of the Court, he would change his plea to guilty of the additional specification if by so doing the young lady would not be embarrassed by being required to appear in the case. Reno then told the Court there were no other witnesses for the defense.

Captain Sanders, an officer of some conscience, wanted nothing further to do with this unhappy farce. Ordered to prosecute the case, he had done his duty, but he was not going to allow Colonel Sturgis or anyone else to place him in the position of persecutor. He advised the Court that he would not make a summation. Major Reno, in his own defense, made a short address which generally followed the lines of his testimony. He stressed the fact that the important thing had been his motives and he felt he had proven to the Court that his intentions had not been dishonorable.

Reno also pointed out it had been his misfortune, "to have attained wide-spread notoriety throughout the country by means of the press . . . and a greater degree of attention will be called to what I do than other officers not so widely advertised."

Thereupon Colonel Wood adjourned the Court.

34

Major Thomas F. Barr, who in 1877 had been the prosecutor of Major Reno on the charges filed against him by Captain Bell, had become Judge Advocate of the Department of Dakota. Under military regulations, after passing across the desk of Colonel Sturgis, the findings of the court-martial at Fort Meade would be sent to him. It would be his duty to prepare recommendations which General Terry, commander of the department, would transmit to the Secretary of War in Washington. Final approval or disapproval of the decision and sentence would rest with the President.

As Major Barr studied the findings of the court-martial he shook his head in disbelief. The verdict was the worst legal hodgepodge he had ever seen in fifteen years of court-martial work. His incredulity increased until he reached a state of almost complete astonishment.

Major Reno had expressed the conviction when the trial ended that he would be acquitted, and most of the officers at Fort Meade held the same opinion. Even Captain Sanders had termed the case a farce. When he was informed that he had been found guilty, and that the court had recommended his dismissal from the Army, he appeared to be dazed.

When Christmas had passed without a decision from Washington, the anxiety of Major Reno had reached a point where

Dr. Irwin feared it would endanger his health. He suggested that the major query General Terry in St. Paul as to the progress of the matter.

Instead of following the doctor's suggestion, Major Reno sent a telegram to Secretary of War Alexander Ramsey. It said:

Don't let me be dismissed. Rather resign if such conclusion be reached.

January and February came and went, with Fort Meade locked in by deep snow and bitter cold. Half of March had passed when casual gossip from St. Paul indicated that General Terry had dismissed the charges against him.

There was no foundation for the report, but Major Reno chose to accept it as authentic. On March 16 he wired Secretary Ramsey:

I withdraw request to resign.

Major Barr had good reason to be dismayed and confused. The court had found Major Reno guilty on the first specification, except for the words "create and," "disreputable," "and did persist in continuing said disturbance until threatened with arrest by Second Lieutenant James S. Pettit," and "to the scandal and disgrace of the military service."

On the second specification, Major Reno had been found guilty, except for the words "in a wanton and riotous manner," and "to the scandal and disgrace of the military service."

On the third specification, the court had found him guilty, except for the words "disgusting" and "to the scandal and disgrace of the military service."

Adding to the confusion, the court had then pronounced Major Reno "not guilty" of the charges brought against him, but "guilty" of "conduct to the prejudice of good order and military discipline."

As if still not content with the legal puzzle they had wrought, the judges then found Major Reno "not guilty" of the words "surreptitiously," "and so stealthily," and "very seriously," which were contained in the charge of which he had been found "guilty."

The recommendation of the court was that "Major Marcus A. Reno, 7th Cavalry, be dismissed from the Military Service of the United States."

After reading that, Major Barr was overcome with amazement. Attached to the verdict was a statement which suggested to him that five of the seven members of the court would have liked to expiate the miscarriage of justice in which they had participated. The five judges had signed a strong plea for clemency.

Major Barr moved cautiously in preparing his recommendations. He wrote General Terry at last:

In my opinion, the Court would have been justified in acquitting Major Reno of the additional charge and its specifications [the tapping on the window]. He was found not guilty of the most serious parts of the specifications, those which characterized the circumstances of his entry to the yard and approach to the window. These eliminated, there is but little left. The simple fact that he looked in the window—which is admitted by him—is not conceived, constructed an act which can properly and justly be held to be conduct which should preclude him from the society of officers and gentlemen, and it is such acts alone which come within the purview of the 61st Article of War.

The fact that the inmates of Colonel Sturgis's were alarmed and affrighted cannot of itself, it is believed, be considered as of convicting force against Major Reno. Such alarm might spring from a natural timidity.

. . . as five of the seven members of the Court unite in a recommendation to clemency, in terms which indicate that the penalty of dismissal was only adjudged because it was mandatory under the additional charge of which the accused was convicted, it is evident that so severe a sentence would not have been agreed upon had the conviction under the original charge and its specifications have been made.

Barr wrote Terry that the findings of the court and the sentence, in view of the majority recommendation for clemency, were inconsistent.

In regard to the altercation with Lieutenant Nicholson, it is to be re-marked that the accused appears to have been repeatedly and grossly insulted by that officer, and while the whole proceedings in the clubroom on that occasion were highly discreditable to both these officers, there was some excuse for the assault made by Major Reno.

Barr pointed out that if the verdict of the court was upheld, a distinguished veteran combat officer would be dismissed from the Army in disgrace for nothing more than participating in a small disturbance in a billiard room and tapping on the window of a young lady with whom he was in love.

Twenty years before he had become commander of the De-partment of Dakota, General Terry had been engaged in the private practice of law in New Haven, Connecticut. Since that time he had scarcely opened a lawbook. He was inclined to order the proceedings against Major Reno dismissed, in accordance with the recommendations of his own Judge Advocate, Major Barr, but nostalgia interfered. He found pleasure in once again assuming the role of a counselor, and he could not resist the temptation to write his own opinion to accompany the findings to Washington.

The results of General Terry's attempt to re-enter the field of law left Major Barr once again confused and appalled.

First, General Terry approved both the court-martial proceed-ings and the finding upon the first charge and its specifications. He then noted that:

The conduct of which Major Reno was found guilty, while unques-tionably very improper and ungentlemanly, does not seem to fall within the 61st Article of War, as that article is interpreted by writers on military law, and as it has been generally construed by courts-martial.

General Terry then submitted:

It is agreed by all hands that it is not *every* ungentlemanly action that subjects an officer to trial under this article. It is action so unbecoming an officer and a gentleman that a person guilty of it is no longer fit to hold a commission.

While the court found Major Reno guilty of the additional charge, it is evident that the large majority of its members who signed the recommendation to mercy, which is appended to the record, did not think that the conduct of which Major Reno had been found guilty was such as to unfit him to hold his commission, for they say that they have *"performed the painful duty of awarding punishment in strict conformity to an Article of War which deprived them of all discretionary power,"* and they *"beg leave to recommend the case of Major Reno to the merciful consideration of the confirming authority* [the President].*"*

Such being the view taken of the case by these members of the court, the finding upon this charge *should not have been guilty with a recommendation to mercy, but it should have been not guilty to the charge.*

Terry expressed the belief that the court, through a misapprehension, had unquestionably committed an error. This, he argued, became abundantly clear when five of the members recommended clemency. It had not been necessary to dismiss Major Reno from the service at all.

Major Barr thought that if the court had committed an error, his commanding officer had helped to compound it by failing to order that the case against Major Reno be dismissed—a simple and justified solution—but he kept the thought to himself.

It did not take General Sherman, Commanding General of the United States Army, long to come to a conclusion after the findings of the court-martial had reached him. Dismissal of Major Reno from the service on the scant evidence, the minor accusations, and the circumstances of the infractions, he declared, would be both unfair and a breach of justice.

General Sherman was required by law to transmit the verdict with his own views to the President, and he wrote cogently to Mr. Hayes:

In view of the recommendation of members of the court-martial in the case of Major Reno, and of the concurring recommendation of the Department Commander, it is respectfully recommended that the sentence of the Court *be modified to a suspension from command for one year with a loss of half pay.*

If Fate had been scheming to deal Major Reno a cruel blow, it could not have done better than to have placed Rutherford Birchard Hayes in the White House in the year 1880.

Hayes had been a political general in the Civil War, but he had displayed uncommon military ability and had emerged with a commendable record. He was an unscrupulous politician, and his ethical standards were made of India rubber. He would sacrifice propriety and morality to make a political gain. He both preached religious bigotry and cried for tolerance of every creed to win votes. He damned carpetbaggers as unconscionable scamps beneath his contempt, and rewarded them with public appointments for election frauds they committed in his behalf. He condemned Grant and the corruption of his Administration, and as a delegate to the Republican Convention of 1872 voted to nominate Grant for a second term. He participated with his dishonest supporters in one of the greatest political swindles in history —the theft of the presidency. Once he had gained the White House, he professed such purity and virtue that, even at diplomatic dinners, he forbade the serving of wine.

As he looked at another case involving Major Reno through the fog of his sanctimony, he saw only an Army officer who obviously had no political influence. Moreover, inasmuch as Major Reno had been born in southern Illinois he probably was a Democrat.

The record of the court-martial, Hayes noted, made it abundantly clear that Major Reno was a heavy drinker. This time he ignored the recommendation of General Terry, General Sherman, the court's plea for clemency, and the War Department.

"Approved," he wrote of the verdict.

Major Reno, after twenty-three years of service, was dishonorably dismissed from the Army.

Preparations for a spring patrol through the Sioux country were under way at Fort Meade when a telegram from St. Paul headquarters brought the news of the President's decision.

Strangely, Major Reno showed no emotion. He packed at once. During the two days he remained at Fort Meade before taking the stage for Rapid City, every officer of the post, with a single exception, made certain that he was seen in the act of turning his back on the disgraced man.

The exception was Fred Benteen.

35

*I*t was Dr. John Brown Hamilton, Surgeon General of the United States Marine Hospital Service, who found Major Reno weak, emaciated, and in critical condition when he called at his rooming house in Washington. He was shown to the major's room by the landlady.

A few moments later he informed both Reno and the landlady that an ambulance would arrive soon to take the major to Providence Hospital. He would arrange for his admittance and give orders for his care.

Dr. Hamilton could look back to his own youthful days in southern Illinois when he had first heard of a brilliant young man named Marcus Reno who had gone to West Point. And he could remember well more recent years when he had read about a Major Reno, whom he had met several times, and who had fought in the Battle of the Little Big Horn, a Major Reno who had been exonerated from a charge of cowardice. And when Reno, an humbled, embittered, and very sick man who had fallen into a haze of delusions, had sought him out and asked that he call, he had been very prompt to respond, although it was not customary for him to treat civilians and he never made private home calls.

Lying in his bed in the sparsely furnished room at Providence Hospital, Reno would have found far more sorrow than comfort in reflecting on the events which had transpired in the last few years.

When he had returned to Harrisburg from Fort Meade, he had

called on Lyman Gilbert at once, but Gilbert did not want to take his case.

Reno had told him that he wanted to get things straightened out as much for Ross as for himself, and Lyman had said that was commendable. He had really needed the thousand dollars he had borrowed from Ross, and his son had been very agreeable about lending it to him. Ross had instructed Lyman to give it to him from the estate account.

Although he wouldn't take the case, Lyman had been friendly, and he had given Reno good advice. He had told him that he needed a political lawyer, preferably a Democrat, because it looked like the Republicans would lose in the fall. Lyman had suggested Scott Lord, who was influential in Democratic political circles and also had good Republican connections. Lord was a brother-in-law of Benjamin Harrison.

Reno had gone at once to New York. Lord had been glad to take the case, and had expressed the opinion there was a good chance of winning it. However, Lord advised that nothing be done until after the nationl election. He had given Lord three hundred dollars, and Lord had said that was enough of a retainer, that he wasn't taking the case only for money. He sincerely believed that Reno had suffered a gross injustice.

From New York Reno had gone to Washington, and had visited his old friend, General McBride. He and Jim McBride had always been good friends. The general had more rooms than he needed. Reno had stayed quite a while. Then he had spent time with several other old Army comrades who lived in Washington.

The Democrats hadn't won, of course. It had been Garfield and Arthur, but only by a slim plurality of approximately ten thousand votes. Scott Lord admitted he didn't exactly know how to proceed with the case. He advised waiting longer. After President Garfield had been murdered and Arthur had become President, Lord went ahead. President Arthur, Lord said, was a member of the stalwarts, not of the liberal or reform factions to which Hayes and Garfield had belonged. Lord knew President Arthur well, and he wrote directly to him, saying:

I have the honor to transmit to you the application of Major Marcus A. Reno, and the addenda sustaining it, and a printed case based on the records found in the Department of War. It seems to me a case requiring as prompt action as your other duties will permit. What induced the then President Hayes to confirm so extreme a sentence, which the court under a mistaken filing was compelled to make (but with a recommendation to mercy), which the Judge Advocate, General Terry the reviewing officer, and General Sherman disapproved need not now be stated. Sufficient to say that when the reviewing officer disapproved the principal findings the proceedings fell, and by the statute the sentence would not be executed; saying nothing of the fact that the findings of the court, saving the one disapproved, were void, I feel a deep interest in the case of Major Reno, who is shown by his record to be a most gallant officer, and is also an honorable gentleman deeply wronged by the action referred to.

In the records he sent to President Arthur, Lord based his case on the actions of General Terry. He made five important points:

First, he noted that under the revised statutes no sentence of a court shall be carried into execution until the whole proceedings shall have been approved by the officer who had ordered the court, and that the execution of the sentence after the disapproval of the reviewing officer was illegal, and all orders subsequent to such disapproval were void, as though no court-martial had been held.

Second, he argued that the formal words, "the foregoing proceedings are approved," had no effect, and in no manner changed the fact of the subsequent disapproval of the principal findings and of the sentence.

Third, that as a matter of law there was no finding against Major Reno, except the finding disapproved by the reviewing officer. *Bevet's Military Law*, sixth edition, said plainly that specifications are only inserted to sustain the charge, and if the charge falls, the specifications fall.

Fourth, that the reviewing officer said that the sentence was manifestly excessive, but as he had no power to modify it, he formally approved it. That was not the confirmation the statute required; rather it was a violation of the statute.

Fifth, that the proceedings before President Hayes being void and of no effect, the confirmation by President Hayes was in turn void. Bevet's said that the power of confirmation contemplates the existence of a sentence in force, not one that had been rendered inoperative by the disapproval of the officer appointing the court.

Scott Lord, and those with whom he conferred, thought he had a strong case. He asked the President to recognize Reno as a major in the cavalry:

The directive that after April 1, 1880, Major Reno should cease to be an officer of the United States was without authority of law. Major Reno was tried upon two charges of conduct unbecoming an officer and gentleman. On the first he was found not guilty. Of the second he was found guilty, and of the specifications as modified, and was sentenced to dismissal from the service, as required by the 61st Article of War. The finding requiring this was disapproved by the reviewing officer, and under Article 104 the proceedings fell, and also because the reviewing officer disapproved of the sentence.

The practical result of disregarding Article 104 has been the execution of a sentence the Court pronounced only because it had no discretion under its mistaken finding, and which finding was disapproved by the reviewing officer.

It was assumed that President Hayes would modify the sentence. How much wiser is the law than such a lottery!

Major Reno has now been suspended from the service six months longer than the extreme limit, suggested by General Sherman. Has not his punishment been more than enough?

President Arthur took the easiest course. He turned the case over to the Secretary of War, Robert Todd Lincoln. Lincoln was an unaccomplished and unimaginative man. He had a memorandum prepared, and in it admitted there had been errors in Reno's case, especially in relation to his dismissal:

It is plain from the recommendations of the court, and the remarks of the reviewing officer, that if Major Reno had been tried on only one charge, the finding which was concurred in by the court and the commanding general would have been less severe than dismissal. The sentence as submitted to the President was, therefore, the artificial result of a rigid form of proceeding, and presented the actual views as to punishment of neither the court nor the reviewing officer.

However, admitting all the arguments of counsel, we reach nothing but error, not nullity.

Secretary Lincoln informed Scott Lord that Captain Edward Ball of the 2nd Cavalry had been named to fill Reno's place in the 7th, and even though Reno had been improperly dismissed, the confirmation of Ball had caused Reno to cease to be an officer of the Army.

Lincoln said:

The sentence of the court-martial, acting within its jurisdiction, which has been approved by the officer required by law, and has been confirmed by the President, is as much beyond appeal or review as is a judgment of the Supreme Court of the United States. A decision made under one President is not liable to be reviewed and annulled under the administration of another.

Therefore, whether the court-martial proceedings are considered or not, Major Reno is out of the Army. If the President afterwards finds that injustice has been done, he cannot undo it by annulling the order of dismissal. That is beyond his recall.

Reno's old friend from the 1st Dragoons, Rufus Ingalls, now a general, attempted to aid him.

In a letter to President Arthur, Ingalls said:

Major Reno's reinstatement to a commission in the Army would be an act of justice to a deserving officer. I have known Major Reno for almost a quarter of a century, both on the frontier and during the late Civil War, and can testify to his zeal and energy and faithful discharge of duty. The sentence is manifestly excessive as a punishment for the acts of which Major Reno was found guilty. The Executive action was harsh almost to the verge of cruelty in depriving Major Reno of a profession for which he had been educated, a profession to which he had devoted the best years of his life.

On his own volition, Reno went to see General Grant. He received a hearty welcome, and when Grant heard what had happened, he immediately wrote President Arthur.

Grant said:

It seems to me, in view of the recommendation of the court which tried Major Reno, of the fact that he was found not guilty of the most serious part of the specifications, and that the reviewing officer, the Department Commander, the Judge Advocate, and the General of the Army concur in the opinion that the court should have found the accused not guilty of the charge under which alone he could have been dismissed from the Army, is full justification for reviewing his case at this late date.

Scott Lord had more talks with Lincoln. The Secretary of War adhered to the position that under the law it was not possible for the President, even with the consent of the Senate, to reappoint Reno. Reno had become a civilian, and a man could be appointed to a majority only through promotion.

Lord informed Lincoln that the Attorney General had expressed serious doubts as to whether that was a correct interpretation of the law.

Lincoln said he didn't care how the Attorney General interpreted the law.

"I certainly fail to see," said Lord, "how the restoration of an officer to the identical rank from which he had been unjustly or illegally dismissed interferes with the promotion."

Lincoln thought the language of the law was very clear, and told Lord:

It gives no authority to the President. As the number of majors of cavalry is limited by law, and the list is full, Major Reno could not be appointed to that grade without removing a major from service.

Lord's next move was to arrange to have a bill for the relief of Major Reno introduced in Congress. It asked for Reno's reinstatement in the Army.

Only a person with strong political influence could have accomplished the move. Congressmen saw in Reno a burden they did not care to bear. The stories Whittaker had concocted had not been forgotten. Moreover, there were men in Congress who considered Custer a military genius, and mourned his loss to the nation.

Scott Lord wouldn't give up. He got the Reno bill dropped in the hopper in each session, until the year 1889.

Ironically, it was Lord's brother-in-law, Benjamin Harrison, who repeatedly got the bill pigeonholed. Harrison was chairman of the Senate Military Affairs Committee. Reno was not a political asset. Harrison was dreaming of becoming President, and it would have done his cause harm to have taken up the fight in defense of a controversial officer—rather, a discredited ex-officer. Harrison was powerful on Capitol Hill, and when other members of Congress learned that he was opposed to the Reno bill, they shied away from it, too.

Restless and discontented by the futility of his efforts to clear his name, and unable to reconcile himself to life as a civilian, Reno moved frequently in Washington. In one of the many boarding-houses in which he lived he met Isabella Ray, a government clerk. Their friendship developed rapidly, and they found mutual interests, undoubtedly encouraged by loneliness, which led them to believe they might know happiness in a life together. How mistaken they were soon became apparent.

They were married in January, 1884.

In February Reno went to Harrisburg and had Lyman Gilbert prepare a will for him. It provided that after repayment of the thousand dollars which Reno had borrowed from his son's estate, any residue should go to his new wife. Actually, the will was little more than a gesture which Reno felt called upon to make. His small savings had been used in his fight for reinstatement in the Army. He was virtually a pauper.

Reno and Isabella Ray lived together in a flat at 601 Eighteenth Street, N.W., for only a few months. Inasmuch as Reno had no income, she continued to work. Although he attempted to secure a post of some kind, he was not successful. Moreover, he was too discouraged and bitter—he had suffered too much disappointment and abuse—to be either a devoted husband or a good companion. They separated, although neither took steps to get a divorce.

At last, on November 19, 1885, Reno secured an appointment as a special examiner in the Bureau of Pensions. The Bureau was in an ornate red-brick building at Fourth and G Streets, N.W., only a short walk from a room he had rented at 316 Indiana Avenue.

Still hoping to restore himself to the position in military history he thought he deserved, and at the same time supplement his small salary, Reno tried his hand at writing about the Battle of the Little Big Horn. The *Weekly Press* of New York indicated an interest in his material, and on December 7, 1885, he wrote the editor:

Your letter of the 5th inst. duly received. My article on the Custer Massacre will be voluminous and will probably make two contributions. I have found a diary kept by myself and written on the battlefield lying in the grass within scent of the dead horses, which were killed in the fight, and from that reason of undoubted reliability and accuracy. I have requested the Chief of Engineers in Washington to send me an official map of the battleground which was made by Lt. McGuire of the Engineering Corps and I have no doubt he will comply with my request. I would be obligated to you if you will inform me what compensation you will give me in case you accept my contribution as I am in need of money.

Reno's talent as a writer was extremely limited. The material he prepared was never accepted for publication.*

*The manuscript was found by his son among his meager possessions. Years later it was rewritten by his son's wife. It appeared in the January-June, 1912, issue of *Americana,* an historical magazine published in New York.

36

A further detailed examination of Major Reno revealed that he had cancer of the tongue. An operation was performed. If in itself it was a success, it afforded no permanent relief. Dr. Hamilton knew that nothing could save Major Reno's life.

The major expressed a wish to see his son, and the doctor sent Ross a letter.

Ross was married to Ittie Kinney, whose family had been in the liquor business in Nashville for many years. The Kinney family home stood at 230 Spruce Street in a pleasant residential area.

Ross had invested a substantial sum in the Kinney liquor business. This had been enough to make him a partner, although the firm name wasn't changed. It remained Kinney, McLaughlin and Company.

When he received Ross' wedding announcement, Major Reno had sent his regrets, pleading that a conflict of engagements and pressure of business made it impossible for him to attend. The truth was that he didn't have the train fare to Nashville, and he no longer possessed proper clothes.

The wedding had been a big social event in Nashville. Reno bought the Nashville papers and clipped the stories about it. One of the clippings said:

The nuptial mass had been dispensed with for the occasion and other concessions had been made, such as marrying the parties after nightfall and by the light of gas.

The ushers for the wedding were selected from the city's leading families. One newspaper said that the guest list read like a Who's Who of Nashville.

Another story said:

The dress worn by the bride was of handsome white rep silk entrained with butterfly drapery. The front was composed of two panels displaying a tracery of fern leaves and marguerites embroidered in Japanese gold thread, gold bullion and seed pearls and garnished with white and gold lace.

Ittie Kinney also wore diamond solitaire earrings, a gift from her father and mother, a cross of eleven large solitaires, a gift from the bridegroom, and an ornament brooch made of a slender bar of gold supporting a small diamond butterfly thickly studded with diamonds and finished with solitaires of diamonds and pearls. The brooch had belonged to the bridegroom's mother, Mary Hannah Ross Reno.

Mr. and Mrs. Ross Reno left for a five-months tour through the East that might extend to Europe.

When Dr. Hamilton realized that Major Reno could live only a few more days, he sent a telegram to Ross in Nashville.

Erysipelas was spreading its scourge, breaking down the major's blood and sapping the little strength he possessed. Then suddenly pneumonia sent its destructive fire through his wasted body.

Throughout the night of March 29, 1889, Nursing Sister Beatrice remained beside the bed of the dying soldier in Providence Hospital. The light of a small gas jet caught on the gleaming white of her starched habit, and shadows flickering about the room magnified its dreariness and emptiness.

The first faint light of March 30 had spread its grayness over the rooftops of Washington when Sister Beatrice arose, gently placed Major Reno's arms on his chest, and drew a sheet over his face.

The Washington *Evening Star* said:

RENO—In this city died, Marcus A. Reno, late Major and Brevet Lt. Col., U. S. Army.

Ross Reno, hurrying up from Nashville, gave J. William Lee's Sons Company $128 for a casket and the hire of four hacks.

The magnificent Washington spring was in full bloom as the

four vehicles and clopping horses moved along a driveway in Glenwood Cemetery.

The landlady of Major Reno's rooming house stood beside a young cemetery minister and Ross Reno as the casket was lowered into the grave by the hack drivers.

The grave was in a common lot owned by the undertaker. Ross Reno paid eighteen dollars for it, but he did not order a stone, and it was never marked.

BIBLIOGRAPHY

PUBLIC RECORDS CONSULTED

Bureau of Vital Statistics, Washington, D.C.
  Records of the death of Marcus A. Reno, March 29, 1889.
Glenwood Cemetery, Washington, D.C.
  Record of the burial of Marcus A. Reno, April 2, 1889.
Harrisburg Cemetery, Harrisburg, Pa.
  Records of the burial of Mary Hannah Reno, July 12, 1874.
National Archives, Washington, D.C.
Pennsylvania Military Archives, Indiantown Gap Military Reservation,
  Indiantown Gap, Pa.
Providence Hospital, Washington, D.C.
  Records of Private Patients, 1889.
Register of Wills, Harrisburg, Pa.
  The Will of James Ross, 1861.
  Administration of the Estates of Mary E. Ross, 1873.
  The guardianship of Robert Ross Reno.
Register of Wills, Washington, D.C.
  The Will of Marcus A. Reno dated, February 4, 1884, probated
    May 18, 1889.
  Petition for the probate of the Will of Marcus A. Reno, June 6,
    1889.
United States Military Academy Archives, West Point, N.Y.
  All orders concerning Cadet Marcus A. Reno.

NEWSPAPERS CONSULTED

Army and Navy Journal, 1862-1889.
The *Banner* (S.C.)
Billings *Gazette,* Billings, Mont., Sept. 18, 1960.

Carolina Spartan, Spartanburg, S.C., May 4, 1865, and issues 1870-1872.

Chicago *Times*, Chicago, Ill., Sept. 22, 1876; Jan. 19, 1879.

Chicago *Daily Tribune*, Chicago, Ill., Jan. 13, 14, 15, 17, 1879.

Evening Star, Washington, D.C., Nov. 22, 1886; Mar. 30, 1889; Apr. 1, 1889.

Fargo *Forum*, Fargo, N.D., Dec. 23, 1956.

Greensboro *Daily Record*, Greensboro, N.C., Apr. 27, 1924.

Nashville *American*, Nashville, Tenn., Jan. 1 and 6, 1888.

New York *Daily Tribune*, New York, N.Y., Nov. 1, 1871; July 23, 1876; Sept. 21, 1876.

New York *Tribune*, New York, N.Y., May 15, 1889.

Patriot, Carrollton, Ill., Feb. 7, 1889.

Patriot, Harrisburg, Pa., July 11, 1874; Apr. 1, 1889; May 5, 1914.

Pittsburgh *Gazette*, Pittsburgh, Pa., Mar. 25, 1872.

Rocky Mountain News, Denver, Colo., Dec. 17, 1864.

Springfield *News-Sun*, Springfield, Ohio, Sept. 13, 1959.

Washington *Post*, Washington, D.C., Sept. 1, 1901.

LIBRARIES CONSULTED

Arlington County Department of Libraries, Arlington, Va.

The Army Library, The Pentagon, Washington, D.C.

Army and Navy Club Library, Washington, D.C.

The Library of Congress, Washington, D.C.

National War College Library, Washington, D.C.

Fort Lesley J. McNair Library, Washington, D.C.

National Archives Library, Washington, D.C.

Selective Service System, National Headquarters Reference Library, Washington, D.C.

Public Library of the District of Columbia, Washington, D.C.

Pennsylvania State Library, Harrisburg, Pa.

Tennessee State Library and Archives, Nashville, Tenn.

U.S. Military Academy Library, West Point, N.Y.

The Wofford College Library, Spartanburg, S.C.

Henry E. Huntington Library and Art Gallery, San Marino, Calif.

Public Library, City of Wilmington, N.C.

Public Library, New York, N.Y.

A

Adjutant General's Office, *The Official Army Register;* 1867-1885, Washington, D.C.

Africa, J. Simpson, *History of Huntingdon and Blair Counties, Pennsylvania,* Philadelphia, Pa., 1883.

Alexander, Holmes, *The American Talleyrand,* New York, N.Y., 1935.

Vol. VII, *Americana,* "Brief Biography of Major Marcus Reno," New York, N.Y., 1912.

American Guide Series, *North Dakota,* New York, N.Y., 1950.

Armes, Colonel George A., *Ups and Downs of an Army Officer,* Washington, D.C., 1900.

Armstrong, V.S., Dr. Nelson, *Nuggets of Experience,* San Bernardino, Calif., 1906.

Association of Graduates of the United States Military Academy 14th Annual Reunion, *Major Marcus A. Reno,* West Point, N.Y., 1889.

B

Babst, Earl D., and Vander Velde, Lewis G., editors, *Michigan and the Cleveland Era,* Ann Arbor, Mich., 1948.

Baldwin, Alice Blackswood, *Memoirs of the Late Frank D. Baldwin,* Los Angeles, Calif., 1929.

Barnard, Harry, *Rutherford B. Hayes,* Indianapolis, Ind., 1954.

Bates, Samuel P., *History of Pennsylvania Volunteers, 1861-1865,* Harrisburg, Pa., 1871.

Biographical Directory of the American Congress 1774-1944, Washington, D.C., 1944.

Boatner III, Mark Mayo, *The Civil War Dictionary,* New York, N.Y., 1959.

Bomar, Sr., Rev. E. E., "What Happened When the Yankees Came to Town," manuscript, Kennedy Library, Spartanburg, S.C., N.D.

Bourke, John G., *On the Border with Crook,* New York, N.Y., 1891.

Bowers, Claude G., *The Tragic Era,* Cambridge, Mass., 1920.

Bowles, *Our New West,* Hartford, Conn., 1869.

Boyd, William H., editor, *Directory of the District of Columbia,* 1880-1890.

Boynton, Captain Edward C., *History of West Point,* New York, N.Y., 1863.

Bradford, Gamaliel, *Lee the American;* Boston, Mass., 1912.

Bradford, West, *Battles and Leaders of the Civil War*, New York, N.Y., 1956.

Bradley, James H., (Stewart, E. I., editor) *The March of the Montana Column*, Norman, Okla., 1961.

Brady, Cyrus Townsend, *Indian Fights and Fighters*, New York, N.Y., 1904.

Brimlow, George Francis, *Cavalrymen out of the West, Life of General William Carey Brown*, Caldwell, Idaho, 1944.

Brinstool, E. A., *The Custer Fight, Captain Benteen's Story of the Battle of Little Big Horn*, Hollywood, Calif., 1933.

Britt, Albert, *Great Indian Chiefs*, New York, N.Y., 1938.

Brooks, Noah, *Washington in Lincoln's Time*, New York, N.Y., 1958.

Brown, Jesse, and Willard, A. M., *The Black Hills Trail*, Rapid City, S.D., 1924.

Buel, Clarence C., and Johnson, Robert Underwood, editors, *Battles and Leaders of the Civil War*, New York, N.Y., 1956.

Burdick, Usher L., *The Army Life of Charles "Chip" Creighton*, Paris, Md., 1937.

Burdick, Usher L., *Last Days of Sitting Bull*, Baltimore, Md., 1941.

Burdick, Usher L., *The Last Battle of the Sioux Nation*, Fargo, N.D., 1929.

Burdick, Usher L., *Tales from Buffalo Land*, Baltimore, Md., 1940.

Burdick, Usher L., *Tragedy in the Great Sioux Camp*, Baltimore, Md.

Burdick, Usher L., editor, *David F. Barry's Indian Notes on the Custer Battle*, Baltimore, Md., 1937.

Burt, Struthers, *Powder River*, New York, N.Y., 1938.

Byrne, P. E., *Soldiers of the Plains*, New York, N.Y., 1926.

C

Carlisle Barracks, Pennsylvania 1857-1954, A Brief History of, Carlisle, Pa., 1954.

Carlisle, Jr., James H., "Memoirs of Wofford College," manuscript, Wofford College Library, Spartanburg, S.C., 1935.

Carpenter, Francis, editor, *Carp's Washington*, New York, N.Y., 1960.

Carter, Hodding, *The Angry Scar*, Garden City, N.Y., 1959.

Casey, Robert J., *The Black Hills*, New York, N.Y., 1949.

Catton, Bruce, *Glory Road*, Garden City, N.Y., 1954.

Catton, Bruce, *Mr. Lincoln's Army*, New York, N.Y., 1959.

Catton, Bruce, *This Hallowed Ground*, Garden City, N.Y., 1956.

Chandler, Lieutenant Colonel Melbourne C., *Of Garry Owen in Glory*, Annandale, Va., 1960.

314

Clapp, Clement L., *History of Greene Country, Illinois*, Chicago, Ill., 1879.

Cleaves, Freeman, *Rock of Chickamauga*, Norman, Okla., 1948.

Commager, Henry Steele, editor, *The Blue and the Gray*, Indianapolis, Ind., 1950.

Crane, Charles Judson, *The Experiences of a Colonel of Infantry*, New York, N.Y., 1923.

Custer, Elizabeth B., *Boots and Saddles*, New York, N.Y., 1885.

Custer, Elizabeth B., *Following the Guidon*, New York, N.Y., 1890.

Custer, Elizabeth B., *Tenting on the Plains*, New York, N.Y., 1893.

Custer, George A., *My Life on the Plains*, New York, N.Y., 1874.

D

Daniels, Jonathan, *Prince of Carpetbaggers*, Philadelphia, Pa., 1958.

Dauphin County, Pennsylvania, Commemorative Biographical Encyclopedia of, Chambersburg, Pa., 1896.

Davis, Joel, compiler, *Nashville Directory*, 1888, Nashville, Tenn., 1888.

DeBarthe, Joe, *Life and Adventures of Frank Grouard*, Norman, Okla., 1958.

DeForest, John William, *A Union Officer in the Reconstruction*, New Haven, Conn., 1948.

Deibert, Chaplain Ralph C., *A History of the Third United States Cavalry*, Fort Myer, Va., N.D.

DeVine, William J., editor, *The Harrisburg City Directory*, Harrisburg, Pa., 1867.

Dodge, Colonel Richard Irving, *33 Years Among Our Wild Indians*, New York, N.Y., 1959.

Downey, Fairfax D., *Clash of Cavalry*, New York, N.Y., 1959.

DuBois, Charles G., *Kick the Dead Lion*, Billings, Mont., 1954.

Dunn, J. P., *Massacres of the Mountains*, New York, N.Y., 1958.

DuPont, H. A., *The Campaign of 1864 in the Valley of Virginia and the Expedition to Lynchburg*, New York, N.Y., 1925.

Dupuy, R. Ernest, *The Compact History of the United States Army*, New York, N.Y., 1956.

Dupuy, R. Ernest, *Men of West Point*, New York, N.Y., 1951.

Dupuy, R. Ernest and Trevor N., *Brave Men and Great Captains*, New York, N.Y., 1956.

Dustin, Fred, *The Custer Fight*, Hollywood, Calif., 1936.

Dustin, Fred, *The Custer Tragedy*, Ann Arbor, Mich., 1939.

Dyer, Frederick H., *A Compendium of the War of the Rebellion*, Des Moines, Iowa, 1908.

E

Eisenschiml, Otto, *The Celebrated Case of FitzJohn Porter*, Indianapolis, Ind., 1950.

Eskeurode, H. J., *Rutherford B. Hayes: Statesman of Reunion*, New York, N.Y., 1930.

Eskew, Garnett Laidlaw, *Willards of Washington*, New York, N.Y., 1954.

Esposito, Colonel Vincent J., editor, *The West Point Atlas of American Wars*, New York, N.Y., 1959.

F

Ferree, Rev. P. V., *The Heroes of the War for the Union*, Cincinnati, Ohio, 1864.

Field, Staff, and Officers of the 1st Regiment of Cavalry from March 4, 1833 to June 1, 1900, Fort Meade, S.D., 1900.

Finerty, John F., *War Path and Bivouac*, Chicago, Ill., 1890.

Fisher, Clay, *Yellow Hair*, Cambridge, Mass., 1853.

Fiske, John, and Wilson, James, editors, *Appleton's Cyclopedia of American Biography*, New York, N.Y., 1894-1900.

Forman, Sidney, *West Point*, New York, N.Y., 1950.

Forsyth, General George A., *Thrilling Days in Army Life*, New York, N.Y., 1900.

Fougera, Katherine Gibson, *With Custer's Cavalry*, Caldwell, Idaho, 1940.

Fourth Cavalry, United States Army, History of the, Fort Meade, S.D., 1930.

Fry, James B., *Brevets in the Armies of Great Britain and the United States*, New York, N.Y., 1877.

Fry, General J. B., *Comments on Godfrey's Narrative*, New York, N.Y., 1892.

Fry, James B., *Military Miscellanies*, New York, N.Y., 1889.

Fuller, George W., *A History of the Pacific Northwest*, New York, N.Y., 1931.

G

Garlington, Major E. A., *Historical Sketches, Army of the United States*, Washington, D.C., 1894.

Godfrey, Brigadier General Edward S., *After the Custer Battle*, Missoula, Mont., 1939.

Godfrey, General Edward S., *General George A. Custer and the Battle of Little Big Horn*, New York, N.Y., 1892.

Godfrey, Brigadier General E. S., *Some Reminiscences, Including the Washita Battle*, Washington, D.C., 1928.

Goplen, Arnold O., *The Historical Significance of Fort Lincoln State Park*, Bismarck, N.D., 1946.

Graham, Colonel William A., *The Custer Myth*, Harrisburg, Pa., 1953.

Graham, Colonel William A., *The Reno Court of Inquiry*, Harrisburg, Pa., 1954.

Graham, Colonel William A., *The Story of the Little Big Horn*, Harrisburg., 1941.

H

Haines, William Wister, *The Winter War*, Boston, Mass., 1961.

Hamersly, L. R., *Records of Living Officers of the United States Army*, Philadelphia, Pa., 1884.

Hanson, Joseph Mills, *The Conquest of the Missouri*, Chicago, Ill., 1909.

Hart, William S., *Injun and Whitey*, Boston, Mass., 1922.

Haskin, William L., and Rodenbough, Theo F., *The Army of the United States*, New York, N.Y., 1896.

Haupt, General Hermann, *Reminiscences*, Milwaukee, Wis., 1901.

Hazelton, Joseph P., *Scouts, Spies and Heroes*, Jersey City, N.J., 1892.

Hazen, General W. B., *A Narrative of Military Service*, Boston, Mass., 1885.

Heitman, Francis B., *Historical Register and Dictionary of the United States Army, 1789-1903*, Washington, D.C., 1903.

Hergesheimer, Joseph, *Sheridan*, Boston, Mass., 1931.

Herr, Major General John K., and Wallace, Edward S., *The Story of the U.S. Cavalry 1775-1942*, Boston, Mass., 1953.

Hicks, Major James E., *U.S. Firearms*, Beverly Hills, Calif., 1957.

History of Greene and Jersey Counties, Illinois, Springfield, Ill., 1885.

Hoig, Stan, *The Sand Creek Massacre*, Norman, Okla., 1961.

Holden, Edward S., editor, *The Centennial of the United States Military Academy at West Point, N.Y.*, Washington, D.C., 1904.

Holloway, W. L., editor, *Wild Life on the Plains and Horrors of Indian Warfare*, St. Louis, Mo., 1891.

Horan, James D., *The Great American West*, New York, N.Y., 1959.

Hughes, Colonel Robert P., *The Campaign Against the Sioux in 1876*, Washington, D.C., 1896.

Hyde, George, *Red Cloud's Folks*, Norman, Okla., 1937.

I

Indian Wars, Proceedings of the Annual Dinner of the Order of 1920-1930, Washington, D.C., 1931.

International Border Commission, *Report*, Department of State, Washington, D.C., 1937.

J

Jackson, Helen, *A Century of Dishonor*, Boston, Mass., 1886.

Johannsen, Albert, *The House of Beadle and Adams*, Norman, Okla., 1950.

Johnson, Roy P., *Jacob Horner of the Seventh Cavalry*, Bismarck, 1957.

Johnson, Virginia W., *The Unregimented General*, Boston, Mass., 1962.

Jones, Nard, *The Great Command*, Boston, Mass., 1959.

Jones, Nard, *Swift Flows the River*, New York, N.Y., 1940.

Jones, Virgil Carrington, *Ranger Mosby*, Chapel Hill, N.C., 1944.

K

Kennedy, Fronde, Supervisor W.P.A., *A History of Spartanburg County*, Spartanburg, S.C., 1940.

King, Captain Charles, *Cadet Life at West Point*, New York, N.Y., N.D.

Kline, M. M., compiler, *Nashville Directory 1887*, Nashville, Tenn., 1887.

Knight, Oliver, *Following the Indian Wars*, Norman, Okla., 1960.

Kuhlman, Charles, *Legend into History*, Harrisburg, Pa., 1951.

L

Lane, Lydia Spencer, *I Married a Soldier*, Philadelphia, Pa., 1910.

Lavender, David, *Bent's Fort*, New York, N.Y., 1954.

Leech, Margaret, *Reveille in Washington*, New York, N.Y., 1941.

Leonard, John W., editor, *Who's Who in America 1903-1905*, Chicago, Ill., 1903.

Living Church Annual, New York, N.Y., 1903.

Lloyd's Clerical Directory (Episcopal), Minneapolis, Minn., 1898.

Lounsbury, Colonel Clement A., *Early History of North Dakota*, Washington, D.C., 1919.

Lounsbury, Colonel Clement A., *North Dakota History and People*, Chicago, Ill., 1917.

Luce, Edward S., *Keogh, Comanche, and Custer*, privately printed, 1939.

Lunt, James D., *Charge to Glory*, New York, N.Y., 1960.
Lynch, Denis Tilden, *An Epoch and a Man*, New York, N.Y., 1929.

M

MacKay, Douglas, *The Honorable Company*, Indianapolis, Ind., 1936.
Malone, Dumas, editor, *Dictionary of American Biography*, New York, N.Y., 1936.
McBarron, Jr., H. Charles, and Parker, Tom, *1st. U.S. Dragoons 1856-1861*, Washington, D.C., 1957.
McCartney, Clarence Edward, *Little Mac, the Life of Gen. George B. McClellan*, Philadelphia, Pa., 1940.
McLaughlin, James, *My Friend, the Indian*, Boston, Mass., 1926.
Medal of Honor of the United States Army, The, Washington, D.C. 1948.
Merington, Marguerite, *The Custer Story*, New York, N.Y., 1950.
Mickie, Peter S., *Life and Letters of General Upton*, New York, N.Y., 1885.
Miles, Nelson A., *Serving the Republic*, New York, N.Y., 1911.
Miller, David Humphreys, *Custer's Fall*, New York, N.Y., 1957.
Monaghan, Jay, *Custer*, Boston, Mass., 1959.
Moore, Frank, *The Portrait Gallery of the War*, New York, N.Y., 1864.

N

Nelson, William H., and Vandever, Frank E., *Fields of Glory*, New York, N.Y., 1960.
Neuder, Charles, *The Great West*, New York, N.Y., 1958.
Nevins, Allen, *Hamilton Fish*, New York, N.Y., 1936.
Nye, W. S., *Carbine and Lance*, Norman, Okla., 1937.

O

Ordinance, Chief of, *Annual Report—1873*, Washington, D.C., 1873.

P

Parsons, John E., and DuMont, John S., *Firearms in the Custer Battle*, Harrisburg, Pa., 1953.
Patch, Joseph Dorst, *The Battle of Ball's Bluff*, Leesburg, Va., 1958.
Pearl, Jack, "The Red Man's Last Stand," *Saga Magazine*, New York, N.Y., November, 1960.

Peirce, Paul Skeels, *The Freedmen's Bureau,* University of Iowa, Iowa City, 1904.
Potomac Corral of the Westerners, *Great Western Indian Fights,* New York, N.Y., 1960.
Powell, Colonel William H., *List of Officers of the Army of the United States,* New York, N.Y., 1900.
Preston, Wheeler, *American Biographies,* New York, N.Y., 1940.
Prince, William H., *The Civil War Centennial Handbook,* Arlington, Va., 1961.

R

Rachlis, Eugene, and Ewers, John C., *Indians of the Plains,* New York, N.Y., 1960.
Randall, J. G., *The Civil War and Reconstruction,* Boston, Mass., 1937.
Randall, Ruth Painter, *Lincoln's Sons,* Boston, Mass., 1955.
Rawling, G. S., "Custer's Last Stand," *History Today,* Vol. XII, No. 1, London, England, January, 1962.
Reno, Ittie Kinney, *Miss Breckenridge,* Philadelphia, Pa., 1890.
Reno, Ittie Kinney, *An Exceptional Case,* Philadelphia, Pa., 1891.
Reno, Major Marcus A., *Report on the Battle of Little Big Horn,* (Report of the Secretary of War), Washington, D.C., 1876.
Rhodes, Charles Dudley, *History of the Cavalry of the Army of the Potomac,* Kansas City, Mo., 1900.
Rhodes, Charles Dudley, *Robert E. Lee, the West Pointer,* Richmond, Va., 1932.
Rickey, Don, *War in the West,* Crow Agency, Mont., 1956.
Rister, Carl Coke, *General Phil Sheridan in the West,* Norman, Okla., 1944.
Robinson, Duane, *Encyclopedia of South Dakota,* Pierre, S.D., 1925.
Roe, Brigadier General Charles Francis, *Custer's Last Battle,* New York, N.Y., 1927.
R.O.T.C. Manual, *American Military History 1607-1958,* Washington, D.C., 1959.
Russell, Charles Edward, *Blaine of Maine,* New York, N.Y., 1931.
Russell, Don, *One Hundred and Three Fights and Scrimmages,* Washington, D.C., 1936.

S

Schaff, Morris, *The Spirit of Old West Point,* Boston, Mass., 1907.
Schmitt, Martin F., editor, *General George Crook, His Autobiography,* Norman, Okla., 1946.

Schouler, James, *History of the United States of America,* Vol. IV, Washington, D.C., 1889.

Scott, Hugh L., *Some Memoirs of a Soldier,* New York, N.Y., 1928.

Sellers, Charles Cotman, *Lorenzo Dow,* New York, N.Y., 1928.

Sherman, General William T., *Annual Report, 1876,* New York, N.Y., 1876.

Shiflit, Kenneth, *The Convenient Coward,* Harrisburg, Pa., 1960.

Shirk, George H., "The Case of the Plagiarized Journal," *The Chronicles of Oklahoma,* Oklahoma City, Okla., Winter, 1958-1959.

Silph, Ralph, *The Story of the Confederacy,* New York, N.Y., 1931.

Simpson, Colonel Harold P., *Brawling Brass,* Waco, Tex., 1960.

Stackpole, Edward J., *They Met at Gettysburg,* Harrisburg, Pa., 1961.

Stanley, Major General D. S., *Personal Memoirs,* Cambridge, Mass., 1917.

Stewart, Edgar I., *Custer's Luck,* Norman, Okla., 1955.

Stewart, Edgar I. and Jane R., editors, *The Field Diary of Lt. Edward Settle Godfrey,* Portland, Ore., 1957.

T

Tanner, George C., *Fifty Years of Church Work in the Diocese of Minnesota 1857-1907,* St. Paul, Minn., 1909.

Tebbel, John, and Jennison, Keith, *The American Indian Wars,* New York, N.Y., 1957.

Terry, Alfred H., Field Diary of, "On the Sioux Campaign of 1876," Manuscript Division, Congressional Library, Washington, D.C., 1876.

Todd, A. L., *Abandoned,* New York, N.Y., 1961.

Tousey, Thomas G., *Military History of Carlisle and Carlisle Barracks,* Richmond, Va., 1939.

Tucker, Glenn, *Hancock the Superb,* Indianapolis, Ind., 1960.

Twinning, Captain W. J., *Report of the Chief Astronomer, International Border Commission, 1874,* Washington, D.C., 1874.

U

Utley, Robert M., *Custer and the Great Controversy,* Los Angeles, Cal., 1962.

V

Van de Water, Frederick F., *Glory Hunter,* Indianapolis, Ind., 1934.

Vaughn, J. W., *With Crook at the Rosebud,* Harrisburg, Pa., 1956.

Vestal, Stanley, *Sitting Bull,* Boston, Mass., 1932.

Vestal, Stanley, *Warpath and Council Fire,* New York, N.Y., 1948.

W

Waldo, Edna La Moore, *Dakota*, Caldwell, Idaho, 1936.

Walker, Judson Elliott, *Campaign of General Custer in the Northeast*, New York, N.Y., 1881.

Wallace, David Duncan, *The History of South Carolina* (3 vols.), New York, N.Y., 1934.

War of the Rebellion, The. A Compilation of the Official Records of the Union and Confederate Armies, Washington, D.C., 1901.

Warner, Ezra J., *Generals in Gray*, Baton Rouge, La., 1959.

Wellman, Paul I., *Death on Horseback*, Philadelphia, Pa., 1934.

West Point Alumni Foundation, *The Register of Graduates and Former Cadets*, West Point, N.Y., 1955.

Wheeler, Colonel Homer W., *Buffalo Days*, Indianapolis, Ind., 1925.

Wheeler, Colonel Homer W., *The Frontier Trail*, Los Angeles, Calif., 1923.

Whittaker, Frederick, *A Complete Life of General George A. Custer*, New York, N.Y., 1876.

Who Was Who in America, Vol. I, 1897-1942, Chicago, Ill., 1942.

Wilkins, Robert P. and Wynona H., *God Giveth the Increase*, Fargo, N.D., 1959.

Williams, M.D., Ralph Chester, *The United States Public Health Service; 1798-1950*, Washington, D.C., 1951.

Windolph, Sergeant, Charles A., *I Fought with Custer* (as told to Robert and Frazer Hunt), New York, N.Y., 1947.

Woodward, W. E., *Meet General Grant*, New York N.Y., 1928.

INDEX

324

325

Reynolds, Charles Alexander (1842?-1876) 158, 166
Reynolds, Joseph Jones, Gen. (1822-1899) 127-128
Richardson, William Alexander, U. S. Cong. (1811-1875) 21-22
Richmond (Va.) 35-37, 38
Robinson, W. W., Lt. 205, 207-208
  involved in Reno-Bell controversy, 211, 215, 216, 218, 219, 222, 224-225, 226-227
Rocky Mountain News (Denver, Colo.) quoted, 116
Rosebud, Battle of the, 140-143, 144
Ross, Mary (Haldeman) (?-1874) 31-32, 40, 48, 49, 84
  death, 87
Ross
  Jacob, 32
  Mary Hannah *see* Reno, M. H.
  Robert, 32
  Robert James, 32
  Roberta 32 *see also* Orth, B.
Rosser, Thomas Lafayette, Gen. (1836-1910) 200-203, 205
Royal Austrian Military Academy 95
Royall, William Bedford, Maj. (1825-?) 141, 235
Ryan, John, Sgt.
  quoted, 193

St. Louis *Democrat* (Mo.) 11
Sanborn, John Benjamin, Gen. (1826-?) 117-118
Sand Creek Massacre, 114-116
Sanders, William W., Capt. 288, 289, 290-291, 293, 294
Sante Fe (N. Mex.) 3, 13, 14, 70
Schofield, John McAllister, Gen. (1831-1906) 13
Scott, Douglas Marshall, Lt. 281, 289
Scott, Gustavus Hall, Adm. (1812-1882) 289
Scott, Hugh L., Gen.
  quoted, 73
Scott, Robert Kingston, Gov., S. C. (1826-1900) 79-81, 82
Scott, Winfield, Lt. Gen. (1786-1866) 24
Shafter, William Rufus, Col. (1835-1906) 287
Sharrow, William H., Sgt. Maj. 163
Sheridan, M. V., Lt. Col.
  quoted, 259

Sheridan, Philip Henry, Gen. (1831-1888) 51, 66, 103, 124, 126, 180, 196, 277
  appraisal of Indian situation, 8-9, 12
  Civil War service, 53-55
  quoted, 276
  quoted on Reno's military tactics, 173n
Sherman, William Tecumseh, Gen. (1820-1891) 99, 122, 134, 196, 277, 303
  approves findings of Court of Inquiry, 275
  denounces Court-Martial, 298
  intercedes for Custer, 131-132
  on Indian treaty committee, 117-118
  on Sand Creek Massacre investigating committee, 116n
  quoted in re Reno, 199
  quoted on Little Big Horn battle, 260
  recommends mercy for Reno, 299
Simpson, James M., Dr. 17, 21, 30
Simpson, Jane (Hopkins) 20
Simpson
  Martha, 20
  Mary, 20
  Samuel, 20
Sitting Bull (Indian chief) (1834?-1890) 92, 118, 127, 143, 146, 157, 159, 160, 186-188, 190-191, 198
Slavery 16 *see also* Negro
Slocum, Herbert J., Lt. 205, 208, 209, 212, 215, 218, 225, 226, 227
Smith, Algernon E., Lt. 162
Smith, Andrew Jackson, Col. (1815-1897) 4
Smith, Edwin W., Capt. 138, 150, 180
Smith, William Farrar, Gen. (1824-1903) 47-48, 49, 56
Smyth, Joseph 281, 288, 289, 292
Spartanburg (S. C.) 77-83, 108
Spilman, Baldwin D., Lt. 284, 289
Spotted Horn Bull 187n
Spotted Horn Bull, Mrs. 187n
Spotted Tail (Indian chief) (c. 1833-1881) 282
Stab (or Stabbed) (Indian scout) 156
Stanley, David Sloan, Col. (1828-1902) 120-121
Stanton, Edwin McMasters, Secretary of War (1814-1869)
  Civil War policies, 34, 35, 36
  political appointments, to Army, 76, 94, 96, 99, 289

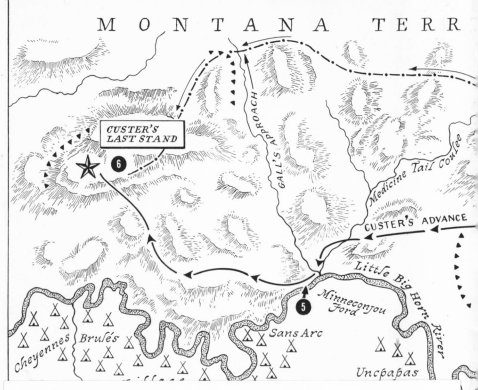

MONTANA TERR

CUSTER'S
LAST STAND

6

GALL'S APPROACH

Medicine Tail Coulee

CUSTER'S ADVANCE

Little Big Horn River

5

Minneconjou Ford

Cheyennes   Brulés   Sans Arc

Uncpapas

Terrell, John Upton, 1900-
   Faint the trumpet sounds; the life
and trial of Major Reno, by John
Upton Terrell and George Walton. New
York, D. McKay Co. [1966]
   xi, 332 p. illus., map (on lining
papers) ports. 22 cm.
   Bibliography: p. 311-322.

   1. Reno, Marcus Albert, 1835-1889.
2. Little Big Horn, Battle of the,
1876. I. Walton, George H., joint
author. II. Title.

The line of dots and dashes moving northward (to the left) in the upper quadrant
reveal Lt. Edward Godfrey's version of Custer's line of march. The heavy arrows below
indicate the route that the Indians and most historians believe Custer followed to his
rendezvous with death.